THE RULER OF

THE RULER OF CHESHIRE

Sir Piers Dutton, Tudor Gangland and the Violent Politics of the Palatine

Edward Dutton

In memory of Sheila May Saxl, née Dutton, (1921-1997)
and John Foster Dutton (1943-2014).

ISBN 978-1-901253-57-3
First published November 2015

Cover illustration © Patricia Kelsall, 2015.
*Portrait of Sir Piers Dutton based on the roundels at Dutton Hall,
signature of Sir Piers Dutton from illustration 7, and coat of arms
from illustration 10.*

Published by:
Léonie Press
an imprint of
Anne Loader Publications
13 Vale Road, Hartford,
Northwich, Cheshire CW8 1PL
Gt Britain
Tel: +44 (0) 1606 75660   e-mail: anne@leoniepress.com
Websites: www.anneloaderpublications.co.uk
www.leoniepress.com

'We care not ... for Cheshire, for the rulers there, Sir William Brereton and Sir Piers Dutton, cannot agree.'

Leaders of the Pilgrimage of Grace,
October 1536

'Sir Piers' friends openly report that he can do as he likes in this county. If he is not punished it will be so supposed by the whole shire.'

Sir William Brereton to Thomas Cromwell,
29th August 1537

Edward Dutton

About the author

EDWARD DUTTON read Theology at Durham University before researching a PhD in the Divinity Department at Aberdeen University which was published as *Meeting Jesus at University* (Ashgate, 2008). He is Adjunct Professor of the Anthropology of Religion at Oulu University in Finland.

Dutton has written many articles on genealogy and history for the magazine *Family Tree* as well as for *Cheshire History* and *History Today*. He is two generations removed from Cheshire.

His grandfather was born in Birkenhead in 1912 and attended the Kings School in Chester, before moving to the Midlands.

Dutton can be found online at edwarddutton.wordpress.com.

He also runs the genealogy service Dutton's Genealogy at duttonsgenealogy.wordpress.com

Contents

List of Illustrations   viii

Acknowledgements   ix

Map of Cheshire   x

Prologue   1

Chapter One: England in 1536   3

Chapter Two: The Rank Society   16

Chapter Three: Family, Youth, and Prison   24

Chapter Four: The Riotous Mayor   40

Chapter Five: Criminal and Courtier   48

Chapter Six: The Disputed Legacy   59

Chapter Seven: High Sheriff of Cheshire   69

Chapter Eight: Dutton Hall and Her Minstrels   88

Chapter Nine: The Deathbed Confession   101

Chapter Ten: Dutton's Papist Heirs   107

Appendix   114

Notes   127

Bibliography   161

Index   179

List of illustrations

1. Coat of Arms of the Duttons of Dutton. Tomb in St Peter's Church, Waverton (Courtesy of Peter Williams of Waverton).
2. Tomb of Sir Randolph Brereton and Eleanor Brereton at St. Oswald's Church, Malpas (Courtesy of Craig Thornber, www.thornber.net).
3. St Werburgh's Abbey (now Chester Cathedral). (Wikipedia).
4. Agricola Tower, Chester Castle (Wikipedia).
5. Lawrence Dutton of Dutton. Part of a picture of a stained glass window in Great Budworth church, drawn in 1568 by Randolph Holme. The window included a Latin statement indicating that the male figure was Lawrence Dutton and it had been made in 1526. (*Memorials of the Duttons of Dutton*, Ch. 4).
6. Sir John Savage (1493-1528). Tomb at Macclesfield Church. (Courtesy of Craig Thornber, www.thornber.net).
7. Letter from Dutton to Cromwell in 1535 *(Memorials of the Duttons of Dutton)*.
8. Sir Thomas Audley, Lord Chancellor. Painted in 1804, based on a contemporary print (Wikipedia).
9. Dutton Hall entrance porch, part of an architectural drawing by Maurice B Adams *(The Building News, October 8, 1886;* courtesy of Mr John Chesworth).
10. Coat of Arms at Dutton Hall *(Memorials of the Duttons of Dutton)*.
11. Dutton Hall in 1899 *(Memorials of the Duttons of Dutton)*.
12. Sketch of the roundel depicting Sir Piers Dutton (Copyright: Edward Dutton).
13. Print of a portrait, supposedly of Sir Piers Dutton (J. H. Hanshall's *The History of the County Palatine of Chester)*.

Acknowledgements

I BECAME interested in Sir Piers Dutton, who is my 11 x great-grandfather, while tracing my broader family tree. I would not have been able to do this without the help of Miss Anne Lawton, Mr. Jeff Wood, the Church of Jesus Christ of Latter Day Saints, and my uncle, the late Mr. John Dutton, so I would like to thank them. A synopsis of this book has been published as 'Sir Piers Dutton of Dutton and Hatton, ca. 1480-1545: Mayor of Chester, High Sheriff of Cheshire and Knight of the Body of Henry VIII' in *Cheshire History*, No. 55 (2015-2016). I would like to thank the editor - Dr. Graeme White of the University of Chester - and the anonymous peer-reviewer for their comments on the article. Parts of Chapter Ten originally appeared in 2014 in the article 'Recusants' in the magazine *Family Tree* and I would like to thank the editor for allowing me to reuse these.

I would also like to thank Mr. Gregor Forbes, of the Aberdeen Avant-garde Association, for digging out an obscure book for me, Mr. Robert Steele (Church historian of Great Budworth), Mr. Tom Hughes of Norton Priory Museum, Mr. Craig Thornber (www.thornber.net), the Boydell Press for sending me on old review copy of *Cheshire and the Tudor State*, Dr. Steven Gunn of Merton College, Oxford; Dr. Robert Tittler of Concordia University, Mr. Ian Morris, Mr John Chesworth and, last but not least, Mrs. Anne Loader, who saw the publication potential in this book, and her husband, Dr. Jack Loader, both of Léonie Press.

Map of Cheshire

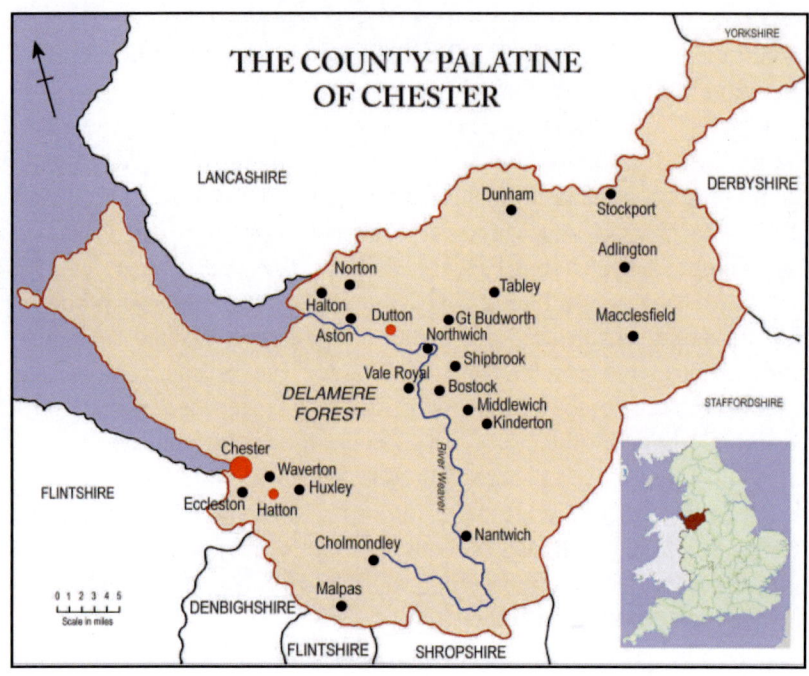

Main map based on those of Cheshire by Christopher Saxon (1540 – c.1610) and Robert Morden (1650-1703). Inset map of former counties of England based on Wikipedia Commons.

Prologue

IN 1519, a farmer called William Bostock, of Huxley in Cheshire, complained to the Court of Star Chamber that his land had been invaded by an armed gang, his produce stolen, and his livestock killed. As a consequence, he had fallen into poverty and he was so frightened that he was seriously contemplating fleeing the county.

In 1535, Randle Brereton, Cheshire's deputy Chamberlain, found himself under arrest for passing on fake coins, a crime which was treason. Despite being completely innocent, he realised that there was a realistic threat of him being hanged, and he made his will accordingly.

In 1540, Thomas Long was standing by a church in Clerkenwell when somebody attacked him with a long-sword and almost cut his hand off. His assailant then came at him with a dagger. Long would have been stabbed to death if it hadn't been for the quick thinking of a passerby.

Bostock, Brereton and Long had one thing in common: they had got on the wrong side of Sir Piers Dutton. Where the history books comment on Dutton at all, he is remembered for putting down a rebellion against the dissolution of Norton Abbey when he was High Sheriff of Cheshire, winning a protracted court case in which his inheritance was contested, and building Dutton Hall. Histories of Cheshire provide slightly more depth, examining the power politics pursued by Sir Piers Dutton. They imply that he was a complex, even unscrupulous, character who used violence, intimidation and even murder, to become the ruler of the semi-autonomous 'Palatine' of Early Tudor Cheshire.

As such, it is surprising that nobody has yet pieced together Dutton's entire life. In *The Ruler of Cheshire*, I present the first ever detailed biography of Sir Piers Dutton.[1] For general historians, this is the first full biography of a figure from Henry VIII's reign who held significant local (but not national) power, from a time when life was far more local than now. It is also a contribution, more broadly, to 'gentry studies'. For local historians and genealogists with connections to Cheshire, I aim to provide in-depth analysis of one of the county's most significant sixteenth century figures.

Quotations from original sources have been changed to modern spelling and years altered so that they begin on 1st January, unless stated otherwise. Surnames have also been changed to modern spelling where there is a clear modern version of the surname.

Appendix One is the surviving letters to and from Sir Piers Dutton, included such that this is a fully comprehensive examination of him.

Edward Dutton
15th June 2015
Oulu, Finland

Chapter One
England in 1536

*'Ye shall not enter this our Pilgrimage of Grace for the
common wealth, but only for the love ye bear to God's
faith and church ... '[2]*

1536 WAS A tumultuous year in England.[3] Having broken with Rome
in 1533 over the divorce of Catherine of Aragon, Henry VIII and his
ministers began the dissolution of the Monasteries. Commissioners
were sent to value the ancient institutions, some of them Pre-Conquest
in origin, so that they could be shut down, their wealth appropriated by
Henry VIII, their works taken over by the state, and their assets sold
off. It's difficult to understand now just how central religious houses
were to the lives of people in England up until 1536. There were 900
monasteries, friaries, priories and nunneries operating in England in
that year, with about 12,000 members. This meant that about 1 in
50 English men were members of religious orders.[4] Virtually every
sizeable town had at least one monastery or convent while the smaller
settlements homed the priories and abbeys. People genuinely believed
in Purgatory, feared the millions of years that might be spent there to
pay for their mortal sins, and accepted that prayer and masses said for
them could reduce their divine sentence. As such, they were at least
grudgingly happy to fund an army of (in theory) holy men and women
to spend all of their time at prayer, so reducing the years of agony prior
to the Day of Judgment for everybody else.[5]

Wealthy patrons might pay for a 'chantry' – a specific group of
monks and their successors – to spend all their time praying for the
souls of them and their family,[6] agricultural labourers did a certain
number of unpaid days of work per year on monastic lands,[7] and

townsfolk gave donations to mendicant friars who wandered about preaching and providing religious services.[8] And it wasn't just a reduction in Purgatorial pain that the laypeople received in return for their outlay. Almost all of the hospitals were run by monks,[9] monks and nuns gave donations to the needy,[10] and, in some cases, even offered free education to local children.[11] Of course, these holy men raped, murdered, stole, and didn't exactly pursue Godly poverty.[12] Even so, the religious houses were central to English life and, in 1536, these institutions began to be dismantled.

But there was far more to 1536 than the dissolution of the monasteries. Much of Henry VIII's reign saw government policy swinging back and forth from pro-Catholic, to pro-Protestant, to pro-Catholic again, as different court factions vied to influence him.[13] In 1536, the Protestant faction was in the ascendant. It was the year in which a particular Protestant dogma was officially accepted in England. For Catholics, salvation was by the Penitential Cycle. You lived your worldly and sinful life but regularly confessed your sins to the priest. He then forgave you (perhaps on condition of some kind of penance), you were in a 'state of grace' and then the process began all over again.[14] This was important because those who died 'un-shriven' (not having recently confessed their sins) would spend more time in Purgatory. However, the 'Ten Articles' of 1536 stressed that you could also be saved by 'faith alone', a radical idea, which implied that you did not need the Confession at all.[15] Even so, more pronounced Protestantism was still heresy in England and in October 1536 Bible-translator William Tyndale (1494-1536), who left England for Protestant Northern Germany in 1524, was strangled at the stake and burnt at Antwerp.[16] 1536 was the year in which the 'See of Rome Act' was passed. Chancellor Sir Thomas More (1478-1535) and Bishop of Rochester John Fisher (1469-1535)[17] had both been executed the previous year for refusing to accept that Henry VIII was 'head of the Church in England'.[18] The 'See of Rome Act' went even further than demanding the assent of senior politicians and ecclesiastics. Anybody who wanted to join a religious order, study for a degree, or hold any religious or secular office had to take an oath stating that they accepted the spiritual authority of the crown and rejected that of Rome. And refusing to take the oath was high treason until 1547.[19] The Pope had formerly wielded such authority over English life that hundreds of English knights, and even its king, fought to regain the Holy Land on his command.[20] Now it was a capital crime to suggest he had any authority in England at all.

In January 1536, Henry VIII's former queen, Catherine of Aragon (1485-1536), died. Her passing provoked an outpouring of grief for the Spanish princess, showing just how unpopular many of the government's policies were.[21] And in the same month, her replacement as queen, Anne Boleyn (c.1501-1536), had yet another miscarriage, further conforming that she was unlikely to be able to produce the healthy son and heir which Henry VIII[22] was so desperate for. This failure was an acute problem because it could be argued that Anne Boleyn was the catalyst behind the English Reformation. Henry VIII was in love with her, but wily Anne was not prepared to simply be the king's mistress. Spellbound by the French-educated beauty, this compelled Henry VIII to divorce his by-now barren wife in favour of Anne. She was deeply unpopular with the people, suspected of being a Protestant, and was a critical and violent-tempered woman.[23] When Henry's new favourite, Jane Seymour (c. 1508-1537), Anne's servant, began opening and shutting a locket which Henry had given her containing his picture in front of Anne, she ripped it off Jane with such force that Anne's fingers bled.[24] Henry VIII soon tired of his new queen, eventually declaring that he had been 'bewitched' by her.[25] She had to be replaced with a wife who could produce a healthy son, a role which Jane Seymour[26] fulfilled. Accordingly, in a scheme engineered by the king's chief minister, Thomas Cromwell (c.1485-1540), that would also rid him of troublesome political enemies, Anne Boleyn was executed for adultery in May 1536, as were five men found guilty of having had sexual relations with her.

The Pilgrimage of Grace

1536 also saw a violent reaction against Henry's religious revolution, especially in the more conservative northlands. In October 1536, a serious rebellion began in Lincolnshire, vociferously protesting against the break with the Roman Catholic Church and the dissolution of the monasteries. The rising was sparked on 2nd October after the closure of Louth Park Abbey and by 14th October, the number of rioters had swelled enormously. They marched on Lincoln and even occupied its cathedral, though the uprising was eventually quelled and its leaders, including the vicar of Louth, were executed. On 13th October another rebellion broke out, this time in Yorkshire. Infuriated by the treatment of Catherine of Aragon, concerned by what had happened to Anne Boleyn, and resentful of the power of the low-born Thomas Cromwell and the Tudor monarchy's increasing centralization of power away from local magnates, a number of Yorkshire gentry, such as Robert Aske (1500-1537), led the so-called Pilgrimage of Grace.[27] For ordinary supporters, this was far less ideological. They were motivated by anger at the enclosure of common land[28] (when there had been a poor harvest in 1535),[29] fury (in the case of some landowners) over the 1535 Statute of Uses' closing of a legal loophole which allowed them to avoid certain taxes,[30] and opposition to any religious reform. The closing of the lesser monasteries highlighted the spread of central government power into the provinces,[31] the threat of further enclosure,[32] and a threat to traditional religion.[33] In addition, many would have been forced to join the rebellion by their feudal masters.

Nine thousand people marched on York, forced the king's new tenants out of the confiscated religious houses they had been rented and arranged for the expelled monks and nuns to be returned. By the time the Duke of Norfolk, Thomas Howard (1473-1554), arrived at Doncaster to fight the insurgents there were about 40,000 of them. In that the English population was only three million, this represented 1.3% of all Anglo-Saxons. The rebellion was too strong to simply be crushed. Fearing a bloodbath, the government's representatives had to deceitfully negotiate. Norfolk promised the pilgrims a pardon, the restoration of the abbeys, and a parliament, to be held in York, if they dispersed, which they did. Then, when a smaller rising, Bigod's rebellion, broke out in Westmorland in February 1537, Norfolk mobilized huge force against it and executed 216 people, displaying their body parts around the country.

Meanwhile, Aske met with the king in London, and was promised action against the pilgrims' grievances and safe passage back to Yorkshire. But as Aske was leaving London, Bigod's rebellion[34] – which was not authorised by Aske – broke out and the king used this as an excuse to arrest Aske and the other pilgrim leaders for treason.[35] Robert Aske was executed by being hanged in chains until he died and his body rotted.[36]

Sir Piers Dutton in 1536

1536 was an earthquake of a year for England. But it was a dramatic year in Cheshire as well; the finest hour of the county's High Sheriff, Sir Piers Dutton of Dutton and Hatton. A small, inter-marrying group of clans – including the Breretons and Duttons – had long battled for control of Cheshire, competing to exploit its wealth, control its land, and keep its lucrative public offices within their families, as they had been since the Norman Conquest.[37] Events in 1536 ensured that, for a time, Dutton was effectively ruler of Cheshire. By 1535, it was clear that Henry VIII so trusted that Dutton would be his enforcer (in a county which, as we will see, was semi-autonomous) that he rejected the three candidates shown to him to replace Dutton as High Sheriff and wrote in Dutton's name himself.[38] Until the 1540s, when some of the functions of the sheriff were taken over by the newly created county 'Lord Lieutenants',[39] the Sheriff was the king's representative in a county, responsible for keeping the peace, enforcing the law and empanelling juries.[40] Dutton was reappointed High Sheriff in 1536 and, crucially, William Brereton (c.1500-1536), Dutton's nephew and rival for supreme political power in the county, was beheaded in May 1536 for carnal relations with Anne Boleyn. In October 1536, Dutton wrote to the Lord Chancellor claiming that he had quelled a rebellion at Norton Abbey in which 200 rioters had threatened the lives of two of the king's commissioners. He was thanked for his swift actions by both Thomas Cromwell and Henry VIII. And in the same year, Dutton's disputed, and enormous, inheritance was confirmed by Act of Parliament.

In some ways, Sir Piers Dutton and Thomas Cromwell were similar characters. Both men ascended the Tudor social hierarchy. Cromwell was the son of a Putney blacksmith who had been 'a ruffian in his young days'.[41] Becoming a successful merchant and barrister, he rose to be a Member of Parliament and, ultimately, the king's chief minister. Clearly, Dutton's rise was far less dramatic. He was born into the gentry, though not into its very richest ranks.[42] As a young man, Piers Dutton had even spent time in jail before becoming Mayor of Chester and then, after inheriting a hugely valuable estate from a distant relative, High Sheriff of the county. Both men were corrupt, having their opponents killed and innocent people unfairly punished if it meant they could better line their coffers and augment their status. Cromwell and Dutton possessed considerable wealth, with Dutton displaying this with his ostentatious rebuilding of the Medieval Dutton Hall between 1539 and 1542. The two politicians were seemingly Protestant, in an age in which complete Protestantism remained heresy in England.[43] Cromwell vied with other ministers to rule England while Dutton feuded with other local magnates to become, at various points, the effective ruler of Cheshire. And both men fell from power. Cromwell's enemies conspired to have him beheaded for treason in July 1540, in the wake of his disastrous arranged marriage between Henry VIII and Anne of Cleves (1515-1557).[44] Dutton's corruption meant he was not re-appointed Sheriff in late 1537, although, unlike Cromwell, he was able to rise back to power again.

Sir Piers Dutton's Significance

The life of Thomas Cromwell is well documented in numerous biographies[45] and even the popular novel and television series *Wolf Hall*.[46] The lives of other famous Early Tudor courtiers, such as Sir Thomas More,[47] Cardinal Thomas Wolsey,[48] Thomas Cranmer,[49] Thomas Howard, Duke of Norfolk[50] and Charles Brandon, Duke of Suffolk[51] have also received book-length treatment.[52] At the other extreme, the discipline in Early Modern History known as 'gentry studies' has produced two book-length biographies of obscure members of the early Tudor or late Medieval gentry, which are useful as works of social history because they document what life was like for everyday members of the lower ranks of the English aristocracy

8

during a dramatic period in the country's history. The first of these biographical subjects is Humphrey Newton of Pownall, near Wilmslow in Cheshire (1466-1536).[53] The author justifies Newton's biography by virtue of the large amount of records relating to this very 'ordinary' gentleman despite the fact that he never held any public office.[54] The second is John Hopton (1430-1478), a Suffolk gentleman who was briefly county sheriff, and so of slightly greater significance than Newton.[55]

The lives of the nationally important and ordinary gentry of Early Tudor England have, thus, been presented in depth. But, what about those who were in the middle of these two extremes, those who were very powerful at a regional level? This biography will be the first book-length examination of such a figure from Early Tudor England. In Tudor England, political power and life in general were extremely localized, meaning it seems odd that an in-depth biography has not been written of such a figure until now.[56] Most people didn't travel more than about eight miles from their place of birth.[57] In this context of localism, Dutton was extremely powerful and influential in five key ways. Firstly, he controlled a significant retinue (a kind of gang) with which he could enforce his will. Secondly, Cheshire was semi-autonomous, meaning that the ruler of Cheshire was more powerful than the leading magnate in most other counties. Thirdly, he was extremely wealthy and had court connections. Fourthly, his family were extremely ancient. And, fifthly, he effectively introduced Protestantism to Cheshire.

Let us begin with Dutton's power as a gang leader. Key to Dutton's power was the feudal system combined with the way in which England was not yet a state in the modern sense. The London government had only very limited control over the provinces. Especially in the North, they relied on local magnates, such as Dutton, to keep order and these magnates would vie with other magnates to increase their sphere of influence. Thus, parts of northern England, and especially Cheshire, were effectively under gang rule.[58] The feudal system had fallen apart after the Black Death in the mid-fourteenth century. Under this system, all land was owned by the king. Portions of it were held from him by 'tenants in chief' ('barons') in return for providing the king with an army of knights. These barons attended the Royal Court. 'Mesne tenants', known as Lords of the Manor, held their land from barons and did knightly service in the barons' own private armies in return for land and protection. They attended the baron's 'court', where grievances could be aired and networking pursued. Smaller scale farmers held their land from the Lords of Manor (who held a Manorial Court) and constituted a private army, or an armed gang, for their manorial lord. Beneath these were the serfs, who were attached to the lord's land and were not free to leave it.[59]

But, despite the collapse (for reasons we will explore shortly) of the feudal system, a form of 'bastard feudalism' developed whereby the local magnate would protect a farmer from disorder in return for that farmer fighting for him in one of his power struggles with another magnate or paying him protection money.[60] Law courts aside, there were two kinds of 'court' in Early Tudor England. Firstly, there were the formal feudal courts, as feudal ownership still operated even though more and more people had freehold land and serfdom had been abolished. Secondly, there were 'courts' or, as they were known, 'retinues' surrounding individuals. The higher layers of Tudor society involved paid retainers. Those whom the king favoured would become part of the royal court (and they would be banished from court if they fell into disfavour). Given some official position at court, they would be granted an annuity in return for which they had to serve their monarch in whatever way he saw fit.[61] Not all peers of the realm or even crown office holders were courtiers. Courtiers were the favoured few. In much the same way, the nobility would maintain a retinue composed of groupies whom they paid to do things for them. And powerful gentry, likewise, would employ groups of retainers.[62] Influential figures would use their retinue to pursue disputes over land ownership, rent or inheritance. They would use them to organize riots, land occupations, theft from occupied lands, and even murders, especially of their enemies' retainers. Retinues were employed to ensure biased juries or nobble unbiased ones when their leaders found themselves in court. And, in addition, lords would intervene to help members of their retinue in their own disputes. Retinues corrupted Medieval England.[63] As part of a broader policy of centralizing power and disempowering provincial magnates, Henry VII[64] attempted to curb retinues.[65] He outlawed livery (retainers wearing uniforms advertising their lord's coat of arms),[66] maintenance (perverting judicial proceedings on a retainer's behalf), and he made nobles and gentry pay sureties for their retainers and obtain a license for them.[67] However, he did not outlaw retaining itself, meaning that Early Tudor England, and especially Cheshire, where the crown's authority was particularly weak, was, in some respects, a kind of gangland.

In this sense, at the height of his power, Sir Piers Dutton was effectively the ruler of a county living in which would have felt a little like living in separate country today. And not only was he the High Sheriff, but he had the hereditary right to license all of the minstrels of Cheshire, a right confirmed by Act of Parliament in 1499[68] which meant that he retained them as well. This right had supposedly been granted to the Lord of the Manor of Dutton in the thirteenth century by the Constable of Cheshire who had, himself, been granted it by the Earl of Chester for leading an army of minstrels, thus repelling the Welsh who were besieging the Earl.[69] By Sir Piers Dutton's time the minstrels were responsible for producing ballads, often about political events and important news. Even the lower ranks of the Cheshire gentry, such as Humphrey Newton, paid to have minstrels perform in their homes to entertain their guests.[70] Minstrels were, in many ways, both the journalists and pop stars of their day[71] and, within Cheshire, they were controlled by Dutton.

Controlling the minstrels also provided Dutton with an important piece of symbolic power. In addition to feeling like a separate country, there is an extent to which, in 1536, Cheshire was one. Along with Durham and Lancashire, Cheshire was a 'County Palatinate', established as such around the 1200s because it sat on the hostile borders of crown authority. These three counties were semi-autonomous within the wider English state. They were ruled directly by a nobleman rather than by the king, and the nobleman, not the king, was their head of state.[72] In the case of Cheshire, the hereditary ruler was the Earl of Chester, a title which was first bestowed on Hugh Lupus by William the Conqueror but which was in the hands of the Prince of Wales by 1301.[73] The people of Cheshire felt themselves to be distinct from the English. Cheshire even had its own myths, relating to its origins and traditions. William the Conqueror had placed a belt, with a sword, around the waist of Hugh Lupus to symbolize the transfer of power over the Palatinate to him. This very sword held pride of place in Chester Castle, the seat of Cheshire.[74] The idea that the minstrels would protect Cheshire from the marauding Welsh armies was also burnt deep into the Palatine's collective psyche. Accordingly, Cheshire's minstrels were a symbol of her independence and the Dutton family played a central part in this, by licensing the minstrels in an annual ceremony in Chester, a piece of drama that asserted Cheshire's independence, reaching back into local mythology. Hugh Lupus had, so it was said, appointed eight barons to depute for him. Their descendants were regarded as lords within Cheshire, they held sway over specific areas of the county, and as late as 1597 Hugh Swinger was executed for murder on the orders of one of the courts which answered to one of the barons who, by hereditary right, deputed for the Earl of Chester (by then the monarch).[75] These baronies, like manorial lordships, sometimes passed through the female line in the case of there being no male heir. By the early sixteenth century they were: Halton (which by the Tudor period was part of the Duchy of Lancaster and thus held by the crown), Montalt or Harwarden (reverted to the crown), Nantwich (Fouleshurst family), Shipbrook (Vernon family), Malpas (Brereton family), Dunham (Massie family), Kinderton (Venables family) and Stockport (Warren family). The Duttons had married into most of these families.

In early Tudor England, Cheshire retained its own parliament. This was composed of the eight (or by the fourteenth century, six) Cheshire barons and assorted palatinate officers. They were responsible for collecting semi-regular 'mises' (grants of money to the crown) and upholding the privileges of Palatine. In 1450, Henry VI had accepted most of a petition by Cheshire's representatives demanding that its autonomy be respected. Cheshire was not to pay direct taxation to the crown and its people could only be made to attend the London courts in extreme circumstances, though Cheshire's leaders had argued that they should never have to.[76] Cheshire paid no direct taxation until 1534, doing-so then as a one-off for reasons that remain obscure because the records do not survive.[77] Cheshire was not represented at Westminster until 1543 either by Knights of the Shire or by Peers of the Realm. There were no Cheshire peerages other than Chester and for much of the early sixteenth century the peers whose families had historical or land connections to Cheshire – the Earls of Derby (Stanley family), the Dudley family, and the barons Audley – were either attainted, not of full-age or suffering from financial problems.[78]

The appointments of Cheshire's officers were unfettered by restrictions that applied elsewhere, meaning they could be 'for life' or 'during pleasure', rather than annual. Although Cheshire's legal officers were appointed by the crown (as Earl of Chester) its courts, though they ultimately administered English Law, were more powerful than those in other counties. The palatine's semi-autonomy meant that it could jail and execute people on the authority of its barons and their officers, deputing for the Earl of Chester, and thus without recourse to the crown.[79] In addition to a High Sheriff, the county also had its own Chamberlain. He was primarily responsible for Cheshire's finances but he also presided over the Exchequer. This was Cheshire's court of equity; its highest court. In addition, Cheshire had its own Chief Justice, who dispensed justice in the name of the Earl of Chester.[80] Both of these officers had powerful deputies. Cheshire's County Court met about nine times each year and grand juries of gentlemen would decide which cases would go to the Assizes.[81]

Accordingly, when he was Sheriff, Sir Piers Dutton was, in some ways, akin to one of the leaders of a client state, evidencing the extent of his power. And he used this power to remove, and even execute, those who caused him problems. As we will see, Dutton was not the only person in Cheshire who abused the power of the palatine, so he reflects, again, a broader historical pattern. Dutton reached his position, rather like his enemy and nephew William Brereton,[82] by combining a local powerbase with a position at court, so he reflects a wider trend in this way as well. The semi-autonomous county of Cheshire reached into a broader region known as the Marches which was composed of the border areas of Wales. The Cheshire Palatinate, for example, controlled Flintshire, on the other side of the border. A Council of the Marches had a kind of authority over the Marches, including over parts of Cheshire, such as the city of Chester. This council was composed of the holders of certain offices, such as the Chamberlain of Cheshire.[83] Dutton, as we will see, came into conflict with the leader of this council.

In addition to this power, the Dutton family, and eventually Sir Piers Dutton, was extremely wealthy. The Manor of Dutton, which Piers Dutton inherited in 1528 and which was confirmed upon him by Act of Parliament in 1536 after a literally violent legal battle that gained national attention, was, at that time, the largest estate in the country.[84] Having inherited it, Dutton became the largest land owner in Cheshire. The family were also one of the richest in Cheshire. Between 1539 and 1542, Dutton lavishly rebuilt Dutton Hall, leading to it being described as 'the finest Tudor mansion in the north west of England',[85] although, in 1933, it was moved piece by piece to East Grinstead in Sussex by the eccentric whisky magnate John Dewar, 2nd Baron Forteviot (1885-1947).[86] The Hall's name was changed to 'Dutton Homestall' and from about 1945 until 2009 it was a prep school called Stoke Brunswick School. It was on sale, along with 17.9 acres of grounds, for £4.5 million in 2010.[87]

The family of which Dutton was head was also extremely ancient. In a period in which a very significant aspect of social status was your family history in the male line – this being the difference between being 'patrician' or 'plebeian' and even affecting how long you had to study at university and what clothes you could wear[88] – Sir Piers Dutton's family were one of only five of the important Cheshire families who could trace their line back to the Conquest, specifically to Odard, 1st Lord of the Manor of Dutton. Indeed, according to some sources, Odard's ancestry could be traced back to at least the ninth century.[89] The Tudors couldn't even come close to matching this. Their family records stop at Ednyfed Fychan (c.1170-1246), seneschal to Llywelyn the Great, King of Gwynedd in North Wales.[90] Even Queen Elizabeth II's male line stops with Theodoric of Wettin in the 10th century.[91] Sir Piers Dutton only inherited his wealth from an extremely distant relative in this, even by that time, ancient family. This story, and Dutton's life in general (including his political disputes), fascinated people at the time.[92] Where modern celebrities are written about in the newspapers, Dutton's exploits were sung about in the ballads of the minstrels: '*Piers Dutton* is up/ And young *Brereton* is nigh/ And *Ffytton* is over ye river/ From *Gawsworth* to *Vernon*/ One and all!' is the cry/ And 'the king and old *Mynshull* for ever![93]

Dutton was also influential on religion in Cheshire. In effect, he sowed the seeds of Protestantism in Cheshire by putting down a pro-Catholic rebellion and arresting those who criticized the new Anglican orthodoxy. His zeal in so-doing has led at least one historian of Cheshire, Tim Thornton, to conclude, in his book *Cheshire and the Tudor State*, that Sir Piers Dutton was probably a Protestant. As such, Protestantism had arrived in Cheshire earlier than originally thought, not in the reign of Edward VI (1537-1553, r. 1547-1553) but in that of Henry VIII (r. 1509-1547).[94] And, as we will see, there is a large body of circumstantial evidence for the conclusion that Dutton was a Protestant; one of the first in Cheshire.

But before examining Dutton's life it would be useful to understand the 'rank system' around which Tudor social life was significantly constructed. Sir Piers Dutton was a member of the 'gentry', born into this class, while Thomas Cromwell had to work his way up into it. But, what was the nature of the Tudor social hierarchy?

Chapter Two
The Rank Society

'Where I believe it reasonable to state
Something about these pilgrims, to relate
Their circumstances as they seemed to me,
Just who they were and each of what degree.'[95]

THE CONCEPT of social class is a mixture of educational, occupational, and financial position combined with one's background.[96] The Tudor social system was slightly more clear-cut in that it was essentially based around money. Everybody had a rank (a 'degree'); just as everybody has an educational rank (their highest qualification) today, though there was still ambiguity on the rank borders. Tudor England was a 'rank society',[97] as was Chaucer's England around 100 years earlier. But Tudor England involved even more ranks that did Chaucer's England and terminology for them had changed.

In the General Prologue of the *Canterbury Tales*, Chaucer describes his pilgrims in approximate rank order: Knight (an aristocratic mounted warrior), esquire (his son, an aspirant knight) and yeoman (their non-aristocratic foot soldier). Eventually, after looking at the ecclesiastical characters and a law officer, he turns to the Franklin. Chaucer's Franklin was a very wealthy man who had been a sheriff and a Knight of the Shire (Member of Parliament). This is rather confusing because a Franklin, by definition, would not have been knighted and there was never a Franklin who was a Knight of the Shire.[98] A more realistic Franklin would have been akin to a Tudor 'yeoman farmer' or possibly non-armigerous gentleman: a wealthy though not aristocratic farmer. We then meet a series of merchants and craftsmen, before we reach the boorish and drunken Ploughman. By the Tudor period, the 'ploughman' would be the 'husbandman', still relatively wealthy but one who takes to the plough himself and lacks the refinement of the average yeoman. So, in *Canterbury Tales* we see a rough, though less graded, approximation of the Tudor rank system. The key difference is that by the Tudor period knight, esquire, and yeoman were essentially social ranks, substantially divorced from military service or fee in lieu thereof. Those at the very top and bottom of late Medieval Society are not represented in *Canterbury Tales* at all.

Who were the Tudor Gentry?

At the top of the Tudor hierarchy was the king. Beneath him was the peerage, the heads of the great noble families who held peerages. With this rank came certain privileges, including the right to sit in the House of Lords and legislate. In 1485, there were 41 peers.

Below the peers of the realm were the so-called 'gentry'. There were two kinds of gentry, those who had the right to use coat armour ('armigerous' or 'county' gentry) and those who did not (non-armigerous or 'parish' gentry).[99] The armigerous gentry were: (1) All legitimate male line descendants (other than the eldest line) of peers of the realm (2) Knights and all of their legitimate, male line descendants and (3) Anyone simply granted coat armour by the heralds, and all of their legitimate male-line descendants. Possession of coat armour was an important status symbol. Armigers would adorn their houses, carriages, and graves with their coats of arms, because it proved they were 'genteel'.[100] Privileges of 'gentility' included the right to settle disputes by duel, the right to wear foreign furs, the right to wear silk shirts, the right to graduate from university in three rather than four years,[101] and, in 1543, the right to own a Bible written in English.[102]

However, the most closely guarded privilege was the use of coat armour. Some people would play for status by using coat armour to which they were not entitled. Shakespeare-era actor Thomas Pope (d.1603) simply purchased a painting of the arms of one Sir Thomas Pope, who was not a relative, and passed them off as his own.[103] The College of Arms had therefore been established in 1484 to regulate the use of coat armour.[104] In so called Visitations, the heralds from this college would periodically descend upon counties and demand that the gentlemen in the county, and anyone found to be displaying coat armour, attend a public meeting in which their right to use heraldic ensigns would be verified with reference to their pedigrees. And they would have to pay a great deal of money for this service. Anybody whose pedigree was not up to scratch could be 'disclaimed' as *'ignobilis'* (non-noble).[105] However, the Visitations were notoriously poorly organized and corrupt, meaning that heralds would accept fake pedigrees from wealthy aspirants in return for bribes and give anybody a coat of arms if they paid them enough money.[106] Elizabeth I's one-time Secretary of State Sir Thomas Smith (1513-1577)[107] cuttingly summarized that:

> 'Ordinarily the king doth only make knights and create barons or higher degrees: for as for gentlemen, they be made good cheap in England. For whosoever studieth the laws of the realm, who studieth in the universities, who professeth liberal sciences, and to be short, who can live idly and without manual labour, and will bear the port, charge and countenance of a gentleman, he shall be called master. And (if need be) a king of heralds shall also give him for money arms, newly made and invented, the title whereof shall pretend to have been found by the said herald in perusing and viewing of old registers, where his ancestors in times past had been recorded to bear the same.'[108]

Though the word 'noble' is usually reserved in modern England for peers of the realm, Tudors divided between the 'higher' or 'titled' nobility (the peerage) and the 'lower nobility' (the gentry). Herald William Camden (1551-1623), Clarenceux King of Arms, asserted, 'The lesser noblemen are the knights, esquires and those whom we commonly call gentlemen.'[109] Due to the corruption of the 'gentleman' and 'esquire' categories, European nobles – most of whom have a male-line ancestor who was granted noble status by Letters Patent from the monarch – have often been reluctant to accept that the English 'gentry' are 'untitled nobility' and thus 'noble'. This was especially complained about in the early nineteenth century when European nobles still maintained privileges and English 'gentry' expatriates on the Continent, therefore, wanted 'noble' recognition.[110]

The distinction between 'noble', 'gentle' and 'plebeian' has only really existed since the 15th century. Under the feudal system, there was a distinction between the 'tenant in chief' ('the baron') who held his land directly from the king and the 'mesne tenant' (the Lord of the Manor) who held his land from the tenant in chief. The tenants in chief became the peers of the realm and the mesne tenants became the knights and thus members of the House of Commons (where members were 'Knights of the Shire').[111] The Black Death, in killing about 40% of the English population, led to huge social change and the collapse of feudalism. There was such a shortage of labour (about 80% of serfs died)[112] that the remaining serfs, who had traditionally farmed the Lord of Manor's land unpaid in return for the right to their own small holding, were able to leave and go to a place where the Lord of the Manor understood that the labourers were now in demand and wanted to be paid.[113] This led to rapid social ascent – from serf to Justice of the Peace in one generation in one case – and, in the following century, a counter-reaction; a so-called 'Age of Deference'.[114] The barons distinguished themselves from the rest by asserting that they were 'noble' while the 'mesne tenant' knights were merely 'gentle'.[115] Knighthood was once solely a matter of wealth and fighting ability: in 1247 every able man who earned at least 40 shillings per annum from his land had to be knighted, meaning he was in the reserve cavalry.[116] After the Black Death, knighthood had lost much of its military significance and became a mark not just of wealth but of gentility. A rich armiger could be a knight but an even richer non-armiger could not be, as he was not 'gentle'.[117]

Within this category of armigerous gentry there was a further hierarchy. The highest rank was the knights, the knight being the first person described by Chaucer. In the Tudor period, as already indicated, a knighthood, though it could be a means of patronage like today, was really more of a compulsory status symbol. If you were armigerous and your income was over a certain level – at the time of Henry VIII this was £40 per year[118] – then you had to be knighted if a summons to become knighted was sent to you, or you had to pay a fine. As a knight, your social rank was higher but you were also encumbered with expensive obligations, including more unpaid public service[119] and even more 'bearing the port', meaning the obligation to live lavishly, fund good works and even entertain the monarch (on his regular 'Royal Progresses' around the country) at huge expense. Accordingly, many gentry increasingly regarded knighthood as an unfair imposition and did their best to avoid being dubbed and avoid paying the fine for avoidance. In some cases, they would even pretend that they were not armigerous at all.[120] Usually, the summons to be knighted would only occur at coronations or if the monarch was particularly hard up. Fines were poorly enforced, especially in Cheshire.[121] Otherwise, a person would be knighted if they were a favoured courtier and wanted to be knighted.

The rank below knight was 'esquire', the next person described by Chaucer. In Chaucer's time, an esquire was an aspiring knight but this had changed by the Tudor period. According to one time Lord Chief Justice Sir Edward Coke (1552-1634),[122] anybody who was armigerous but not a knight was an 'esquire'[123] while according to other sources an esquire is the descendant of a knight but only in the eldest male line, the younger line descendants being merely 'gentlemen'.[124] In reality, it appears that the richest non-knight armigerous gentry were referred to as 'esquires' while the less wealthy ones were 'gentlemen'[125] Beneath these, there were the 'gentlemen of paper and wax' who had been given coat armour by the heralds but lacked a noble family history.[126] Beneath these there were the non-armigerous gentry. These people were gentleman by acclamation. They had the lifestyle of the gentry, socialized with the gentry and, therefore, were regarded as such by the general population, whether they had coat armour or not. And if they'd lied about having coat armour then they could have their lies officially declared fact. As Penelope Corfield has summarized: '...although in Tudor and Stuart times the College of Arms toured the counties to adjudicate heraldic claims and to disgrade impostors, there were subtle and not-so-subtle pressures upon them to give recognition to plausible newcomers. These visitations were relatively infrequent – every 20 or 25 years – and imperfectly administered, which allowed ample leeway for social invention.'[127]

In addition, although, in theory, any armiger was a 'gentlemen', he would not necessarily be *accepted* as such. You would not be accepted as a gentleman if you did not have a gentlemanly lifestyle. In about 1620, Eusebius Andrewes, in prison in the Fleet for debt, insisted that he and his wife be treated as the gentry which they were. The warden responded by loading Andrewes with chains, placing him in a worse cell and confiscating his precious 21-generation pedigree.[128] Primogeniture in all land-owning classes meant that younger sons often descended socially, ending life at a lower rank than their father's.[129] In the diocese of Durham in the 1560s, 59% of the gentry could write their names on their wills.[130]

A Society of Social Descent

More generally, Tudor England was by necessity a society of social descent. Wealth strongly predicted how many of your children would reach adulthood. The fertility of the richer 50% of those who left wills in Essex in the early seventeenth century was 40% higher than that of the poorer 50%.[131] Accordingly, esquires' sons became gentlemen while gentlemen's sons became yeoman farmers and merchants. Yeomen were the next rank down. By 1500 this military dimension was lost and the word 'yeomen' referred to wealthy farmers who did not 'take to the plough' themselves but who were not as wealthy as gentlemen, earning less than about £20 per year during Henry VIII's reign.[132] Merchants were those apprenticed to city guilds who became freemen of the city. They were ranked the same as yeomen. In the 1560s in the diocese of Durham, 37% of yeomen could sign their wills.[133]

In addition, yeoman and merchants' sons became husbandmen, who did take to the plough, and craftsmen. Again, these two were ranked together and, in Durham in the 1560s, 16% of tradesmen and 6% of husbandmen could sign their wills.[134] Husbandmen's and craftsmen's sons became smallholders and smallholders' sons became shepherds and landless labourers,[135] of which only 5% could sign their wills.[136] The financial boundaries between these ranks were unclear, meaning that people would be 'husbandman' on one document but 'yeoman' on another.[137] To avoid mockery, 'gentlemen by blood' were best advised to go by their financial rank, and generally did so.

By the Tudor era, this distinction between 'gentry' and 'non-gentry' even extended to the clergy and it is illustrated by a rather confusing paradox in terms of clerical forms of address. As we will see, Sir Piers Dutton had a relative who was called 'Sir John Dutton, priest'. This did not mean that the priest had been knighted. The majority of priests were not graduates. Graduate priests were the elite in the Tudor era and would go on to the more senior positions, including vicar or rector.[138] 'Sir' was the Tudor form of address for non-graduate clerics[139] and reflected the old belief that the priest was of the same social rank as a knight.[140] Knights would, therefore, be distinguished from non-graduate clerics with the post-nominal 'Knight'. Graduate clerics were addressed as 'Master', just as gentlemen were in the Tudor era. Later, 'Mister' became the form of address for gentlemen, with 'Master' relegated to those of low social status and eventually simply to child males.[141] But, in the Tudor era, 'Master' was the form of address for gentlemen. As graduate priests were graduates, they were indeed 'gentlemen' and were addressed accordingly.

The letters of Thomas Cranmer, for example, reflect this clear difference in how clerics are addressed. Cranmer refers to 'Sir John Fleming, curate of St. Nicholas in Bristol'. However, the Dean of the Arches is 'Master Dean', the Chancellor of York is 'Master Doctor Downes', the 'Parson of Bingham' is 'Master Stapleton' and the 'Parson of St. Dunstan's' in London is 'Master Palgrave'.[142] In line with our discussion of the post-Black Death 'Age of Deference', it would seem that prior to the Black Death knighthood was conferred on all those with a certain income and clergy were regarded as having the same rank as knights and so took the title 'Sir'. By the late fifteenth century, there was a much clearer distinction between non-gentry and the gentry, the lower ranks of which used the title 'Master'. The younger sons of the nobility, and to a lesser extent of the gentry, would go to university, become priests and were distinguished from their (more likely plebeian and, anyway, non-graduate) colleagues by the form of address 'Master'. Thus, they were being associated, with this form of address, with the gentry, even though 'gentleman' is a lower rank than 'knight'. As graduates they were 'gentlemen', even if non-armigerous. When non-graduate clerics began to be addressed as 'Sir', likely before the establishment of universities, a knighthood would have had lower status than in the sixteenth century and would have been less clearly associated with the aristocracy. Thus, the usage of 'Sir' with regard to them was an anachronism which, ironically, demonstrated their lower status than priests who were 'Master'.

Sir Piers Dutton's 'rank' by birth was gentry. He is 'Master' in earlier documents and his grandfather, to whom he was heir, was an esquire who paid a fine to avoid being knighted.[143] But Piers Dutton's grandfather was nothing like as wealthy as his grandson became and he presumably paid the fine precisely in order to avoid the expense of being a knight. His grandson had no need to avoid this expense. Sir Piers Dutton moved upwards socio-economically at a time when only about 11% of people attained a higher rank than their father's[144] and most moved down.[145]

Chapter Three
Family, Youth, and Prison

*'Sir Piers Dutton is the only name in the Dutton
pedigree which requires particular attention.'* [146]

WE HAVE already met some of Sir Piers Dutton's ancestors. Odard,
1st Lord of the Manor of Dutton, was mentioned in the Domesday
Book of 1086 and there is some evidence that he and his brothers, who
also came to England, were distantly related to William the Conqueror.
Odard held the Manor of Dutton, in the parish of Great Budworth
which is four miles north of Northwich. He held a third of the village
of Dutton directly from the Earl of Chester (meaning he was a baron)
and the villages of Aston, Weston, Whitley and Halton from William
Fitz Nigel, Baron of Halton, a man who some sources claim was his
nephew. The Domesday Book entry can be seen below:

In noting Odard's own ancestry, it should be remembered that from
about the 1630s it began to be fashionable for the gentry to accept
fabricated pedigrees which went back not just to the Conquest but
even further, especially if their families had only emerged from
obscurity after the Black Death. [147] Odard is described as a 'cousin of
W. Conqueror' on a draft of the 1580 Cheshire Visitation, [148] but this
idea may not yet have developed during Sir Piers Dutton's time.

Hugh Fitz Odard de Dutton was one of the benefactors of Norton
Priory in 1115. [149] This was an Augustinian order of Canons Regular;

priests, living communally, who engaged in public liturgy and the ministry of sacraments.[150] Another Hugh (5th Lord of Dutton) was granted the right to license the Cheshire Minstrels in the early thirteenth century. Nineteenth century gentlemen found this quirky piece of history fascinating and discussions of it were published in various journals. Readers of the *New Monthly Magazine* in November 1818 may well have been enthralled by the article 'On the Peculiar Custom of Licensing the Minstrels of Cheshire'.[151]

Sir Thomas Dutton (1314-1381), 10th Lord of Dutton, was moderately noteworthy insomuch as he managed to combine a successful civic career with being a murderer and a rapist. According to the Cheshire antiquary Sir Peter Leycester (1614-1678), in about 1352:

> 'It seems *(Sir Thomas Dutton)* was indicted, for that he and others came with armed power, (when King Edward the Third, was out of England) within the verge of the lodging of Lionel the King's son, Protector of England and assaulted the Manor of Geaumes, nigh Reading in Wiltshire, and there slew Michael Poynings, the uncle, and Thomas Le Clerke of Shipton, and others, and committed a rape on Margery the wife of one Nicolas de la Beche.'

Luckily, Edward III (r. 1312-1377) pardoned Sir Thomas Dutton. Indeed, he made him responsible for 'apprehending of certain Malefactors, Robbers and Disturbers of the Peace in Cheshire)'.[152] Edward III was clearly impressed by the results because he appointed Dutton High Sheriff of Cheshire in 1357 and 1360 and knighted him in 1362. In 1379, Sir Thomas Dutton paid for a chantry in Warrington Priory so that monks could pray for his soul, and those of his descendants, forever.

Sir Thomas Dutton was Sir Piers Dutton's 4 x great-grandfather. With his 3 x great-grandfather, Edmund, the family split in two. Edmund's eldest son became Lord of Dutton, a line which died out in 1528, three generations later, with the death of Lawrence Dutton, 17th Lord of Dutton (c.1474-1528). Edmund's younger son (Sir Piers Dutton's great-great-grandfather) Hugh Dutton (c.1370-1440), who was Sheriff of Cheshire in 1422, became Lord of the Manor of Hatton in place of his heiress wife. Hatton is in the parish of Waverton, three miles south of Chester. Sir Piers Dutton became Lord of Hatton and Dutton as the closest male legitimate relative of Lawrence Dutton. Cheshire antiquary George Ormerod (1785-1873) bluntly asserts in his *History of Cheshire*, with reference to the entire family, that: 'Sir Piers Dutton is the only name in the Dutton pedigree which requires particular attention.'[153]

1. *Coat of Arms of the Duttons of Dutton. Tomb in St Peter's Church, Waverton (Courtesy of Peter Williams of Waverton).*

Family and Recent Ancestry

Piers Dutton was the son of Peter Dutton, Junior, of Hatton (c.1454-1503), the son of Peter Dutton, Senior, of Hatton (1432-1503), the son of John Dutton (c.1400-1464), the son of Hugh Dutton (c.1370-1440), already mentioned.

We know little of the early life of Piers Dutton. We cannot even be sure of the year of his birth. However, he was definitely of full-age (21 for males) by April 1503, when he legally inherited his lands upon the death of his grandfather, Peter Dutton of Hatton, Senior (1432-1503). Piers' grandfather was, according to those who knew the man, born in 1432,[154] and the average age for elder line gentry to father children in late Medieval England was about 22,[155] and, as we will see, Piers seemingly had two older sisters, so circa 1480 would appear to be a sound estimate of the year of Piers Dutton's birth. His life began towards the end of the bloody Wars of the Roses.

Between 1455 and Henry Tudor's victory at Bosworth Field in 1485, the Houses of York and Lancaster had battled for the throne. This complex dynastic conflict went all the way back to 1399 when Henry of Bolingbroke (Henry IV) (1367-1413) had seized the throne from his cousin Richard II (1367-1400) who was the grandson of Edward III. Bolingbroke's son, Henry V, died aged just 35 in 1422, leaving the throne to his baby son Henry VI (1421-1471). Richard of York (1411-1460) was a maternal line great-great-grandson of Edward III, via Edward's second son. Henry IV was descended via Edward's third son, arguably giving Richard a better claim to the crown. Richard of York became Henry VI's protector and, later, *de facto* ruler of England during the king's period of insanity in 1454. When Henry recovered, his powerful wife, Margaret of Anjou (1430-1482), forced Richard of York from court. York mustered his forces and so began the Wars of the Roses. A significant battle near the beginning of the wars was Blore Heath in Staffordshire on 23rd September 1459. It was a Yorkist triumph in which 2000 Lancastrians were slain, including Piers Dutton's relative Sir Thomas Dutton, Lord of the Manor of Dutton.[156] Eventually, the Yorkists reigned under Richard of York's son[157] Edward IV (1442-1483). His younger brother, Richard III, lost the throne to the Lancastrian claimant, Henry VII, in 1485.[158]

Piers Dutton's mother was Elizabeth Fouleshurst, daughter of Sir Robert Fouleshurst of Crewe (c.1418-c.1498), whose seat was Nantwich Castle, on the site of which now stands the Crown Inn.[159] In 1870, this was run by one Thomas Piggott, great-grandfather of the world-renowned jockey Lester Piggott.[160] Fouleshurst had been Sheriff of Cheshire 1470-71, was a Lancastrian in the Wars of the Roses, and had been a courtier as 'esquire to the body' (a minor courtly position) of Prince Edward, Henry VI's son.[161] Fouleshurst was one of the Cheshire barons. Elizabeth Fouleshurst's mother was Jane Vernon, daughter of Sir Richard Vernon (1390-1451).[162] He was MP for Staffordshire and then Derbyshire from 1419 to 1433 and Speaker of the House of Commons in 1426. He was also Marshal of England and Sheriff of various counties.[163] So, Piers Dutton was connected to some of northern England's most prominent gentry families.

There are some discrepancies in the records of Piers Dutton's immediate ancestors that do not appear to have been previously noticed. Most obviously, Sir Peter Leycester recorded that Piers Dutton's grandfather was 'Peter Dutton of Hatton, Senior', who *'married'* in *'1464'* to 'Elizabeth Grosvenor'.[164] His son, 'Peter Dutton of Hatton, Junior' (the father of Piers), had, according to Leycester, a daughter called Eleanor who married 'Randle Brereton of Malpas', though other sources termed him 'Randolph Brereton of Malpas'. According to a manuscript of Cheshire's 1580 Visitation, Sir Randolph Brereton, Chamberlain of Chester, married 'Eleanor, daughter of Piers Dutton of Dutton'.[165] Various historians of the period, such as Eric Ives (1931-2012) also assert that Sir Randolph Brereton married Eleanor, daughter of 'Piers Dutton of Halton *(sic.)*'[166] and observe that Randolph was 'Knight of the Body of Henry VII' and later 'Knight-banneret',[167] these being minor courtly positions. (It should be noted that 'Peter' and 'Piers' are often used interchangeably in the records).

However, 1464 seems a very unlikely year for Peter Dutton, Senior, to have married in, at least if Ives' estimate for the year of birth of Eleanor and Randolph's son William Brereton, who was executed for adultery with Anne Boleyn in 1536, is correct. Assuming that 'Peter Dutton, Junior' was born in 1465, he would have been about 26 when his own grandson, William Brereton of Malpas, was born in 1490. This grandson was the sixth or seventh son of his mother.[168] So, Peter Dutton, Junior, would have been about 16 (at the oldest) when his first grandson by that particular daughter was born. This is obviously impossible.

The Cheshire Recognizance Rolls are court records, especially with regard to keeping the peace, inquisitions post mortem and official appointments. An inquisition post mortem was an enquiry held upon the death of a royal feudal tenant to establish his heirs, the nature of his lands and thus what income and rights were due to the crown. These rights would include the right to run the estate until the male heir was 21 (before which he would be a royal ward, raised by the appointed Master of the Wards) or the right to a payment, known as a relief, so that a full-age heir could access his estates. The inquiry would

2. Tomb of Sir Randolph Brereton and Eleanor Brereton at St. Oswald's Church, Malpas (Courtesy of Craig Thornber, www.thornber.net).

be organised by a royal commissioner and a jury, who were charged with discovering the necessary information.[169] Looking through the Cheshire Recognizance Rolls, we can start to work out with more certainty the years of birth of Piers and his ancestors and, so, resolve this anomaly.[170] It can be seen that a Hugh de Dutton (of Hatton) is first mentioned in a court case 1403[171] and he died in 1440.[172] His son 'John de Dutton of Hatton' is first recorded as being married to 'Margaret his wife' in 1419.[173] John was bound over to keep the peace in 1454, and in 1455 and on both occasions his son 'Peter' was mentioned,[174] implying that Peter was at least around 12, the approximate age of criminal responsibility.[175] This 'John de Dutton of Hatton' disappeared from the records in 1464[176] and later the same year 'Peter de Dutton of Hatton' was mentioned as being the husband of 'Elizabeth'.[177] Leycester appears to have assumed that Peter, therefore, married in 1464, but he may have married considerably earlier, there being no reason to mention his wife in the court entries until 1464.

In a Court of Star Chamber case in 1528, which we will explore below, William Ryder, said to be 100 years old, was called upon to testify that Sir Piers Dutton was descended from Edmund, brother of a Lord of the Manor of Dutton. Ryder stated that Hugh Dutton, son of Edmund and later Lord of the Manor of Hatton by marriage, had been given Moldsworth for life by his brother, Sir Peter Dutton (1367-1433), Lord of the Manor of Dutton. Hugh had married the heiress to Hatton and had a son called John Dutton (ca. 1400-1464). This John had fathered a 'Piers' (Peter) 'who was eight years old when this Hugh Dutton departed and went to dwell at Dutton during his life'.[178] This may mean that Peter was eight when his grandfather moved to Hatton, presumably either when he married or when his own father-in-law died, or that Peter was eight when his grandfather died, which seems more likely. This means that Peter Dutton of Hatton, Senior (Piers' grandfather) was born in 1432. Ryder claimed he knew John Dutton for the first 40 years of his (Ryder's) life (which would fit with John dying in about 1464) and Ryder's father had been a servant to Hugh Dutton (who had been Sheriff of Cheshire in 1422) and then to his son John. Ryder did not mention another generation, as Piers' father predeceased Piers' grandfather. However, the Act of Parliament in 1536 which awarded the disputed Manor of Dutton to Sir Piers Dutton specifically refers to Piers as 'son of Piers Dutton, son of Piers, son of John, son of Hugh'.[179]

A record from between 1473 and 1483 refers to a 'Piers Dutton, the younger' who was a 'felon' and was married to 'Eleanor, daughter of Sir Robert Fouleshurst' and a 'Piers Dutton, the elder'.[180] There is also a record of the outlawry of 'Peter Dutton, Esq., lately of Hatton, junior' in 1481 wherein 'Ralph Dutton, Gent., lately of Hatton' was also outlawed, this possibly being Peter's brother as he had a brother of this name.[181] Returning to the recognizance rolls, an inquisition post mortem in 1472 stated that Elizabeth Dutton née Grosvenor was 41, approximately the age William Ryder would have estimated her husband to be in that year.[182] In 1477, 'Peter de Dutton of Hatton' began to be marked as 'senior', implying he had a grown-up son of the same name.[183] 'Peter Dutton of Hatton, senior' disappeared from the recognizance rolls in 1488 when he had to pay a surety of £100 to keep the peace to Sir William Stanley.[184] He was mentioned again in April 1503, when he died.[185] As such, it may well be the case that Piers' father was born in the 1450s, which would line up with his widow remarrying, in 1507, to Thomas Leycester of Tabley (1444-1526) as his third wife,[186] as it would make them a roughly similar generation. Piers' grandfather, Sir Robert Fouleshurst, married Piers' grandmother in 1439,[187] so his mother may have been born in the mid-1450s.

The anomaly of Peter Dutton, Junior's, daughter marrying Sir Randolph Brereton and having William Brereton of Malpas as her 'sixth son' can be resolved if we estimate Brereton's year of birth at 1500, assume that he had no older sisters and assume that the six sons were produced once every year or so, quite possible if wet nurses were employed as they generally were by the Early Modern gentry.[188] If this was the case then Peter Dutton, Senior (1432-1503) may have fathered his eldest son when he was about 22 meaning that Peter Dutton, Junior, lived about 1454 to 1503. He was last specifically mentioned in the recognizance rolls in 1489[189] but was fined 6s 8d for assaulting Elias ap Daye in Chester in early 1503,[190] clearly before April when we know he was already dead and his father died. 1454 is perfectly possible as a year of birth as 22 to 24 was the average age that late Medieval gentry males got married,[191] while 21 was the average marriage age for the gentry's eldest sons.[192] Peter Dutton, Junior (c.1454-1503), in turn, could have fathered Eleanor at about 24 (1478), as she is the second daughter on the 1580 Visitation. If she began having children at around 14 (1492) then it is quite possible that Peter's grandson, William Brereton, was born in 1500. The average age of marriage for late Medieval English women was 17,[193] but the daughters of the gentry were usually married younger, often below the canonical age of 12.[194] This also fits better with William Brereton's marriage date, 1529,[195] as he would have been 29 rather than almost 40. In addition, there is no record of a crown office being held by William Brereton before 1522, that is to say, the new date of birth does not render him a minor while holding a crown office.[196]

Piers Dutton's grandfather, Peter Dutton of Hatton, Senior, appears to have used violence to deal with turf and financial disputes, just like his grandson later did. Between 1453 and his death in 1503, 'Peter

Dutton of Hatton, (senior)' was bound over to keep the peace against assorted complainants numerous times, either as part of his father John's gang, the gang of Roger Dutton, Lord of Dutton, or as leader of his own gang.[197] By 1496, Peter Dutton, Senior, had been made Lieutenant Governor of the Isle of Man.[198] He was fined in early 1503 for refusing to be knighted.[199] He died on 8th April 1503, leaving the Manor of Hatton and other lands to his grandson and heir, Piers.[200]

Peter Dutton's son, Peter Dutton, junior, was outlawed for a felony, specifically for a raid, in 1481; presumably on the land of one of his rivals for local power.[201] In theory, outlawry was one of the harshest penalties that could be passed in a society with no police system. It meant that Peter Dutton, Junior, could be killed with impunity. But in practice it was a temporary indignity which a wealthy person could easily endure, and he could also easily buy any confiscated property back.[202] He also had three daughters, according to the surviving manuscripts of the visitations.[203] As the final visitations themselves were only concerned with dynastic claims they tend to be streamlined versions of these manuscripts, only recording the eldest son. These daughters were Elizabeth, who married Sir George Calverley of Lea; Eleanor Brereton (c. 1478-1522), whom we have already met, and Jane, who married George Leech, Esq., Sheriff of the City of Chester.[204] However, as we will see later, Piers Dutton mentioned that he had three sisters who were nuns. As discussed, Peter Dutton, junior, predeceased his father.[205]

Childhood and Education

We only have hints of what Piers Dutton's youth may have been like. He was probably baptized on the day of his birth, possibly in the private chapel at Hatton Hall. It was common practice to baptize babies as soon as possible, as the unbaptized were believed to spend eternity in limbo. Piers and his family would have regularly attended that chapel and, as he learnt to read, he would have read Latin graces aloud while his elders ate.[206] Hatton Hall was a quadrangular plaster and timber manor house inside a 20-yard wide square moat, which had mostly fallen down by the nineteenth century.[207] Like most manor houses in the late fifteenth century, Hatton Hall would have had a Great Hall with a minstrels' gallery. It is not entirely clear where Piers lived as a young child. However, the fact that his father was always referred to as 'of Hatton' would seem to imply that he lived at Hatton Hall as part of an extended family.

Piers would have been used to his grandfather and father entertaining guests almost daily: clergy, passing friars and senior workers on their estates. As they talked and listened to the minstrels play, mutton and salted fish would have been the standard meal. At one end of the hall would have been his grandfather's chamber, complete with four-poster bed, while storage rooms would have surrounded the hall. The inventory of the descendant of Piers Dutton, his grandson Rowland Dutton (c. 1550-1605)[208] who lived in Hatton Hall in 1605, describes a four poster bed with blue and yellow curtains,[209] which may have been an heirloom. Above these rooms would have been communal rooms for servants or family members and a couple of rooms for other guests. The rooms would have been decorated liberally with tapestries.[210] Tapestries would also have been stored in the 'ancient' cypress chest, which was coated in silk and marked with the Hatton arms, which was mentioned in Rowland Dutton's inventory. It is likely that this chest was already at Hatton Hall when Piers Dutton was a child.

The education of the sons of the gentry in the late fifteenth century would tend to follow a set pattern. They would begin by being educated in their own household, by their mother or a local clergyman.[211] By the age of around 10, they would be sent to the household of another family, a system which was ubiquitous until the late fifteenth century when it was beginning to be replaced by education at grammar schools.[212] The family to which they were sent was often a family of higher status, meaning that gentry sons might be sent to a noble household or even a royal household.[213]

There were then two main 'further education' options open to the sons of the gentry in the late fifteenth century: University or the Inns of Court. Both were effectively secondary schools and it must be remembered that the students were around the age of 14 when they began.[214] Oxford and Cambridge, Spartan places modelled on monasteries, continued to teach grammar right up until 1570 and 'business education' was a big part of the curriculum. The Inns of Court taught history, scripture, music, even dancing, and enough law, Latin and Norman French to help students run their own lands or obtain lucrative positions running the lands of others.[215] In addition, the Inns of Court became increasingly popular among the gentry from the mid-fifteenth century because a legal education meant that gentry had less of a need to employ lawyers in their own frequent legal disputes.[216]

We cannot know whether Dutton attended a grammar school but it is probable that he did not because this option was only just rising in popularity among the gentry in the late fifteenth century and, as of 1487, Cheshire only had one school; in Stockport.[217] Accordingly, Dutton may have been educated, as a child, in another household, of higher status than the Duttons of Hatton. One possibility is that of Thomas Stanley, 1st Earl of Derby and King of Mann (1435-1504).[218] A peer with extensive landholdings in Cheshire, Piers' grandfather, Peter Dutton, Senior, was part of his retinue and was appointed Lieutenant Governor of the Isle of Man in 1496. The Stanley family were dominant in Cheshire in the late fifteenth century, with Stanleys being Cheshire's High Sheriffs continuously between 1463 and 1495.[219] A surviving letter from Edward Stanley, 3rd Earl of Derby, (1509-1572) to Dutton, written in 1536, is in an extremely informal and friendly style, implying that the two men were on very friendly terms.[220]

As for higher education, Piers Dutton is not recorded as having attended Oxford or Cambridge.[221] This is unsurprising, as the universities were dominated by the (higher) nobility, and those training to be priests, until well into the next century,[222] however the majority of priests, as we have discussed, were not graduates; graduate priests were the elite.[223] Likewise, none of Piers Dutton's sons attended university but Hugh Dutton, son of Piers' son Ralph, matriculated from Hart Hall, Oxford, in 1580.[224] It seems likely, therefore, that Dutton attended an Inn of Court. He cannot be found in the records of Middle Temple[225] or Lincoln's Inn and the records of Gray's Inn and Inner Temple only go back to 1521 and 1547 respectively.[226] However, there were certainly other Duttons who were known to have trained at Inner Temple in senior legal positions, such as Thomas Dutton who was made Clerk of the Peace in Flintshire in 1542,[227] so Inner Temple is a possibility.

Indeed, Inner Temple tended to attract gentlemen's sons from the north, the Midlands, and London while Middle Temple attracted those from the West country.[228] The records of the now defunct Inns of Chancery, which prepared students for the Inns of Court, are often very poorly maintained[229] so it would be impossible to ever prove the hypothesis that Dutton attended one of those. However, Piers Dutton's grandson Rowland Dutton entered Lincoln's Inn in 1564.[230] And Piers Dutton pursued exactly the kind of work that a spell at an Inn of Court was designed for. Dutton was Steward of Halton Castle.[231] Legal knowledge was vital for a steward, some stewards were attorneys in the Medieval period,[232] and the steward was effectively a kind of lawyer. The steward presided over the manorial court and appointed other manorial officials, such as the reeve or bailiff. In addition, there were cases in this period of trained barristers being stewards, such as Henry Heydon, who was appointed steward to Cecily Neville (mother of Edward IV).[233] Contacts made through the Inns of Court were one way that Protestantism spread in the early sixteenth century gentry,[234] so education at an Inn of Court would be congruous with Dutton's apparent Protestantism. Finally, Dutton's grandfather was steward of Chester's Court of Histronics in 1481, so legal training ran in the family.[235] As such, there are grounds for a reasonable inference, if no more than that, that Dutton attended an Inn of Court, probably Inner Temple.

In general, students would begin their training with a year at one of the Inns of Chancery, where they would be schooled in Latin and grammar, though this could also be achieved through private tutors. They would then be admitted to Inner Temple as a so-called 'inner barrister'. There, they would study plea rolls, listen to lectures, take part in moots (mock court cases), and attend court cases at Westminster Hall. The Inn also served as a finishing school for the sons of gentry, teaching them scripture and courtly manners as well as the law. Those who actually became barristers would stay at the inn for seven years but most, probably including Piers Dutton, stayed there for three years and never qualified as barristers.[236]

It is possible that Dutton was apprenticed as a merchant in London. However, this seems extremely unlikely because, as we will see, he was regarded as embodying non-merchant dominance of the Corporation of Chester. In addition, he certainly was not a draper – as their records survived the Great Fire of London – and this is the only London craft we know he had contact with, as we will see shortly. Likewise, the records of the Mercers (a similar trade to drapery) survive and he is not on those.[237] Moreover, only later, in the sixteenth century, did an apprenticeship as a London merchant start to become a normal education option of the sons of gentry (though mainly the younger ones) and it remained the least popular option.[238] In the fifteenth century, a London apprenticeship was the further education choice for wealthy yeomen's sons. For example, between 1480 and 1500 a total of 46% of those admitted as apprentices by the Skinners and Merchant Tailors were from north of the Trent.[239] In general, by the seventeenth century, apprenticeship was for the younger sons of the gentry, who would not inherit and needed a trade by necessity.[240] The fact that Dutton did not become a freeman of Chester until just before becoming Mayor (see below) would further imply that he was not apprenticed as a merchant in Chester either.

A Wayward Youth

Dutton possibly first appears on the records on 6th September 1496, when a 'Piers Dutton of Hatton' was indicted for having 'retained' William Ryder at Waverton in 1495.[241] As we have seen, this same family servant (or, possibly, his elderly relative) testified for Dutton in 1528. We have no further details. This would have been at a time when Henry VII was attempting to restrict the ability of magnates to retain. However, in that the names 'Piers' and 'Peter' are often used interchangeably this record may refer to Piers' grandfather; the most important 'Piers or Peter Dutton of Hatton' in 1496. At this time Piers Dutton would have been around 16 and would have been encouraged to learn to hunt, hunting being a crucial form of exercise and social activity for people of his rank.[242] However, he would have hunted stags, not foxes. Yeomen hunted foxes. Gentlemen did not begin to do so until the late seventeenth century.

3. St Werburgh's Abbey (now Chester Cathedral). (Wikipedia).

Piers Dutton comes to prominence in April 1503 when his grandfather died and he inherited Hatton. He comes to prominence again in 1504.[243] This time there was a dispute between the Abbot of St. Werburgh's, Chester, one John Birchenshawe (c. 1463-c.1538), and Piers Dutton. The Abbot of St. Werburgh's was, by this time, an increasingly powerful figure in Chester and was asserting his authority. His character has been described as 'insufferable',[244] and thus likely to provoke conflict. Also, the abbey owned Waverton church, the church for Piers Dutton's manor of Hatton, requiring tithes from all local farmers,[245] and it was the feudal master of other lands which Dutton had inherited via his grandmother Elizabeth Grosvenor. Dutton had also inherited Hatton by 1504. Accordingly, we can understand why Dutton, a major land owner in the parish of Waverton, would have disliked the abbot and wanted a more docile one.

In late 1504, Sir Randolph Brereton (c. 1470-1530) (Dutton's brother-in-law), newly appointed Chamberlain of Chester, demanded that Dutton pay a surety of the peace against one John Coddington, despite the fact that this man hadn't made a complaint against him. He then demanded that Dutton pay a surety to ensure he and his servants behaved peacefully towards the Abbot of St. Werburgh's and his servants. Without any lawful reason to do so, so claimed Dutton, Randolph Brereton, with the assistance of his deputy Randle Brereton,[246] kept Dutton in prison for three weeks in Chester Castle because of this demand and intended to keep him there throughout Christmas. Brereton brought the Abbot to testify about Dutton's behaviour before the Chester Exchequer at night while Dutton was locked up in his cell, asleep. Dutton complained that they deliberately did this to stop him testifying in open court against the abbot and so that Dutton could not demand bail. Dutton was released and then when he turned up at 'Candlemas' (2nd February) to pay the surety, he was held in prison for a further month until he was released by order of the 'king's commissioners.[247] This term, in this context, would appear to refer to assize judges commissioned to preside over cases.

We cannot really know for sure what had been happening but in light of Dutton's later conduct, it seems unlikely that he was an entirely innocent party. By 1516, Dutton was invading the lands of those who owed his patrons money and stealing their property as a means of recovering the debt. He also maintained a gang of retainers to do his bidding and was prepared to protect them from legal process. Accordingly, it is likely that in 1504, being now Lord of the Manor of Hatton, Dutton was behaving in a similar way, possibly intimidating the Abbot and his people, instructing his servants to steal from the abbey lands if there was some boundary or financial dispute, attempting to use force to takeover the abbot's lands, which would have bordered his own, or similar menacing behaviour.

As for the spell of imprisonment in early 1505, this would appear to be connected to a series of events which came to light in the Court of Star Chamber in 1518. Richard Done – father of Sir John Done (c.1501-1561) whom we will meet later – seemingly an enemy of Dutton's, had his brother, an outlaw called William Done, and a number of other servants, badly beat up and almost murder a servant of Dutton's called William Fletcher. Done's people then alleged that Piers Dutton had one Ralph Dutton (c.1456-1517), presumably Piers Dutton's father's

38

4. Agricola Tower, Chester Castle (Wikipedia).

brother, murder Hugh, the servant of Richard Done. They added that Dutton had sent an armed mob of 120 people to the area where the Dones lived, such that they were afraid to leave their property. It is seemingly in connection with this that Piers Dutton was held in early 1505, though he insisted that Hugh's murder had taken place while he was in prison, presumably in 1504. Dutton later alleged that while he was in prison in 1505, William Done assembled 140 armed men, rode into Chester, and attempted to seize Dutton and lynch him.[248] 'Ralph Dutton, Gent.' was outlawed for murder on 5th August 1511, with an inquisition into his property taking place at Chester in 1517. It was found that he owned no property whatsoever,[249] so he had presumably rented land or transferred ownership to relatives. Convicted felons who could read, as Ralph presumably could, would claim 'Benefit of the Clergy', allowing them to avoid a death sentence.

Chapter Four
The Riotous Mayor

'...the citizens thought good and put Sir Piers out of his mayoralty and chose by free election John Raborne in his place.'[250]

IN ABOUT 1503, Dutton married Eleanor Legh, daughter of Thomas Legh, Lord of the Manor of Adlington in Cheshire (1452-1519). Certainly, their first son, Peter, married in 1520[251] and it is unlikely that he was younger than about 16. In marrying Eleanor Legh, Piers Dutton wed into a family that was not only rich but almost as ancient as his own. Robert de Legh (1308-1370), ancestor of Dutton's father-in-law, was descended from Gilbert Venables, who came to England with William the Conqueror. Thomas Legh's great grandfather, Robert, had fought at Agincourt and died of plague a few days later.[252] Dutton's new mother-in-law was Katherine Savage, a matrilineal descendent of King Edward I and sister of Thomas Savage, Archbishop of York between 1501 and 1507. Their mother was the daughter of Thomas Stanley, 1st Baron Stanley, King of Mann.[253] Over the next 13 or so years, Piers and Eleanor had 10 children: seven daughters and three sons, one of whom, Ralph – a religious dissenter – we will get to know later. Being a suspected Roman Catholic or 'Papist' during the reign of Elizabeth I (r. 1558-1603)[254] severely damaged the political prospects of Ralph Dutton. However, Piers Dutton had no reputation for being a dissident and, accordingly, his political rise was swift, though his first fall from power equally so.

King Henry VII and Cheshire

Dutton always seemed to have had a knack for reaching his political zenith in 'interesting times'. The background to Dutton's mayoralty of Chester was three ongoing conflicts: between the city and the county, between the city and its abbey, and the between the king and the county.

With regard to the king, Cheshire support, led by Sir William Stanley (1435-1495) who switched to the Lancastrian cause at the last minute, was decisive in Henry VII's victory at Bosworth Field in 1485. But in 1494, Sir William Stanley, the Chamberlain of the Palatinate, had spoken in favour of the pretender to the throne Perkin Warbeck (1474-1499) who had claimed to be Prince Richard of York, one of the Princes in the Tower, nephew of Richard III and the younger son of Edward IV.[255] This led to Stanley's execution in 1495, something which cast serious doubt on the loyalty of the Cheshire gentry and, even more so, its nobles. Cheshire's nobility, anyway, was particularly weak, meaning Cheshire's gentry were particularly strong.[256] Henry VII made a point of promoting gentry at court[257] which in turn augmented their local power base. On 5th December 1536, two fishmongers testified that they had overheard the leaders of the Pilgrimage of Grace refer to Sir Piers Dutton and Sir William Brereton of Brereton as the 'rulers' of Cheshire,[258] despite the fact that the Earl of Derby owned estates in Cheshire. Indeed, in 1535, two Cheshire monasteries (Norton and Birkenhead) rejected the Earl of Derby and the Earl of Shrewsbury, respectively, as their stewards in favour of Cheshire gentry.[259]

Support for Warbeck clearly extended to other important Cheshire magnates, including Dutton's future father-in-law, Thomas Legh. In June 1494, Legh had led a gang of 40 men to the house of Lancastrian-supporter Robert Grosvenor, at Eccleston, at about 4am and 'ploughed up the land around with ploughs, shouting all the while and terrifying the king's lieges'. Other riots were led by other gentry families, such as the Aldersleys.[260] Henry VII's response was to appoint people from outside Cheshire to key posts, such as Chief Justice of Chester, and to ensure that Cheshire appointees were absolutely loyal. It may be relevant that, in 1506, Henry VII gave the City of Chester a new charter which effectively made the city (with the exception of the castle) independent of the county. Although the city council was increasingly dominated by the gentry, this move would have empowered an organization that was still significantly mercantile. As we will see, Dutton epitomized attempts to compromise this independence. Also, in 1508, the Palatine was asked to pay a 'mise;' a contribution to crown funds. Piers Dutton was granted a small salary to ensure that this mise was raised and led the negotiations that culminated in it, especially investigating what Cheshire landowners who lived outside the county should pay.[261] He seemingly had inherited this position from his grandfather, who led the negotiations over the Cheshire mise of 1497.[262] The 1508 mise may have helped to demonstrate anew Cheshire's (and Dutton's) loyalty to the Tudors.

The City-Abbey Conflict

Turning to the abbey, as long ago as 1478, there was clearly a state of animosity between the Corporation of Chester and the Abbot of St. Werburgh's over who ran parts of Chester and who enforced laws and issued fines. The abbot at that time, Richard Oldham, was bailed for £1000 to keep the peace; one of his guarantors was Peter Dutton of Hatton, Senior, the grandfather of Piers.[263] Monks were accused of murder and rape and the abbot embezzled money left to the abbey to perform masses.[264] By the beginning of the sixteenth century, the Archdeaconry of Chester was effectively independent of its diocese (Coventry and Lichfield) and the Abbot of St. Werburgh's since 1493, John Birchenshawe, was the most powerful baron in the Palatinate. Possibly because of the silting of the River Dee, trade in Chester had suffered throughout the fifteenth century. For example, in 1410-20 around 2000 tones of wine had been imported into Chester. By 1460-70 this was down to 600. However, the tide began to turn by around 1500 and trade substantially improved.[265] At the same time, St. Werburgh's also began to recover from a period of decline. St. Werburgh's was a Benedictine Order, focused heavily on prayer and long periods of silence.[266]

In 1507, the abbot asserted his authority by ordering 'securities of the peace' to be taken from Rauff Banastre and John Adknave (alias Harrison)[267] who had been involved in a brawl outside the Northgate. Outraged by this interference in city territory, the mayor, recorder and aldermen had the abbot brought before the king's commissioners. The abbot denied that 'recognizance' had taken place, that is to say he denied that he had taken a surety from the two brawlers. However, an investigation by the commissioners found that he had. In 1509, the year Henry VII died and the 17-year-old Henry VIII succeeded, they made an award of complete victory to the mayor and the city and declared that the abbot only had jurisdiction within the abbey. They also took away the abbot's right to hold his 'baron's court' during the annual St. Werburgh's Fair.[268] A 'fair' lasted for weeks and was a crucially important centre for local and even international trade in Medieval England.[269]

In 1510-11, there was, in consequence, a violent conflict between the abbey and the city over boundary disputes. It is reported that: 'It was in connection with this dispute that Peter *(Piers)* Dutton, Esquire, of Hatton, was committed to the Castle at the instance of the abbot, but he escaped.'[270] As we have seen, Dutton was already an enemy of the abbot. In 1504, Sir Randolph Brereton had supported the abbot against Dutton and imprisoned Dutton in Chester Castle. The fact that the abbot was able to pressure Sir Randolph Brereton to imprison Dutton, that Dutton was able to escape (very possibly with the connivance of a prison insider) and that it was not possible for Brereton to return him to prison only underlines how corrupt and lawless early sixteenth century Cheshire was.

The City-County Conflict

Turning to the tension in the city and the county influence within it, we have two groups who would be likely to have separate interests. On the one hand, there were the merchants of Chester. By the terminology of the time, these people were understood as the 'middling sort'.[271] Though some were very wealthy, they were not members of the minor nobility. They were apprenticed into Chester's guilds, became freemen of the city (allowing them to trade within it) and got themselves elected onto the 'Common Council' or co-opted as Aldermen, eventually, in some cases, becoming sheriffs or mayors of the city. As of 1506, the rules of the Corporation of Chester were clearly formalized. There were to be 24 Aldermen, a co-opted group, and 40 Common Councillors, elected by the freemen of the city. The mayor was to be elected by the Aldermen. His deputies, the two city sheriffs, were to be elected by the Aldermen in one case and by the entire assembly in the other. The city's courts would be presided over by the mayor, former mayors, the recorder, and designated senior Aldermen. In 1506, Chester was legally affirmed as independent of the Cheshire Palatinate.[272] In theory, the Corporation of Chester was run by merchants, for merchants, and it aimed to ensure that only those who had been made free of a city guild, or had paid for their freedom, could trade within the city. It was thus the preserve of mercantile – 'middling sort' – families. This was the theory, but it was not the reality.

There was a lot of money to be made out of civic offices. Some of the younger sons of gentry, or even the younger sons of yeomen who were nevertheless of recent gentry stock, would apprentice in London or even Chester, become freemen, and get themselves co-opted as Aldermen when a vacancy arose. Civic office meant influence which in turn meant money and social ascent. By the 1450s, there is evidence of an increasing number of people who were landed gentry serving as aldermen and mayors. Once the process – of gentry becoming freemen and being co-opted as Aldermen – started it would have been difficult to stop. The gentry relatives of merchant Aldermen would have purchased their freedom and been co-opted and this would have continued until a tipping point was reached and the Aldermen were mainly gentry. Once this happened, the mayors and sheriffs would have been likewise. Thereafter, civic office was held by members of established county families such as the Aldersleys, Balls, Davenports and, of course, Duttons. Office holders would maintain contact with merchants but also with the county grandees to whom they were related. Indeed, they could go so far as running the city in the interests of their own county families rather than in the interests of its merchants. By the early sixteenth century, there was an established system whereby the Mayors and Aldermen were composed of gentry or the wealthiest civic families, the Sheriffs were mainly from wealthy civic families, while only the Common Councilman were likely to be drawn from the ranks of ordinary merchants.

As early as the late fifteenth century, there is evidence that the most senior positions were being taken by the gentry and this was undermining the power of the Chester corporation. It was therefore undermining the power of merchants and their ability to maintain a monopoly on trade and thus prosper. Men arrested by the city sheriffs for debt or illegal trade had successfully appealed to the Exchequer (which was largely composed of gentry) on the grounds that they were 'avowry' men under the specific protection of the palatinate. The sheriffs of the city had to appear before the Exchequer to explain their actions, and the Chief Justice and Chamberlain eventually overturned their right to jail privileged tenants of the Earl of Chester, though they accepted their right to fine those who had practised a craft without freedom of the city. Those imprisoned by the sheriffs would increasingly sue them for mistreatment and force them before the Palatinate courts.[273] The increasing dominance of the city's Aldermen (many of whom were ex-mayors or co-opted by them) by the gentry meant that those with power had little interest in defending the independence of the city or even the interests of its ordinary merchants. Their interests lay in defending the power of the large land owners in the county, among whom they often numbered, and even extending this power into the city itself.

Mayoralty of Chester

Dutton was made a freeman of the City of Chester in October 1511.[274] He was presumably co-opted as an Alderman in the same year. Dutton was then elected Mayor of Chester himself in 1512. The accounts of his two sheriffs for the year 1512-13, Thomas and David Middleton, give a flavour of what life was like in Chester at the time. There were numerous assaults, affrays, and cases of illegal trading. Thomas Savage was fined 40s for 'heaping filth on the highway', Richard Dayner was fined 13s 4d for allowing servants to play 'spirula and other unlawful games'. The government wanted men to practise archery, so they could defend the country in a time of war, so any activity seen to compete with this was illegal. A number of butchers were fined for hanging entrails in the street. John Towner, a clerk,[275] was fined 40s for assaulting a shearman, William Lancaster had to pay 6s 8d for laying in wait to murder Thomas Deane, while Agnes Billington was fined 40s for keeping a brothel.[276] Dutton was elected mayor again in 1513. During his second term in office he used his position to make an official complaint about the way in which Sir Randolph Brereton was stewarding the county. The palatinate was at that time £1359 in arrears due to the crown,[277] arrears that Sir Randolph's son, William Brereton, managed to heavily reduce after 1530.[278] Dutton was elected again in late 1514.[279] It was this last election which caused all of the resentment against county interference felt by the freeman and their common councillors to erupt. For a mayor whose interests were very obviously connected to the county and not the city, and who had never been a Chester merchant, to be elected a third time was bad enough, but this mayor allowed county influence to become particularly strong.[280]

It is likely that Dutton knew how strong feelings were against his re-election by 1514 because there is evidence that people were stopped from even speaking against it at the meeting that chose him. When Dutton was elected in 1514 a 'standing counsel' (in-house lawyer) for the Corporation of Chester by the name of 'Harebrowne' stood up and 'pleaded for Mr. Dutton and the Commons against the Mayor and Aldermen'. The supporters of the Mayor and Aldermen managed to bundle Harebrown out of the building.[281] According to a Chester chronicler, there was soon, 'a great discord and falling out between the gentlemen of the shire and the citizens of Chester. The commonalty thought that Mr. Mayor took the country gent. part. By which means the citizens thought good and put Sir Piers *(sic.)*[282] out of his mayoralty and chose by free election John Raborne in his place.'[283] Dutton's election was declared illegal, he and his sheriffs were removed sometime in December 1514, and John Raborne, a draper, replaced him by January 1515.[284]

We can only imagine how Dutton must have felt. Dutton, a minor noble but from one of Cheshire's greatest families, was removed from office by a coup in which the common councilman (who represented the 'plebeian' merchants) illegally selected their own mayor; a decision so overwhelmingly popular among the merchants that the Aldermen had no option but to back down and accept it, possibly for fear of the functioning of the city becoming paralyzed.

However, despite being seen as representing the county, there is circumstantial evidence that Dutton traded in cloth and other fabrics. Dutton had some kind of friendship with draper Henry Patmore of London, married his widow, and then become involved in his business affairs, shipping cloth.[285] Dutton sold land to draper Henry Gee, who had been Mayor of Chester 1533-34 and 1539-40.[286] Dutton also vigorously pursued a Chester leather merchant called Philip Constantine around 1535.[287] Perhaps his motive was that Constantine was a competitor. However, the city of Chester levied a tax on leather and in 1541, as a Justice of the Peace, Dutton presided over cases in which tanned leather was seized.[288] But although, as an ex-Mayor, Dutton could have remained an Alderman and local justice, the coup of 1515 marked the end of Dutton's dominance of the city of Chester.

Chapter Five
Criminal and Courtier

'Your orator is wary of his life to live in such extreme malice
with the said Piers and is fallen in poverty by the occasion
of the said Piers and shall be feign right shortly to flee the
country and dwelling through the said handling of the said
Piers Dutton... [289]

FOR THE next ten years or so, Dutton acted as an enforcer for
various Cheshire magnates, leading gangs onto the land of those who
owed them money and seizing their property. He incurred a 'fine' in
May 1516 for involvement in a 'riot' which included John Baptist
Grymbald, John Dymmock, Simon Browne, Ralph Mainwaring, Sir
John Warburton (Sheriff of Cheshire, 1508-1524), William Smyth and
Peter Stanley[290] (later gentleman usher to King Henry VIII).[291] This
'riot' is seemingly code for their marching onto a tenant's land and
stealing his produce as payment for a disputed debt.

This kind of activity received little more than a telling off until around
1516 when Cardinal Thomas Wolsey (1473-1530), Henry VIII's chief
minister, began an anti-corruption drive, reviving the little-used Court
of Star Chamber. Wolsey allowed people to bypass local courts and
bring their cases straight to the Court of Star Chamber, where they
would be heard by privy councillors and senior judges. This was very
expensive; court fees before the Exchequer in Chester might amount
to £7 where they might be £20 before the Court of Star Chamber.[292]
But, as a consequence of Wolsey's efforts, many local magnates -
who thought they were above the law and had the local courts in their
pockets - found themselves up before the Court of Star Chamber in
London. There were many cases, some of them dating back years,

involving Cheshire, because the palatine had its own legal system and, until Star Chamber's revival, Cheshire's officials and their supporters were, therefore, above the law. With Star Chamber, Cheshire's courts could be sidestepped for the first time. Cheshire's prosecuted gentry were kept in the Fleet Prison while they awaited trial and during their trials. Despite the fact that wealthy prisoners could pay for a spacious cell, pleasant food and bring their servants,[293] this would have been a humiliation.[294] Even the wealthiest prisoners would tend to find themselves in communal cells where they might bond with each other and arrange assistance for each other on the outside.[295] As we will see later, this is exactly what happened in Dutton's case.

Before the Court of Star Chamber

Around 1518, Dutton was brought before the Court of Star Chamber for complicity in the murder of Hugh, one of the servants of Richard Done, and, accordingly, kept in the Fleet. As we have discussed, this incident had probably occurred in about 1504. Dutton was accused of hiring Ralph Dutton, his uncle, to kill the servant. Dutton's defence was that he was in prison in Chester Castle when the incident took place. He also raised the issue of the attempt by William Done (Richard's brother) and his gang to abduct him from Chester Castle.[296] Indeed, while he was in the Fleet on this charge he used the system to take out his own cases. Dutton alleged that Richard Done had ordered his servants to assault one of his (Dutton's) servants, by the name of William Fletcher,[297] and he accused Sir Randolph Brereton of having falsely imprisoned him in 1504 and 1505.

While he was in prison in the Fleet in about 1518, Dutton allegedly had one Thomas Hutchins murdered and had a 'near kinsman' called 'Sir John Dutton, priest'[298] smuggle the murderers out of Cheshire, to Oxfordshire. Piers Dutton then had money conveyed to them via Sir John Dutton, priest. This would seem to be a case of Dutton protecting one of his enforcers. It came to light in a Star Chamber case in 1528.[299] And Dutton appeared before the court on 26th June 1518 in relation to yet another murder case, this time from 1516.

Sir William Brereton of Brereton (c.1480-1541) was, after the removal of William Brereton of Malpas in 1536, Dutton's rival for the dominance of Cheshire. He was the third cousin of Sir Randolph Brereton, the two men sharing a great-great-grandfather. Sir William Brereton married first to Alice, daughter of Sir John Savage, and, secondly, to Eleanor who was the daughter of Sir Randolph Brereton and thus Dutton's niece.[300]

Sir William Brereton, also brought before the court, was examined by Cardinal Wolsey himself in the case of the murder of Lawrence Swettenham.[301] In August 1516 (on the 'Feast of St. Oswald', a day of celebration), Swettenham had been invited to go to Brereton Green and play bowls with the 'gentlemen' John Cotton of Cotton and his brother Harry Cotton, for money. As the game progressed, a number of relatives and acquaintances of the Cottons turned up to watch. During the game, where we can assume all present were fairly drunk, an argument broke out over who was winning. John Breddon, one of the acquaintances and a servant of Sir William Brereton, interfered in the ensuing fight. From behind, he took a 'bill' (a kind of short spear) and hit Swettenham over the head, 'so that his brains came forth by force (from) behind of his head, and there (he) died within less space then a quarter of (an) hour, without speaking of any word'. Sir William Brereton, when told about this, intervened to stop the murderers being arrested, so a complaint was made to the court that he had left them at their liberty. In the meantime, they fled to Shropshire and then to Kent. Brereton and other Cheshire gentry actually had money sent to the fugitives.

Sir William Brereton testified that he didn't particularly like Swettenham, though it is unclear why. Dutton stated on oath that he was instructed by 'the lords' (presumably the Cheshire barons) to arrest one of the murderers (possibly he had such powers as a Chester Justice) and confessed that 'one of the indicted murderers was with (me) in the Fleet' (presumably when Dutton was awaiting a court appearance) and that '(I) paid for part of his costs'. He added that some of the murderers had likely fled to 'Essex'.[302] So, reading between the lines, the leading Cheshire gentry in 1516 employed gangs to deal with problematic people and were prepared to protect those people from the irritant of the Law. Unfortunately, most of the verdicts of the Court of Star Chamber do not survive so, unless reference is made in other documents, we cannot know what punishments were administered or even who won a particular case. However, in this case it is recorded that Brereton had to pay a fine.

Enclosure

Between court cases, Dutton had his own estate to run and he can be found in 1518 having some of his lands enclosed.[303]   Until the Medieval period, English agriculture followed the Open Field System. Each manor had a few very large fields divided into strips spread across the fields, as different parts of the field were of different quality. This meant that the farmers had to cooperate with each other. They also cooperated with each other in the use of the 'common land', which all of the farmers had the right to graze their sheep upon. This land was normally at the borders of a manor. Though something of a simplification, the Tudor enclosure movement can be roughly explained as follows:

Land began to be enclosed as of 1235 but the process accelerated during the Tudor period, as land use began to change from arable to more lucrative sheep farming. In order to achieve this, land had to be enclosed into a smaller number of fields, or the sheep would be uncontrollable. Landowners accomplished this, often by agreement, by enclosing the common land into hedged fields and turning the fields over to sheep. Major land owners also evicted tenants, due to any minor fault, so that the strip system could be dismantled more easily. This allowed them to farm the arable land more efficiently, in small fields, and turn over more land to wool production. The land was farmed more efficiently because everybody was now only contributing to their own land and so they worked more diligently to maintain and improve it. Each field also focused only on a single product, centred in a single, bounded area. However, enclosure also led to a rise in poverty and vagrancy as landless people who had previously relied on it could no longer make use of the now enclosed common land.[304] Sheep farming was also less labour intensive, leading to a rise in unemployment.

His Lord's Enforcer

Dutton was before the Court of Star Chamber again in 1519. This time, a Huxley yeoman, called William Bostock, found himself in a financial dispute with Sir John Savage (c1472-1527).[305] Savage was a major land owner, Dutton's kinsman via his mother-in-law, and Bostock's landlord. Bostock claimed that certain lands were owned by him freehold whereas Savage insisted that they were manorial lands for which Bostock had to pay rent. On 10th October 1518, Dutton, acting on behalf of Sir John Savage, sent a group of heavies to the farm of unfortunate Bostock. The gang stole his cattle. Then on the 18th October, he sent the same group, armed with swords, to beat Bostock up and possibly maim him. He wasn't at home so they chased his animals around the farm and slaughtered one of his mares. When Bostock still wouldn't pay, Dutton led a gang of 20 men to the farm on 9th August 1519. They ploughed up the land, took away all the corn to sell it, and Dutton told Bostock that he would 'occupy' the land if Bostock didn't pay the appropriate rent to Savage. Dutton would also regularly 'menace' Bostock and take his servants prisoner. Bostock was left begging the court to help. According to the abstract of the case:

> 'Your orator is wary of his life to live in such extreme malice with the said Piers and is fallen in poverty by the occasion of the said Piers and shall be feign right shortly to flee the county and dwelling through the said handling of the said Piers Dutton except your most merciful pity to your orator be showed in this behalf.'[306]

So, once more, we have a case in which Cheshire gentry use extra-judicial violence to get what they want and Dutton is heavily involved in it.

It seems Dutton was pardoned for one of his crimes on 28th April 1520. This record refers to 'Peter Dutton', but it clearly means 'Piers' because he is 'of Hatton' and a former Mayor of Chester. It also refers to him being 'of London' (as well as of 'Holt', 'Hawarden' in Wales and of 'Bloxwich' in Staffordshire) and as a 'Squire of the Body'.[307] Accordingly, Dutton was a courtier by 1520 and would have lived wherever the king was staying at any given time.

Dutton the Courtier

'Esquire of the Body' was one of the most junior positions at court. It was outside of the Privy Chamber whereas the more senior positions were inside. There were four esquires of the body, working in shifts. Their main purpose, apart from ceremonial attendance, was serving the king his pottage at dinner and supper. In addition, they helped him put on his underwear in the morning and take it off at night. More senior courtiers, called Gentleman of the Privy Chamber, helped him finish dressing. The Esquires of the Body had control of the royal residence at night and slept under the 'cloth of state'. During the day, they performed menial tasks, such as carrying the king's cloak.[308]   By 1524, Dutton's nephew, William Brereton of Malpas, was Groom of the Privy Chamber.[309] The position was highly prized as it allowed unfettered access to the sovereign. The groom was the king's intimate.[310] Changing the king's underwear and feeding him would have been rather intimate as well, so we can imagine that a bond between the two men could easily be made, boosting Dutton's status with other members of the court and making general promotion more likely.

   In that Dutton was already established in London, he had presumably been a courtier before 1520. It is certainly noteworthy that Dutton disappears from the Cheshire court cases in 1519 and does not appear on them again until 1528. Wolsey's campaign did not abate until 1521.[311]   So Dutton's absence from Star Chamber ties in with him not having spent a great deal of time in Cheshire during this period. He appeared in the King's Book of Payments in August 1521, under Obligations, along with Reignold Digby, Thomas Rotherham, Ralph Neville, Earl of Westmorland (1498-1549), John Townley and Laurence Bonvix.[312] Ralph Neville was definitely a courtier in November 1520, when he attended the king at the Field of Cloth of Gold.[313] This was a meeting between Henry VIII and the French king, Francis I, just outside Calais, a city which, at that time, was English territory. The two monarchs attended with large retinues. However, Piers was not one of the five esquires or knights of the body present.[314] In 1523, Dutton is recorded, under 'Debts Due to the Crown', as owing the king £120. In this entry, he is recorded, for the first time in one of the letters and papers of Henry VIII as 'Sir Piers Dutton'.[315] However, it appears that sometimes there was confusion over whether or not people were knighted. In a letter from William Brereton to Randle Brereton and Richard Leftwich in 1529, William Brereton refers to 'Master Dutton' whereas in another 1529 letter, from William Pole to William Brereton, it is 'Sir Piers Dutton'.[316] Sir Piers Dutton was a Knight of the Body of Henry VIII from 1527 to 1528, according to the Julian calendar.[317] This was, seemingly, one of the more senior 'servants of the body', as it was possible to be an 'esquire of the body' and have a knighthood, meaning that the title 'knight of the body' was more than simply an 'esquire of the body' who had been knighted.[318]

It is unclear how Dutton became a courtier or even when, though there is no record of him being paid anything by the king prior to 1521. The most likely scenario is that he was made a courtier as part of the Tudor policy of recruiting a very large number of, in effect, 'courtiers on paper' from among influential people in the shires. They would be admitted to the household, specifically to the department known as the 'King's Chamber' and would swear an oath to the king in front of the Lord Chamberlain. However, they would only very occasionally attend a court function, bringing them into contact with the king. As such, they could spend almost all their time in their own locality, but they were flattered with courtier status, helping to secure the loyalty of the provinces. These provincial courtiers were unpaid supernumeraries and between 1509 and 1530 around 400 men were recruited in this way.[319] As three-time Mayor of Chester, Dutton would certainly have shown himself to be a man of local influence. Once at court, Dutton's aim would have been to attend courtly events and generally impress people and, in particular, impress the king, who was the ultimate fount of patronage. He must have achieved this by 1519 because he had the paid position of esquire of the body, which would have meant living at court. The court was based around factions. The most powerful men at court would vie for influence with the king and less powerful courtiers would attach themselves to these men out of self-interest, affection or loyalty, thus winning their patronage. They would then rise or fall along with their faction leader and change factions when expedient to do so.

Marriages and Children

Dutton's place at court may help to explain his second marriage. Dutton's first wife, Eleanor, died in about 1520. She last appears in the records on 10th December that year.[320] Dutton had had 10 children by her, according to the Visitations:

(1) Peter Dutton (c.1504-1520). He married Jane Booth in 1520 but the marriage was not consummated.[321] They seemingly married as children. Child marriages were a fact of life for many gentry in Early Modern England. Supposed to cement alliances between families, they were contracted as *verba de futuro* ('words of future consent') and had to be ratified when children reached marriageable age, which was around the age of 12 for girls and 15 for boys.[322]

(2) Hugh Dutton (c.1508-1540), Sir Piers Dutton's heir, who married Jane Booth, his brother's widow, in 1526[323] and had children.

(3) Ralph Dutton (c. 1514-1582), an ardent Catholic who we will meet later.

(4) Katherine, who married, as her second husband, Richard Grosvenor.

(5) Elizabeth, who married William Manley.

(6) Anne, who married Hamlett Massie, of another significant Cheshire family.

(7) Margery, who married John Booth.

(8) Margaret who married Ralph Sherman, a yeoman.[324]

Eleanor bore Dutton two further daughters – Mary and Alice. Records at the College of Arms state that he had an illegitimate daughter, Maud, who married James Cotgrave around 1520, meaning she may have been born before Dutton married. And then, according to an inquisition after Dutton's death, he had two further illegitimate children, perhaps by the same mistress, John and Elizabeth Dutton.[325] We will see below why his having had children out of wedlock is in no way surprising.

Dutton's second marriage, in about 1521, was to Juliana Patmore, the widow of London draper Henry Patmore and daughter of William Poyntz of North Ockenden in Essex,[326] which is 30 miles from Charing Cross. The Poyntz family were also grocers in London.[327] Henry

Patmore was a draper in Colchester and moved to London permanently in 1509.[328] At the time of his death he lived in the parish of St. Peter's, Cornhill.[329] Having married Juliana, and having thus taken control of her inheritance, Dutton even found himself in a legal dispute over cloth which Patmore had shipped to Spain.[330] This was a very unusual marriage choice. In the entire history of the Dutton family up until that point nobody had married into a family that was not from either Cheshire or its neighbouring counties. As such, it may reflect the fact that Dutton was a courtier, spending large amounts of his time in London. It seems that Piers and Juliana had a child in 1526, though this probably died young as it does not appear on the Visitations.[331] They appear to have also had a child around 1521, called Piers. However, the evidence for this is contradictory, so it is worth discussing.

Manuscripts of the 1580 and 1613 Cheshire visitations survive in the Harleian Collection, which was formed by Robert Harley, 1st Earl of Oxford (1661-1724). The manuscripts of the 1580 Visitation (Harl. 1404 and 1505) are within two almost identical, handwritten heraldic books. Many additions have been made to the pedigrees, meaning they much more detailed than the official pedigrees held at the College of Arms. According to an 1808 entry in the British Library catalogue of the Harleian manuscripts, the books were written by the same person, 'the painter-stainer Mr. John Saunders, when he was a young man'.[332] John Saunders was born in about 1617, so we can assume the book was written before the Civil War. Saunders is a reliable source. Heralds who lacked the skills to conduct the heraldic work themselves during this period would often employ painter-stainers as their deputies, though the painters would often never become part of the College of Arms officially.[333] In this regard, Saunders acted as a 'deputy-herald', helping the Windsor Herald, Elias Ashmole, conduct the 1664 Cheshire Visitation.[334] According to Robert Tittler of Concordia University in Canada: 'Saunders was one of the leading herald painters of his time, enjoying patronage at the highest levels and working closely with heralds on sundry visitations. He collected heraldic books, and created copies of others, and managed somehow to gain access to all sorts of pedigrees in various counties.'[335] Tittler added that his work had 'a very high reputation' and 'must be taken seriously'.This source does not record that Piers and Juliana had any children.

The Harleian 1613 Visitation of Cheshire is based on Harleian manuscript 1535, a heraldic book which contains a copy of the visitation. This includes additions and entire pedigrees added by Richard Mundy (a seventeenth century painter-stainer) and others.[336] According to Tittler, Richard Mundy (1588-1640) is also a reliable source. Both he and Saunders were 'amongst the most distinguished in their profession at the time' and Mundy also assisted with Visitations. According to this source, Piers and Juliana had a son called Piers. In 1558, Piers Dutton of Newborough in Great Budworth died. He was a gentleman by rank who held his land from John Dutton of Dutton, the grandson of Sir Piers Dutton. His will implied that one of his daughters was of marriageable age.[337] As such, it appears likely that Piers Dutton of Newborough was born in about 1521 and was the son of Sir Piers Dutton and Juliana.

Protestant Connections

Dutton's unusual marriage choice is also part of Thornton's evidence that Sir Piers Dutton was Protestant. Proto-Protestantism, in the form of the Lollard movement, had been present in England since the fourteenth century.[338] Indeed, the diocese of Coventry and Lichfield, which included Cheshire, housed a strong Lollard movement. In 1512, Seventy-four Lollards appeared before the Bishop's Court accused of advocating heretical views and possessing the Bible written in English. On 4th April 1520, six people were burnt at the stake in Coventry for proto-Protestant heresy.[339] However, there does not appear to have been a strong Lollard movement in Cheshire. The first burning in England for Protestant heresy, specifically, did not occur until 1530, when priest Thomas Hitton was burnt at Maidstone.[340]

The case that Dutton was Protestant has two parts to it. Firstly, Dutton zealously liquidated Norton Abbey, despite the fact his ancestor helped to establish it, it included a chantry to pray for the Duttons, and it was the burial place of a number of his ancestors, and he had critics of new Anglican doctrines arrested, as we will see later.

Secondly, Dame[341] Juliana Dutton was almost certainly a Protestant.

Her son Thomas, a priest who posed as a draper while in London, was sentenced to perpetual imprisonment in 1531 for arguing in front of many witnesses that people should only pray to God (not saints), that the truth of scripture had been hidden until it was translated, and that priests should marry.[342] Thomas Patmore was only released, and restored to his position of Vicar of Much Hadham in Hertfordshire, when the Speaker of the Commons, Thomas Audley (formerly Colchester Town Clerk) pleaded Patmore's case. Patmore had studied in Wittenberg under Martin Luther himself and established a Protestant cell in London called the 'Christian Brethren'.[343] A number of the Poyntz family fled to Protestant states in Germany during the reign of Queen Mary (r. 1553-1558),[344] who brutally restored Catholicism in England, and one of them sheltered William Tyndale in his later years.[345] Essex, the home county of Dame Juliana, had a significant Lollard movement in the early sixteenth century.[346] London was, in comparison to other English cities, the hotbed of Protestantism during the early Reformation[347] while Cheshire, and the north of England more generally, remained more pro-Catholic.[348] People would tend to marry those with similar theological views to their own.[349] Accordingly, it seems reasonable to conclude that Dutton was a Protestant, especially when taken with the fact that Dutton shut down a chantry dedicated to praying for *his* (and all his relatives') soul (at Norton) and thus reducing his years in Purgatory. His closeness to Thomas Cromwell and other suspected Protestants, which we will explore later, would also add credence to this interpretation.

Marrying Juliana was, in many ways, extremely lucky. She was the widow of a wealthy merchant and Dutton inherited, therefore, all her property. But this was nothing compared to the good fortune that would envelop Dutton a few years later.

Chapter Six
The Disputed Legacy

'...such a beast in his living in every point of naughtiness as never was in the whole realm.'[350]

LAWRENCE DUTTON (c.1474-1528), 17th Lord of Dutton, was dying by the autumn of 1527 and he knew it. His wife had never produced any sons, though Dutton had a large number of 'bastard' children as set out in his will. Indeed, this will, which Lawrence Dutton dictated on the 4th October 1527, may have been one of the most controversial wills made during the reign of Henry VIII.[351]

It began predictably enough. Lawrence emphasized that he was of sound mind and that when he will 'depart out of this miserable transitory world' he will bequeath his 'soul to Almighty God'.[352] He desired to be buried with his ancestors at Norton Abbey and left money for every priest, clerk, and 'poor man' who was prepared to turn up at his funeral and pray for his soul. He made bequests to his daughters, Isabel and Douce, a bequest to a priest to sing for his soul, and he left money as a legacy for his servants. But then he turned to the important part of his testament. He had five illegitimate children (three sons and two daughters), so epitomising the immorality which Adam Beconsall (a priest commissioned by the Archdeacon of Chester in investigate life in the county) stressed so characterised Cheshire in his account of the palatine to Cromwell in 1535.[353] Lawrence's 'bastard son' John Dutton (ca. 1500-1542) was left all lands that Lawrence Dutton had bought himself and lifetime use, though not ownership, of some other lands.[354] John Dutton would absolutely not be left these other lands as his property because these should go to Lawrence's male heirs 'lawfully begotten'.

5. Lawrence Dutton of Dutton. Part of a picture of a stained glass window in Great Budworth church, drawn in 1568 by Randolph Holme. The window included a Latin statement indicating that the male figure was Lawrence Dutton and it had been made in 1526. (Memorials of the Duttons of Dutton, Ch. 4).

Likewise, his 'bastard sons' Robert Dutton and Thomas Dutton received land to use during their lives, but not as their property. This was because:

> 'Sir Piers Dutton ... for default of issue male of my body lawfully begotten is my next right heir male as appears by my old evidences...'

Lawrence's will then introduces further children to whom Sir Piers Dutton is obliged to give various rights, such as his 'bastard daughters' Katherine and Anne Dutton. It was crucial that Lawrence explicitly did this because, legally, illegitimate children had no rights to their parents' property. The number of illegitimate children, and the fact that they had taken their father's surname, may be surprising to modern readers.

However, though illegitimacy was stigmatized in early Tudor England, it did not involve anything like the shame which it did in the nineteenth century. It was extremely common, and essentially socially acceptable, for wealthy men in Tudor England to father illegitimate children. Upper class men in Early Modern England would generally have 'roughly as many illegitimate children as legitimate ones',[355] usually by servants. In general, these illegitimate children would be acknowledged by their father, they would take their father's surname, they would frequently be raised in his household, and he would pay for them to be educated. In the early half of the sixteenth century, they tended to be explicitly mentioned in wills rather than simply informally provided for, as starts to occur in the second half of the century.[356] And illegitimate children would be provided for 'to the degree of their mother',[357] with the mothers often being the daughters of men lower down the social hierarchy, such as yeomen.

We should not be surprised that Lawrence Dutton had illegitimate children, that they had taken his surname, and that he made bequests to them. What is bizarre is that he refused to leave them – or his legitimate daughters, or even the daughters (for he had no sons) of his uncle Sir Thomas Dutton who died for the Lancastrian cause at the Battle of Blore Heath in 1459 – any part of the valuable Manor of Dutton and its related estates. Instead, seemingly fixated with some Romantic desire that the Duttons of Dutton, scions of Cheshire since the Conquest, must not die out with him, Lawrence left this enormous inheritance to his third cousin once removed. Due to a series of mishaps, his nearest legitimate, male-line relative was the great-great-great grandson of Lawrence Dutton's great-great grandfather. But there was no legal necessity compelling Lawrence Dutton to leave his property to such a distant relative.

We cannot possibly know the real motivation behind Lawrence's last will. Maybe he disliked his uncle Sir Thomas and his uncle's descendants. It may be that Sir Piers Dutton charmed him. In about 1526, he helped Lawrence move timber from Shropshire to Dutton Hall at which time Lawrence told Piers that he was the 'rightful heir to Dutton' and even let Dutton refurbish the door frame with the wood himself.[358] Clearly, they had been in contact some time before Lawrence died and were on friendly terms. But, whatever his motivations, Lawrence Dutton's last will and testament caused uproar. It became a national scandal and an Act of Parliament was required to put an end to the, at times, violent dispute.

The Family Feud

John Dutton (1403-1445) had been 13th Lord of Dutton. He had inherited the manor from his father, Sir Peter Dutton, 12th Lord of Dutton (1367-1433), who was the son of Sir Piers Dutton's ancestor, Edmund Dutton (ca. 1341-ca. 1383). This Edmund Dutton was the brother of the childless Sir Lawrence Dutton (ca. 1339-1392), 11th Lord of Dutton, and also the father of Piers' great-great grandfather Hugh Dutton (ca. 1370- 1440) who became Lord of Hatton.

With John Dutton's death in 1445, the manor had gone to his eldest son, Sir Thomas Dutton (ca. 1424-1459), and then Sir Thomas Dutton's only surviving son, another John Dutton (ca. 1448-1473), let us call him 'John the Childless'. Sir Thomas Dutton also had daughters: (1) Anne who married Sir Thomas Molineaux of Sefton in Lancashire; (2) Isabel, who married Sir Christopher Southworth of Southworth in Lancashire; (3) Elizabeth, who married Ralph Bostock of Bostock in Davenham, Cheshire, by whom she had Anne Bostock, their heir, who married to Sir John Savage of Clifton in Cheshire; (4) Margaret, who married Thomas Aston of Aston, and later Ralph Vernon, and (5) Eleanor, who married Richard Cholmondley of Cholmondley.

However, when John the Childless died, the 16th Lord of Dutton was his uncle, Sir Thomas Dutton's brother, Roger Dutton (ca. 1432-ca. 1476). This Roger died and left the manor to his son Lawrence Dutton. The daughters of Sir Thomas Dutton had all married, as we have seen. A number of their descendants were allies of William Brereton of Malpas, Sir Piers Dutton's rival. But it wasn't only Lawrence Dutton's closer relatives who had reason to be livid about what he'd done. It infuriated all of Sir Piers Dutton's political rivals for dominance of Cheshire. If Sir Piers Dutton got hold of his inheritance it would make him an extremely wealthy man, boosting his standing at court and his influence within the Palatinate. At stake were eight manors and lands in a further ten, worth 4000 marks (about £2600) per year.[359] And, indirectly, even more was at stake. Sir Piers Dutton could end up running the whole county if he inherited land of such value. Lawrence Dutton's will had to be overturned.

Lawrence Dutton died some time in early January 1528 and Sir Piers

Dutton immediately moved to Dutton Hall. His enemies, however, didn't wait long to act. On the night of 15th January, having waited until Dutton was absent, three men – John Bruen, Esq., John Bostock and William Groves – broke into a house on the manor called the 'Day House' and took possession of it. The three men, it was later discovered, were servants of Sir John Savage (c.1493-1528), the son of Sir Thomas Dutton's heiress grand-daughter, Anne Bostock, and also working for Richard Aston, Esq., another grandson of Sir Thomas Dutton. They ate or destroyed all the food (stored for the winter), smashed up the house, and set up a pavilion.

Dutton refused to vacate the manor in the face of such intimidation. Accordingly, the next day Sir John Savage and Richard Aston assembled a mob of 200 men, armed with swords, bows and arrows, bucklers, and clubs, and marched into the Manor of Dutton, to a place called Hiltley. They stayed in the area for one and half days, proclaiming to the tenants that they were now in charge and generally inciting further riot and disorder.

Many of the 'rioters', including Sir John Savage, were close kinsmen of the chamberlain of Cheshire Sir Randolph Brereton (in three cases they were his grandchildren), or Sir William Pole, who was then the

6. Sir John Savage (1493-1528). Tomb at Macclesfield Church.
(Courtesy of Craig Thornber, www.thornber.net).

High Sheriff. In addition, the Under Sheriff was a retainer of Sir John Savage's. Sir Randolph Brereton's reaction, clearly fearing a counter-attack by Dutton's own gang, was to arrest Dutton and have him bound over to keep the peace, demanding a surety of 1000 marks to guarantee the peaceful behaviour of himself, his servants and all his family. Twenty of Dutton's associates were released without bonds. However, the Under Sheriff then raided their houses in the Manor of Dutton, arrested them again and jailed them in Chester Castle. Sir Randolph Brereton then declared that he would not release them until they paid the new fines which he demanded. In order to protect his followers, and ultimately his inheritance, Dutton complained to the king's commissioners, leading to a case in the Court of Star Chamber.

The response of Savage and his co-defendants was that Dutton had no definite title to the Manor of Dutton. They further argued that when John the Childless died the manor shouldn't have gone to his uncle Roger, anyway, but rather to Sir John Savage, as he was the son and heir of Anne Savage, daughter of Elizabeth Bostock, nee Dutton, sister of John the Childless. A number of other heirs general, descended from sisters of John the Childless, also staked partial claims to the estate.

Dutton's defence was simply to prove that he was descended from Hugh Dutton, Lord of the Manor of Hatton, son of Edmund. It seems to have been suggested that Sir Piers Dutton was descended from a Hugh Dutton of Moldsworth, who was a different person. Dutton called William Ryder who was 'about the age of 100 years'. Ryder testified that he remembered Hugh Dutton and that his father had been Hugh Dutton's servant for 40 years. He was sure that there were not two Hugh Duttons. Hugh had held Moldsworth for life by gift of his brother and inherited Hatton via a branch of the Vernon family, whose heiress he had married. A man of 80 testified the same. Hugh Worrall, aged 73, testified that he had heard Lawrence Dutton say that Sir Piers Dutton was his rightful heir. He had heard Margaret Vernon, sister of John the Childless, assert that she and her sisters had no right to the land and that Sir Piers Dutton was the heir. Worrall further claimed that another distant relative, Lawrence Dutton, Esq. (the childless son of Richard Dutton, brother of John Dutton, the 13th Lord of Dutton) testified that Sir Thomas Dutton was actually illegitimate, and was born by a first marriage to a supposed 'widow' whose husband in fact remained alive. It was revealed in the trial that Lawrence Dutton's wife had begged him to leave his estate to Sir Thomas Dutton's heirs but he wouldn't 'for all the goods in the world' because Sir Piers Dutton was his rightful heir. Robert Massey testified that Lawrence had declared that the land had always passed to the heir male and he wanted to leave the situation as he found it. During this conversation, which took place in 1526, Lawrence had said that he still hoped for a male heir as his wife was two years younger than Sir Piers Dutton's and Dutton's wife had just had a child.[360]

On 13th February, the court decided that, to avoid further riots, the disputed lands would be administered by Sir John Porte, Justice of the King's Bench, and Sir William Leyland, until the issue could be resolved.[361] This, in itself, was a coup for Dutton because Sir John Porte was the executor of Lawrence Dutton's will.[362] By 13th November 1528, it was clear that the judges were minded to find in favour of Dutton. Richard Leftwiche, Brereton's deputy as Escheator (enforcer of the king's feudal rights) of Cheshire and himself a witness to Lawrence Dutton's will, wrote to William Brereton of Malpas to say, 'I doubt how my Lord Cardinal's Grace will accept the findings of Dutton's lands, it is mis-done, you look thereunto considering his decree.'[363] Dutton's friendship with Thomas Cromwell likely helped his case. They certainly knew each other in 1529 when Dutton was listed as owing Cromwell money.[364] Quite why he owed him money is unclear, but it may have been that they were connected via both being Protestant, perhaps through Dame Juliana.

The Rise and Fall of William Brereton of Malpas

In 1530, Sir Randolph Brereton died and his son William Brereton replaced him as Chamberlain of Chester and Baron of Malpas. William Brereton also became Constable of Chester Castle, Steward of Halton Castle, and Rider of the Forest of Delamere. Halton Castle was the administrative centre of the 'Honour of Halton', a semi-autonomous area that maintained its own court and prison at Halton Castle. This so-called 'Fee of Halton' was ultimately under the control of the Duchy of Lancaster, meaning that the Chancellor of the Duchy Lancaster, a government position.[365] But even with these new powers, Brereton's star was falling and Dutton's was rising. Cardinal Wolsey was effectively replaced by Thomas Cromwell, who appears to have had financial dealings with Dutton, making it likely that they were on friendly terms.[366] In addition, now that Brereton was in charge of Cheshire's finances, he began to make himself a powerful enemy at court in the form of Thomas Cromwell. In order to sort out the Palatine's parlous finances, Brereton heavily cut Cheshire's grants to the crown. Then, in 1532, Brereton obstructed Cromwell in his attempts to obtain the revenues from the vacant bishopric of Coventry and Lichfield, which covered Cheshire. This was a problem because Cromwell was negotiating the king's divorce from Catherine of Aragon and had earmarked the money to bribe a particular cardinal.[367] Dutton was now confident enough to start challenging Brereton's authority. In 1528, Sir John Savage died and his young son became a 'ward' of William Brereton. The 'wards' were fatherless children who had inherited feudal land. The land would be run by the state until they attained majority and they would be raised by the Master of the Wards or someone deputing for him. Dutton put information before the Master of Wards, the notoriously Vicar-of-Brayish Sir William Paulet (c.1485-1572)[368] which stated that the uncles of the young Savage, his rival in the lawsuit, were not entitled to a courtly annuity. If this had been accepted, which it wasn't, Brereton would have been forced to pay for the Savages' lands out of his own pocket or lose their support.[369] Then, on 10th June 1531, Dutton mounted another challenge. One Richard Penkethman caught a sturgeon within the Manor of Weston, which was owned by Dutton. Under archaic laws, all sturgeons had to be presented to the king[370] and, as Weston was within the jurisdiction of Halton Castle, they were supposed to be given to the Steward of Halton Castle, William Brereton, so that he could present them to the king. Dutton simply took the fish from Penkethman for himself, possibly with the implication that he would give it to the king. This led to Brereton, who had also been appointed escheator, to complain to the Chancellor of the Duchy of Lancaster, demanding that he intervene to protect his rights as Steward of Halton.[371] Accordingly, Dutton's action can be seen as an indirect challenge to Brereton. Obviously, with an enemy of Brereton's as the *de facto* chief minister (Cromwell was only confirmed in this position in 1534), there were no consequences for Dutton. Indeed, Cromwell began a policy of undermining Brereton by giving Brereton's lesser offices to his rivals when they came up for renewal and, more generally, promoting and helping his enemies.

In June 1533, Dutton, still anxiously awaiting a decision on his land lawsuit, complained to Cromwell-ally Rowland Lee (c.1487-1543), soon to be Bishop of Coventry and Lichfield, about his treatment. Lee, who possibly married Henry VIII and Anne Boleyn and who definitely took part in the divorce proceedings of Catherine of Aragon, promptly wrote to Cromwell praising Dutton and asserting that he 'keepeth and knoweth Jesus'.[372] This seems to imply that he was conveying to Cromwell that Dutton was a Protestant; a man after their own hearts. In July 1533, a resolution of the Privy Council (in many respects the 'cabinet' of the day) declared that Dutton was the rightful heir to the Dutton lands.[373] This was confirmed on 16th May 1534 by award of Henry VIII. The coheirs of Sir Thomas Dutton (c. 1424-1459) were awarded a number of ancestral Dutton manors and lands but Sir Piers Dutton was awarded the lion's share, including the manor of Dutton.[374] Sir Piers Dutton had, essentially, won.

And in the same year, William Brereton made a particularly catastrophic error of political judgement. He was convinced that a Flintshire gentleman called John ap Griffith Eyton had killed one of his retainers. Flintshire was controlled by the Palatinate. Eyton was acquitted by a London court but Brereton was determined to have him found guilty so, with the help of Anne Boleyn (with whom he was on very friendly terms), he had him re-arrested, put on trial in the Holt, in the Dee Valley, and executed. This was possible because the Palatinate, including its legal system, were not controlled by the crown.[375] Cromwell had tried to intervene to save Eyton's life but to no avail. Rowland Lee, now Bishop of Coventry and Lichfield, wrote to Cromwell on 10th July 1534 explaining that Dutton was one of the few significant Cheshire gentry who were absent from Eyton's show trial.[376] The purpose of this trial appears to have been Brereton's desire to assert his authority in the Welsh Marches. But the plan had unintended consequences, because it highlighted, to people like Cromwell who already disliked Brereton, that he was unstable and ruthless and it also stressed his desperation, as his power was clearly in decline. Brereton's power in Cheshire and Wales also meant that he stood in the way of a more general Tudor policy of centralizing power and removing influence from provincial magnates.[377] Brereton was very powerful. Although he was not High Sheriff of Cheshire, by 1535, William Brereton was Controller of Chester and Flint (its financial officer), Chamberlain of Cheshire, Steward of Halton, Steward of Longendale, Keeper of Shotwick Park, Keeper of Mersley Park, Escheator of Cheshire, Ranger of Delamere Forest, Steward of the Holt and various other parts of the Welsh Marches, Sheriff of Flintshire, Sheriff of Merioneth, Constable of Chester Castle, and a major landowner with a significant retinue.[378] His power had to be curbed.

In the long term, Cromwell ensured that the power of the entire Palatine was curbed. In 1535, the Act of Union was passed, which made Wales part of the English state, thus heavily reducing Brereton's, or any other magnate's, powers there by 1536, when it came into force.[379] In 1537, an Act of Parliament asserted that: 'justice had not been before that time indifferently ministered in the palatine of Chester (or in several counties of Wales...' Accordingly, Cheshire would have Justices of the Peace like everywhere else and they would be answerable to the crown.[380] This Act, therefore, reduced the powers of the Cheshire Sheriff and Chamberlain. Cheshire was no longer completely judicially independent as of 1538.

But Brereton's actions also had consequences in the short term. Brereton had to be tamed and then eliminated. Perhaps partly for this reason, on 14th November 1534, Cromwell had Sir Piers Dutton, Brereton's enemy, appointed High Sheriff of Cheshire. Then, in January 1535, it seems that William Brereton was removed as Steward of Halton and replaced by Sir Edward Neville (c.1471-1538), Gentleman of the Privy Chamber. Dutton became his deputy steward, with Dutton recommended by the king to exercise all the powers, though Dutton later complained to Cromwell that Sir William Brereton had intervened to stop Neville accepting a fee from Dutton to purchase the office.[381] Even so, as Sheriff, Dutton could take his revenge.

Chapter Seven
High Sheriff of Cheshire

'...we give unto you our right hearty thanks and shall
undoubtedly consider your faithful service to your singular
rejoice and comfort hereafter.[382]

THE 14th November 1534 must have been a very satisfying day for Sir Piers Dutton. He was finally in a position of power over all the people who had made his life difficult over the years: the abbots, the gentry who wanted to overturn his inheritance, the people who insisted on taking him to court and having him jailed, and the Brereton family. Most usefully of all, as High Sheriff, he was in charge of imprisoning criminals and arranging executions.[383]

Obviously, his enemies could expect little justice. Richard Cholmondeley, one of those who had campaigned against Dutton's inheritance, complained in 1536 that he could do nothing to stop other people's cattle trespassing on his land because Sir Piers Dutton 'beareth (me) no good will'.[384] But as sheriff, Dutton could do much more than simply make his enemies' lives difficult. He began by trying to get someone he could trust put in charge of the Cistercian Abbey in Whitegate (the 'Abbey of Vale Royal'), probably because he held lands from the abbey.[385] (Cistercians were an extreme-contemplative order, known for a focus on manual labour[386]). At the same time, he tried to have William Brereton's deputy-Chamberlain (Randle Brereton[387]) and the Abbot of Norton, Thomas Birkenhead, executed for treason. This would further weaken William Brereton and help Dutton to take control of Norton Abbey, the steward of which was William Brereton. Overtly, both schemes failed, but in reality they achieved their goals of weakening both William Brereton and the Abbot of Norton.

Beginning with the Abbey of Vale Royal: in 1535, John Butler, the

Abbot of the Vale Royal, died. Brereton wanted Ralph Goldsmith to replace him but the monks were granted a free election and, in a sign of his declining power, they completely ignored what the Chamberlain wanted. On 21st June, Dutton wrote to Cromwell recommending 'Dan'[388] Randal Wilmslow for the position and did so again on 3rd August.[389] Indeed, Dutton's candidate offered Cromwell £100 to 'do him further as large pleasure as any man'.[390] In the end, John Harware was elected. Brereton took a £100 bribe and a £20 per annum pension from the new abbot. But he had to negotiate with him to get a bond of 200 marks whereas he had no problem receiving a bond of £1000 from the previous abbot when he was elected.[391] This might be interpreted as evidence that people realised that Brereton's power was weakening.

The Coining Affair

In the same letter in which Dutton recommended Wilmslow to be abbot of Vale Royal, he informed Cromwell that he had arrested the Abbot of Norton, Robert Jannons (one of his bailiffs) and Randle Brereton, Deputy Chamberlain of Cheshire, for illegal coining. The production of counterfeit coins was treason because it had become such a significant problem for the economy.[392] As so-called 'petty treason', it incurred a penalty of death by hanging. This was Dutton's other plan: to have his political enemies or their associates executed for treason. A number of other criminals played a part in this complex scheme which needs to be explained at length.

Henry Broke, a gentleman, later claimed that in 1533 he had been passed false coins by John Wreygth who had himself been passed them by Robert Jannons, servant of the Abbot of Norton.

In 1534, Robert Hale had stolen a chalice from a church in Tame, Oxfordshire, and, with his servant Piers Felday, melted it down to make fake coins. They then distributed these coins around Chester for others to pass them on. On Shrove Sunday 1535, Hale, Felday, and the Abbot of Vale Crucis committed a robbery in Oxfordshire. Hale was arrested while the others successfully fled to London. In Oxford jail, Hale told Sir Walter Stenmore that he would betray to him the names of many thieves if Stenmore would help him. Stenmore agreed but then passed

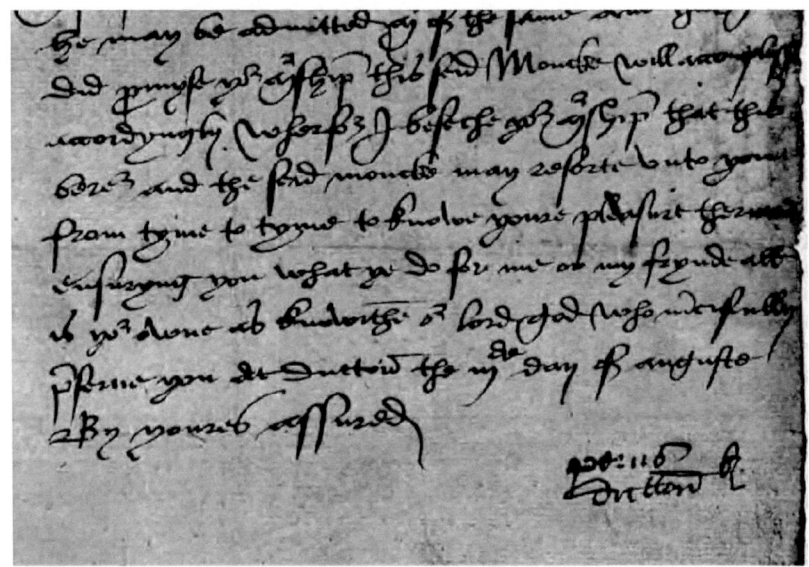

*7. Letter from Dutton to Cromwell in 1535
(Memorials of the Duttons of Dutton).*

the information gleaned from Hale to Cromwell. Cromwell passed the information to Dutton, presumably as the affair related to Cheshire. Hale was moved to Newgate prison where a number of others to whom coins had allegedly been passed in Chester, such as Philip Constantine, also found themselves. Even by the standards of the day, Newgate would be an extremely unpleasant prison, even for those who could pay their way. Built in 1188 and just inside the City of London, Newgate was utterly dilapidated by the end of the sixteenth century and would have been moving that way in the 1530s. It was poorly ventilated, over-crowded, and notorious for 'gaol fever' (typhus).[393]

Meanwhile, as the others languished in Newgate, back in Chester, John Wreygth (who had passed fake coins to Henry Brook) was arrested for treason. According to Brook, who was repeating hearsay, at this time the Abbot of Norton began to employ one Thomas Holfe as his smith knowing that he was a 'cunning workman'[394] – a forger of coins. At about the same time, Felday returned to Chester. Knowing who the people were involved in the coining affair, Dutton arrested

Felday.[395]   So, by June 1535, Hale, Felday and a number of others were being held in Newgate. Dutton and his servants, including Ralph Mainwaring (Dutton's deputy), then visited Felday in prison. Dutton boasted to Felday that he 'was in so great favour with the king and his council' that he could gain him a pardon. However, he would only do so if Felday implicated a number of Dutton's enemies. Dutton told him to implicate 'Randle Brereton' (the deputy Chamberlain) in receiving and using 'false coins' because 'he hath done me many high displeasures',[396] presumably partly a reference to the events of 1504 in which Randle Brereton may have been involved.

Felday should claim that he had sold Randle Brereton partridges as an explanation for having had contact with him, because Felday was known to sell these around Chester. He should also accuse Sir John Done (an ally of William Brereton), Sir William Pole (another Brereton ally), the Abbot of Norton – the Abbot of Norton was a Brereton ally, with Brereton having been the steward of Norton Abbey since 1525[397] – and various others. To sweeten the deal, Dutton added, Dame Juliana Dutton would give Felday a new coat once he was free. Felday obliged and Dutton acted on this in June 1535. Dutton made his arrests, though seemingly did not arrest everyone he demanded Felday name, and Randle Brereton took the situation so seriously that he made his will, which is dated 15th August 1535.[398]

In the end, the plan fell apart. Dutton took his evidence to the Privy Council. Dutton's servants were present at his examination and signalled with two fingers for Felday so he knew to name a person if the possibility of that person's guilt was put to him, which resulted in further people being named, such as Piers Bruen, servant of Sir John Done.[399] But, eventually, Felday was dismissed as an unreliable witness and the other evidence against the abbot was too weak. In August 1536, Felday confessed to coining and was moved to the Tower of London. Bruen spent 18 weeks in the Tower before being released,[400] so perhaps the others who were falsely accused spent a similar amount of time there. As the prisoners were not noble, they would likely have been in a communal cell in the tower and shackled in irons, until somebody paid the jailer to unshackle them.[401]

Sir William Brereton of Brereton's Conflict with Dutton

Sir William Brereton of Brereton was Chief Justice and Deputy Marshall of Ireland and between 1534 and May 1536 he had been in Ireland, suppressing a rebellion by Thomas Fitzgerald, Earl of Kildare (1513-1537).[402] In May 1536, Sir William Brereton of Brereton was called back to England to become Deputy Chamberlain of Cheshire.[403] After William Brereton of Malpas' execution, the position of Chamberlain was first given to Henry VIII's illegitimate son, Henry Fitzroy, Duke of Richmond (1519-1536),[404] but he died in July 1536 and was replaced by Rees Mansell.[405] Mansell was not from Cheshire so a desire to centralize power may have been behind this decision. However, as a navy leader, Mansell was also frequently absent, meaning that his deputy was effectively in charge.[406]

Accordingly, in 1537, Sir William Brereton, as *de facto* Chamberlain, had Felday moved to Chester castle. Felday confessed all his lies, which he said he had told at Dutton's inducement, to Sir William Brereton who wrote and told Cromwell on 8th June 1537.[407] In actuality, Felday should not have come under the control of Sir William Brereton at all. Indeed, Sir Thomas Audley (1488-1544),[408] who had been appointed Lord Chancellor in 1533, wrote to Cromwell on 26th May 1537 saying that Felday should have been delivered to Dutton. According to the abstract, Audley had heard:

> 'that Sir William Brereton, deputy-chamberlain of Chester, has laboured to have the prisoner delivered to him. Does not know for what purpose, but execution does not pertain to his office. Understands that Cromwell has written to the sheriffs of London to deliver him to Brereton, but asks that his previous order may take effect. Suspects that Brereton wishes to save the prisoner, as he saved the abbot of Norton, whom he dares avow to be a traitor.'[409]

That it was Audley who wrote to defend Dutton against Brereton is noteworthy as the letters from Sir William Brereton tend to be to Cromwell while those from Dutton tend to be to Audley. This may imply that Dutton was closer to Audley than he was to Cromwell. One possible explanation for their apparent relative closeness may be that

Audley may have had connections with Dame Juliana Dutton. Audley was born in Earl's Colne in Essex, had been the Colchester town clerk from 1514 to 1532, had been an Essex Justice of the Peace from 1520 and its MP in 1529. He was also regarded as at least cautiously supportive of Protestantism, though this was tempered by his general obedience to the king.[410] And, of course, it was he who persuaded parliament to release Juliana's son from prison.

8. Sir Thomas Audley, Lord Chancellor. Painted in 1804, based on a contemporary print (Wikipedia).

But a significant aim of Dutton's plan back in 1535 was, presumably, to use Felday's evidence as a means of humiliating William Brereton of Malpas. The plan, if successful, would show that there was nothing Dutton's enemy could do to protect his kinsman and deputy chamberlain or his allies. And it came close to linking William Brereton of Malpas with a network of counterfeiters and thus traitors.[411] Its other aim (also achieved) was to damage the Abbot of Norton, the results of which we will explore below. At Michaelmas 1535, Dutton made his way to

London, probably to secure his reappointment as High Sheriff. He was successful, because Henry VIII ignored the three candidates presented to him and wrote in Dutton's name himself,[412] evidencing the king's determination that the loyal Dutton get the position again.

Displacing William Brereton of Malpas

1536 was highly significant in Sir Piers Dutton's continued ascent. An Act of Parliament on 15th February confirmed Dutton's inheritance as Lord of the Manor of Dutton. And with William Brereton of Malpas badly weakened by Dutton, Cromwell made his move to destroy the Chester Chamberlain.

As part of his well-known scheme to depose Anne Boleyn, he had her accused of adultery in April 1536. However, he added William Brereton's name to the list of the accused males.

Brereton was tried on 12th May 1536 before a special commission composed of men who either were beholden to Cromwell, couldn't afford to upset the king, or simply disliked Brereton. Based purely on the word of one of the other defendants, Brereton was found guilty and executed.[413] With the removal of William Brereton, Cromwell wanted to ensure that nobody in Cheshire could be quite as powerful as him ever again, so Brereton's assorted offices were parcelled out. Sir Piers Dutton was the main beneficiary.

As of May 1536, Dutton was more than just Sheriff. He became deputy Steward of Halton Castle.[414] He also took various offices directly from William Brereton, including Ranger of Delamere Forest and Keeper of Shotwick Park.

Unfortunately, the document which lists the appointments, written by Thomas Wriothesley (1505-1550), Clerk of the Signet,[415] is so badly damaged that it is impossible to make out the other offices that Dutton inherited from Brereton.[416]

The Norton Abbey Rebellion

In September 1536, Dutton arrested one John Heseham for treason. Specifically, he had been 'questioning the King's spiritual supremacy'.

Dutton had him locked up in Chester Castle. The sheriff, who must have sworn an oath accepting the king's spiritual supremacy in 1535, wrote to Cromwell that he had arrested him for trying to flee and for, 'divers traitorous and seditious words that he hath spoken, which was that if the spiritual men had holden together the king could not have been head of the church; and also that the Bishop of Rochester and Sir Thomas Moore died martyrs in the quarrel aforesaid'.[417] We might regard this act of zeal as further evidence that Dutton was Protestant.

In October 1536, Dutton grabbed an opportunity to impress Cromwell and the king even more. 1536 was the year in which Cromwell began to enact the dissolution of the monasteries. Commissioners were appointed in Cheshire to carry this out, with William Brereton's name first on the list and Dutton's second. After William Brereton's appointment on Tower Hill, Dutton became the chief commissioner. In February 1536, it was declared that any abbey with a value of less than £200 would be dissolved. The king's commissioners, led by Dutton, had valued Norton Abbey at £260.[418] However, its debts reduced its value to £180.[419] This combined with the fact that the abbot was under investigation for coining persuaded the commissioners that the abbey should be dissolved.[420] Two commissioners, Mr. Coombes and Mr. Bolles, arrived in early October 1536 to do just that.

In a letter to Sir Thomas Audley, Dutton wrote that the two men had been packing away the jewels and other valuables, when the abbot attacked them with a force of between 200 and 300 men. In Dutton's words:

> 'Please it your good lordship to be advertised Mr. Coombes and Mr. Bolles the king's commissioners within the county of Chester were lately at Norton within the same county for the suppressing of the abbey there. And when they had packed up such jewels and other stuff as they had there and thought upon the morrow after to depart thence, the abbot gathered a great company together to the number of two or three hundred persons, so that the said commissioners were in fear of their lives... '

In fear of their lives, Coombes and Bolles barricaded themselves in the abbey tower and somehow managed to send a letter to Dutton explaining the danger they were in. This letter arrived at 9 pm on the 8th October and by 2 o'clock in the morning on 9th October Dutton had arrived at the abbey with his own armed gang, composed of his tenants and assorted supporters.

> 'Which letter came to me about nine of the clock in the same night upon Sunday last; and about two of the clock in the same night I came thither with such of my lovers and tenants as I had near about me and found divers fires made there as well within the gates as without and the said abbot had caused an ox and other victuals to be killed and prepared for such his company as he had then there; and it was thought in the morrow after he had come forth to have had a great number more.'

The abbot's men, claimed Dutton, had made a fire in front of the gates of the abbey and the abbot had found them an ox and other food to roast on it. Dutton claimed that he charged at the rioters and they were so frightened that they jumped into the river and he could not locate many of them in the dark.

> 'Notwithstanding I used some policy and came suddenly upon them so that the company that were there fled and some of them took poles and waters; and it was so dark that I could not find them; and it was thought if the matter had not been quickly handled, it would have grown to further inconvenience, to what danger God knoweth.'

Nevertheless, Dutton managed to arrest the abbot and three of his canons and imprisoned them in Halton Castle. He also restored William Parker, the king's farmer, to ownership of his new abbey.

> 'Howbeit, I took the abbot and three of his canons and brought them to the king's castle of Halton and there committed them to ward to the constable to be kept as the king's 'rebellions' upon pain of £1,000; and afterwards saw the said commissioners with their stuff conveyed thence and William Parker the king's servant who is appointed to be the king's farmer there restored to his possession.'[421]

Henry VIII was extremely excited and pleased by this, which was probably Dutton's intention. He wrote to Dutton and Sir William Brereton on 19th October. With regard to Dutton's actions, he stated: 'we give unto you right hearty thanks, and shall undoubtedly consider your faithful service and comfort hereafter'. Henry directed that if, in

Dutton and Brereton's view, the abbot and his servants were traitors who had incited an insurrection against the crown then, 'you shall immediately, upon the sight hereof, without any manner or further circumstance of law or delay, cause them to be hanged (*) for the terrible example of all other hereafter.' Indeed, he originally wrote, 'hanged, setting up their heads and quarters around the country', but he had second thoughts and crossed those nine words out.[422] Henry wrote to them again 20th October, reiterating his earlier letter. They were to be hanged as 'arrant traitors' and this was to be done as quickly as possible.[423] In effect, Henry was demanding execution without trial.

However, on 30th November, Dutton wrote to Cromwell explaining that he could not execute the abbot because he had received a letter from the Earl of Derby, in which was enclosed a letter to Derby from various nobles then quelling the Yorkshire uprising – the Duke of Norfolk, the Earl of Rutland, and the Earl of Shrewsbury[424] This letter, written on 30th October, demanded that none of the prisoners be executed, presumably because the earls were trying to restore order in the North and didn't want any further unrest sparked. It threatened dire consequences if they were executed: 'And if ye fail not hereof at your peril. And our lord hath your lordship in his governance.' Derby strongly advised Dutton to do as the letter commanded. Even so, Dutton emphasized to Cromwell that he had already signed the death warrant of the abbot, but Sir William Brereton refused to do so (both needed to sign as Henry had instructed both of them). Indeed, Sir William Brereton and Sir Thomas Butler had actually written to Cromwell claiming that, 'the common fame of the county imputes no fault to them' (meaning the abbot and the canons).[425]

There was clearly a significant body of opinion in favour of the abbot's innocence, seemingly with good reason. It is perfectly possible that Dutton exaggerated the events of the 8th-9th October 1536 or even concocted them entirely. Firstly, we know that Dutton was capable of deceit in order to damage political opponents, as seen in the Felday coining affair, which we will return to below. Secondly, he had every reason to hold a grudge against the abbot and want the abbey closed. Dutton's hatred towards the abbot may have been motivated by his feud with the Brereton family. Although the Duttons were traditionally patrons of Norton Abbey, William Brereton had been granted an annuity of 53s 4d by the abbot and by 1535 William Brereton was steward of the abbey, with an annual salary of 60s.[426] In addition, as Dutton's lands bordered those of the abbey, he probably hoped to gain some of its land after its dissolution. In 1535, Dutton had led a campaign of vilification against the abbey, accusing its members, and members of the Benedictine Godstow nunnery, of 'debauched conduct'[427] during his inspections of the religious houses to discern their value and whether they ought to be closed. He was quoted as having said, 'Time disclosed the real character of nuns and friars and it would have been a sin to hold forth with such bad people.'[428] Quelling a rebellion by the abbot would likely impress the king and assist in this aim. He would be the man who stopped a serious pro-monastery rebellion. Certainly, the king was impressed enough, in December, to reappoint Dutton as High Sheriff for 1537.

Thirdly, there are serious holes in Dutton's account and there is no other account to corroborate it. If the two commissioners were able to get a letter, via a messenger, out of the tower to Dutton then, surely, the mob could not have been as ferocious as Dutton implied. If they were in fear of their lives, why didn't they leave by the same route? In the book *Tudor Cheshire*, Joan Beck explains that, 'Somehow, they smuggled a message out to Sir Piers Dutton...'[429] but how? If it was possible to get a message out it seems unlikely that the crowd was overly fierce. Further, how did Dutton's men manage to disperse '200 or 300 people' in the dark and succeed in capturing the supposed ring-leaders but not anyone else? Sir Thomas Butler, Sheriff of Lancashire in 1535, was instrumental in suppressing pro-monastic forces in Lancashire and instituting the new religious policy there. But on 8th November he wrote to Cromwell asking him to intercede on behalf of the imprisoned canons of Norton, 'whereof surely if I had any conjecture that they were in any way culpable I would not then once move your good lordship for their case ... but would to the utterest of my power force their execution.'[430] For these reasons, Cheshire local historian Geoffrey Chesters went so far as to assert, 'a case may be made for the view that the rising only occurred in Sir Piers Dutton's imagination.'[431] This seems far-fetched, not least because of the level of detail in Dutton's description: that they roasted an ox, for example. But it is certainly likely that Dutton exaggerated whatever did occur.

If Dutton was telling the truth then one interpretation is that the Norton Abbey riot was the seeds of a Cheshire Pilgrimage of Grace (this happened later in October, but there had already been a similar rebellion in Lincolnshire) but Dutton tore them from the earth before they could flower. However, the monasteries appear to have been less popular in Cheshire than in Lancashire or Yorkshire; so it seems unlikely that the Pilgrimage of Grace would have spread to Cheshire. Cheshire had fewer *per capita* monasteries than Yorkshire or Lancashire and those few monasteries played a less significant role in the life of the county than did their equivalents in Yorkshire and Lancashire. At Vale Royal, some of the abbey's tenants supported the king in opposing the risings, infuriating the abbot who had declared that the king was 'not lawfully married'. The abbot would have imprisoned the tenants if Sir Piers Dutton had not stopped him.[432] Why would feelings not also be similar in the area around Norton Abbey? Moreover, monks in and around Chester had a poor reputation. For example, Chester's friars were regularly before the city's courts accused of assaults on the monks of St. Werburgh's or on men of the town.[433] The monks themselves were often in trouble during the period for various offences, including murder and rape.[434] Adam Beconsall, the archdeacon's commissioner, reported, in 1535, that the Abbot of Norton had, in the 1520s, been living with a woman and had fathered several children by her.[435] Accordingly, it seems likely that the Abbot and his canons did not incite a rebellion or, at least, not one as serious as that described by Dutton.

The execution of the abbot and his canons was delayed and then called off. Meanwhile, Dutton was reappointed sheriff for 1537 in December 1536. But Brereton reported in a letter to Cromwell on 18th January 1537 that he was trying to arrange a joint enquiry into the 'supposed insurrection' at Norton Abbey, but, despite many requests, Sir Piers Dutton would not co-operate with him. He therefore suggested that the inquiry should be conducted by a commission of 'men from the shire'.[436]

A Fight Over the Forest

In early 1537, Dutton was in London for three months with his Under-Sheriff, Ralph Mainwaring, and made an official complaint to Cromwell about how Cheshire had been run in his absence.[437] Then, possibly with the hubris that comes from success, Dutton made an unwise decision in March 1537. As we saw earlier, one of the positions that Dutton had inherited from William Brereton was 'Ranger of Delamere Forest', a protector of the forest in which only the monarch and those with his permission could hunt. Sir John Done, a member of the household of Princess Mary and Sheriff of Cheshire from 1529 to 1530, held a recognized hereditary right to hunt in the forest and the Dones and Duttons had long been rivals.[438] This rivalry intensified after Dutton inherited Dutton Hall as this sat within the bounds of an area of the Forest of Delamere over which Sir John Done exercised hereditary right of rangership.[439] In 1536, Dutton, his deputy sheriff and 50 of Dutton's servants had stopped Done's men from hunting a stag, fishing and felling trees in the forest. Some time in 1536, Done wrote to the king begging him to prosecute Dutton and his associates. Done was furious that:

> 'Dutton has caused his servants to kill the King's deer, under colour of his rangership of the forest of Mara and Mondrom. His servants caused a riot to be made against the servants of Sir John Done, forester of the said forest, and prevented them from fetching in a strayed hart.'[440]

Dutton responded by taking out a case against Done for misusing the king's forest but Done was able to show that he was legally entitled to use it.[441] Dutton was then accused, by Sir John Done, of illegal stag hunting in the area of the forest of which Done was master, as well as trying to intimidate witnesses. Consequently, despite Dutton still being in favour at court, Dutton ultimately lost the case. Various secondary sources assert that 'it is said that' Dutton was outlawed at this point.[442] However, there appears to be no evidence for this, as the anonymous writer of history of the Dutton family *Memorials of the Duttons of Dutton* pointed out in 1901.[443] In November 1537, the position of High Sheriff passed to Sir Henry Delves (1498-1560).[444]

Dutton's name was not presented as an option to the king but, unlike when this happened in 1535, the king did not write in Dutton's name himself.[445] This decision may have been influenced by ongoing legal proceedings against Dutton.

The Abduction and Execution of Piers Felday

By 1537, Dutton's audacious plan to have associates of the now dead William Brereton (and Dutton's enemies more generally) executed for treason had collapsed. Felday was dismissed as an unreliable witness by the council and all those he had implicated had long ago been freed. And, worse still, Felday was moved to Chester and confessed to Sir William Brereton, in June 1537, that he had been procured by Dutton, by threats and inducements, to give false evidence against Dutton's enemies, especially with regard to coining.[446] However, Dutton heard about Felday's confession, which was made not just before Brereton but the Mayor of Chester and many others.[447] The confession meant that Felday was a threat to Dutton, presumably because he could reveal even more.

Accordingly, Dutton had him abducted from Chester Castle by force, held him hostage at one of his houses (Hatton Hall) and had him executed on Saturday 4th August 1537.[448] Before Felday climbed the scaffold at Boughton, a market town,[449] he asked for a priest other than the one appointed by Dutton, with whom he'd spent the previous day, to hear his confession. There were many monks and friars in the crowd and John Hurleton, Prior of White Friars in Chester, stepped forward. However, Dutton's servants would not let anybody, other than a priest appointed by Dutton, hear the confession. This priest was a friend of Dutton's and was even paid an annuity by him, so could be trusted. Felday climbed the scaffold and began to publicly proclaim that all of the accusations of coining he had made had been untrue.

'Masters, never trust a knight, esquire, nor gentleman, for I was fair promised; howbeit it is an old saying, "Fair words make fools fain!"' he exclaimed. Then Ralph Manning responded: 'Felday, thou did accuse me; is that true or not? God forgive thee, and I do.' Felday made no response to this. Felday then started publicly denouncing various

Cheshire magnates for hiring him to commit violence and asserted that there were people in the crowd who had illegal coining irons. Dutton's servants pushed him off the ladder before he could say any more.[450] On 29th August, Sir William Brereton wrote to Cromwell telling him what had happened. He added that: 'Sir Piers' friends openly report that he can do as he likes in this county. If he is not punished it will be so supposed by the whole shire. I desire to know your mind by the bearer, my son.'[451] Cromwell never acted against Dutton.

Meanwhile, Sir William Brereton conducted his enquiry into the 'supposed insurrection'. The records of the enquiry do not survive but by 26th May 1537, Lord Chancellor Sir Thomas Audeley, one of Dutton's patrons, wrote to Cromwell that, 'Sir William Brereton saved the abbot of Norton, being I dare avow a traitor.'[452] By August 1537, the Abbot and canons were released from Chester Castle and the Abbot was awarded a pension of £24. A number of canons were likewise pensioned off.[453] As stated, in November 1537, Dutton was replaced as sheriff.[454]

De Facto Sheriff?

Even though he'd been removed from office, Dutton was nowhere close to retiring from politics and his new scheme was to attack Sir John Done, whose machinations may have indirectly led to his not being reappointed Sheriff.

In a letter to Cromwell, Brereton explained on 2nd January 1538 that one George Mullington had confessed to killing the king's game in Delamere Forest the previous December. Brereton had sent out an errant to have him arrested and committed to Chester Castle, but Mullington was rescued by Dame Juliana Dutton and was protected by the Dutton family. Brereton appealed to Sir Henry Delves, the new Sheriff of Cheshire, but he refused to do anything about it, because Delves was a friend of Dutton's.[455] Considering Dutton's influence, it seems probable that Delves, who was later MP for Cheshire in 1554,[456] was merely a puppet sheriff and Dutton remained in charge. This is further evidenced by Delves writing to Cromwell objecting to Thomas Hurleton as his deputy,[457] and arguing in favour of Henry Brook, an ally of Dutton's who had assisted Dutton in the Felday case.[458]

However, having not been reappointed Sheriff, Dutton may have been naturally concerned about his status at court and relationship with Cromwell. Cromwell's servant and representative in Chester, Richard Hough (1505-1573), had been promised the Ridership of Delamere Forest, something he wrote to Cromwell about on 27th January 1538, adding that Dutton was in London, not Cheshire, at the time.[459] Dutton was absent because he had gone to London to secure his reappointment, so was obviously concerned about his position with Cromwell.[460] Dutton clearly remained in favour at court, however, as in July 1538 he was granted yet another lucrative stewardship, this time of the Manor of Tattenhall.[461] Hough's overtures towards the ridership were ignored.

Conflict with Bishop Rowland Lee

In 1538, Dutton was also in dispute with Rowland Lee, the head of the Council of the Marches over who really wielded authority. By this time, Lee seemed to distrust Dutton as when, in mid-1537, Audley had instructed Lee to make Dutton a member of the Council of the Marches, Lee had written to Cromwell to argue against the decision.[462] The conflict between Dutton and Lee came to a head due to a complex series of events.

In 1531, Richard Cholmondeley of Cheshire, a Brereton ally, had taken the lease of a vicarage, and been promised an extension on the lease. However, the following year, the lease was given to Randle Mainwaring, also of Cheshire, with the vicar complaining that Cholmondeley had been late in paying his rent. In 1534, there was, therefore, a legal dispute between Cholmondeley and Mainwaring. This became so acrimonious than on 1st December 1537, when Mainwaring was in London, Cholmondeley sent a gang to lie in wait for Mainwaring as he made his way home to Cheshire. There was only one road between London and Chester, Watling Street. They attacked him and his servants and left them for dead, though Cholmondeley insisted that he had been attacked by Mainwaring's men the previous day. Dutton reported the events to Cromwell on 15th December.[463]

In the same letter, Dutton wrote to Cromwell accusing Sir Randolph Brereton's son, Thomas, of trying to rig the jury on his father's inquisition post mortem to deprive the crown of its rightful taxes.[464] Accordingly, he may have been concerned that Cromwell favoured the Brereton faction and may have hoped that drawing Cromwell's attention to a riot, the incident on 1st December, involving Brereton allies, would change Cromwell's mind. In response to Dutton's letter regarding the riot, Cromwell instructed Rowland Lee to jail the two men, which he did in separate prisons.

By March 1538, the men had not yet been indicted so Chancellor Audley, probably at Dutton's request, demanded that they be sent to London. Dutton, therefore, was attempting to undermine the authority of Lee and the Council of the Marches to get his enemy prosecuted. Lee responded by going to Chester where he jailed a grand jury, appointed by Dutton, for being corruptly lenient to Dutton's allies. He told Cromwell that they found murderers guilty of manslaughter and gave lenient sentences to, or found not guilty, members of Dutton's retinue who had committed crimes of violence during disputes. Lee presented violence and corruption as endemic in Cheshire, pressurising Cromwell to appoint outsiders to run the county.[465] Rowland Lee wrote to Cromwell on 16th March 1538 saying: 'The dissension between Brereton and Dutton destroys order in Cheshire; if I might give counsel, neither of them should be officers of the chamberlainship.'[466] Clearly, in the wake of the Pilgrimage of Grace, shire leaders had to be able to act decisively in the government's cause, meaning political disorder in Cheshire was the last thing Cromwell needed. It might even be argued that this conflict was one factor motivating Cromwell to integrate Cheshire more fully into the Tudor state.

Sidelined from Power

On 28th November 1538, Dutton was leading an inquisition post mortem into the lands and heirs of Peter Stanley and William Massey. On 30th November, he was in Westmorland conducting an inquiry into the late Ralph Leycester.[467] But in early 1539, his political opponents led a coordinated, and successful, attack. Dutton's enemies, including

Brereton, accused him of discharging his duties as a commissioner 'with too much zeal and some dishonesty'.[468] Sir John Done accused him of rigging juries at Halton Castle manorial court, including appoint a number of his 'servants' as jurors. These included John Dutton of Helsby (c. 1470- Before 1544) whose kinship with Piers is unclear.[469] Done also accused Dutton of leading a riot against him (in the forest, as discussed), and inducing Felday to falsely accuse his servant Piers Bruen, meaning that Bruen had to spend 18 weeks in the Tower of London.[470] Thomas Aston, in a letter to the Earl of Southampton, William FitzWilliam (1490-1542), Chancellor of the Duchy of Lancaster,[471] accused Dutton of appointing his own corrupt officials to look after Halton Castle's records, making frivolous allegations against enemies to drain them of money through legal fees, and jury rigging at court hearings.[472] Dutton was summonsed to Chester Castle to answer the charges before the Exchequer.

Evidence of Dutton's continued power and popularity at court, however, could be seen in July 1539 when Cheshire's 'Commission for the Peace' was appointed. Of 33 names, beginning with Audley (the Lord Chancellor), Dutton was in 11th position, with first seven names being peers such as the Duke of Norfolk, the Duke of Suffolk and Cromwell. In terms of gentry only Sir William Sulyard (Justice of the Common Pleas, who died in 1540),[473] Sir John Porte and Sir Edward Croft (sometime High Sheriff of Hertfordshire) were placed ahead of him. Sir John Done was placed far behind.[474] Further evidence of his continued influence behind the scenes can be seen in a letter from Sir William Brereton to Cromwell on 9th October 1539:

> 'Although your Lordship set a loving end between my cousin Dutton and me, I fear he bears no favour to some of my friends and may handle them severely if now, in my absence, he can obtain a sheriff to his mind. I beg your Lordship therefore (the rather as by the King's commandment I must endeavour myself to do his Grace's service) to see that there be an indifferent sheriff appointed for the coming year.'[475]

Sir William Brereton was Chief Justice of Ireland so he may have been referring to going there.[476] In addition, it should be noted that the word 'cousin' could be used in this period to mean even a distant kinsman.[477] (Sir William Brereton was the son of Agnes Legh, sister of Dutton's father-in-law Thomas Legh and thus Dutton's deceased wife's cousin). But, clearly, if the Sheriff of Cheshire was remotely friendly with Dutton then his influence would be further heightened. Seemingly due to concern over the damage conflict between Cheshire's warring families was doing to the county, a series of outsiders, with interests in Lancashire and Shropshire, were appointed as Sheriffs after Sir Henry Delves. These were Sir Robert Needham (1538-9), Sir Alex Radcliffe (1539-40), Edmund Trafford (1540-41) and the newcomer but local John Holcroft (1541-42). As such, Dutton's direct power, in the sense of holding a powerful office, was reduced and he seems to have focused on more indirect forms of playing for status.

Chapter Eight
Dutton Hall and Her Minstrels

'Somewhat reluctantly I leave Dutton (Hall);
few places are more interesting in the county.'[478]

IN 1539, Dutton decided to focus his attention on rebuilding Dutton Hall. The half timber, quadrangle construction that was produced – which also connected the Dutton's chapel to their house – is regarded by some as one of the finest examples of mid-Tudor architecture in the North West.[479] The chapel had fallen down by 1900.[480] But, even so T. A. Coward wrote in 1903 that, 'Somewhat reluctantly I leave Dutton (Hall); few places are more interesting in the county.'[481]

Dutton Hall

Sitting, originally, in 1400 acres of meadow, Dutton Hall must have been an impressive site for any visitor. It is now in East Grinstead in Sussex and has been put back together, though not entirely faithfully.

Above the main door, Dutton has carved 'S. P. D. K' ('Sir Piers Dutton, Knight') while on the lower beam is a true love's knot entwining the letters 'P' and 'J' ('Piers and Juliana'). On the lintel is written: 'Sir Piers Dutton, Knight, Lord of Dutton, and my lady Dame Julian his wife made this hall and building in the year of Our Lord God 1542. Who thanketh God of all.' 1542 was the year the building work was completed and 'Who thanketh God of all' was the motto of the Duttons of Dutton.

As you walk into the porch, you come to a further archway, the entrance proper to Dutton Hall, protected by an imposing studded door, above which is inscribed, 'Who thanketh God of all, 1539.'

9. Dutton Hall entrance porch, part of an architectural drawing by Maurice B Adams, The Building News, October 8, 1886. (Courtesy of John Chesworth.)

Beneath the archway are ranged six shields carefully carved into the woodwork, the two centre shields displaying the arms of Hatton and Dutton. As we have seen, gentility – and the right to a coat of arms – was highly significant to status in Tudor England and there was no attempt to be subtle. At the top left-hand, and right side of the archway, Dutton had an opulent display of his coat of arms carved (combining the Dutton and Hatton arms, as he descended from the Hatton heiress), with two griffins as supporters, and helmets atop. Always aware of how important it was to seem religious, he had a wreath carved beneath the left-hand coat of arms in which was the sacred monogram, 'I. H. S' (the first three letters of the Greek word for Jesus). A sacred heart was carved beneath the one on the right.

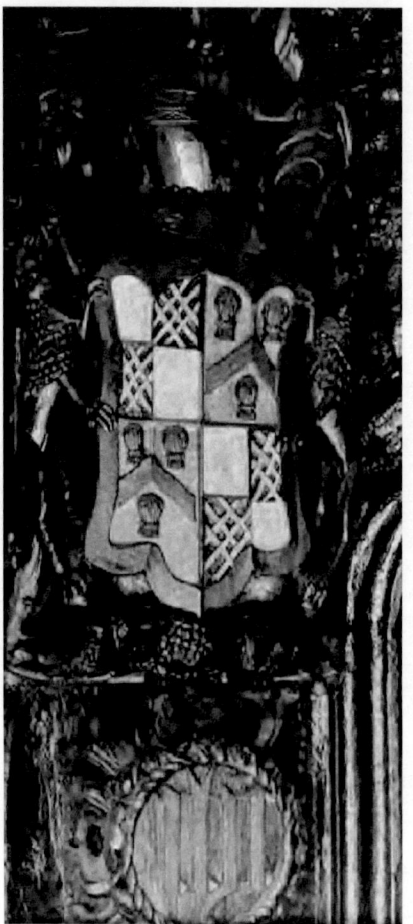

10. Coat of Arms at Dutton Hall
(Memorials of the Duttons of Dutton).

On the left of the archway is another carving, of a Tudor Rose, encircled with a garter. Below this is a crown of thorns with five Tudor roses and another carving, of a sacrificial lamb. A number of historians have argued that Dutton stole these decorations from Norton Abbey. For example, Coward averred that 'Dutton Hall is fine' and that it was 'a mansion of no mean importance in the days of Henry VIII'. However, he added that, 'There can be little doubt that Dutton Hall was built on the spoils of the priory and the rewards of the king... There is a diversity of opinion about the decorations of the entrance and about the inner door... There is something very ecclesiastic about this door ... I am afraid that this doorway and many other good bits of work formerly stood in the looted priory at Norton.'[482]

11. Dutton Hall in 1899 (Memorials of the Duttons of Dutton).

Eventually, we reach a great dining hall, above which was a minstrel's gallery,[483] and at one side of which was a fireplace measuring eight by fourteen feet. There is a screen across the minstrel's gallery upon which are many carvings, including three roundels. The left hand roundel is a chubby, squarefaced, thinly bearded man wearing a John Knox cap. It is supported, on either side, by two men wearing plumed hats, who may well be minstrels as the stereotypical Medieval minstrel typically wore such headgear.[484] Beneath the roundel appears to be carved 'SPDK' ('Sir Piers Dutton, Knight'). This same carving was above Dutton Hall's main door before the hall was moved. So this, as we will see below, would seem to be the only certain representation of Sir Piers Dutton that survives. The central roundel contains the top three quarters of a man wearing a doublet. It is also supported by minstrels. The right-hand roundel is a right-facing profile supported by two female forms. This, together with the shape of the head dress, may mean that it is Dame Juliana.

*12. Sketch of the roundel depicting Sir Piers Dutton
(Copyright: Edward Dutton).*

At the upper end of the Great Hall's ceiling, there is another inscription, carved in letters four inches deep stating that 'after a long suite made by the heirs of Dutton against Sir Piers Dutton then of Hatton' all the judges of the realm agreed that Dutton was the rightful heir. A retinue of 50 servants were employed to run the house and, as Dutton was their hereditary master, the house was always known to be full of the music of minstrels. However, there was a sinister side to the minstrels. Dutton used his minstrels to eject Thomas Pyllyn from his house in Chester. He had two men break down the door with an iron bar and then entered with 200 minstrels.[485] Pyllyn, a shoemaker, was later was Feodary of Cheshire in 1556 and one of the city sheriffs in 1561.[486] Dutton Hall allows us to read a lot into the psychology of Sir Piers Dutton. He had to struggle bitterly to keep his inheritance and possibly knew, even in 1539, that his right to it was questionable, so we see him literally carving his right to it into the building. Courtier status is also emphasized, with the carved Tudor rose. Dutton Hall is Dutton's monument, his way of casting his success in stone and wood for all to see.

The Minstrels and the Marriages

As we have already discussed, the Duttons of Dutton exercised a 'curious jurisdiction' over the minstrels and other vagrants of Cheshire. This was granted by the Constable of Chester to Hugh de Dutton sometime towards the end of the reign of King John, in about 1215. Randle, Earl of Chester, had to police constant border raids from the Welsh. On one occasion, the Welsh overwhelmed him and he had to retreat to the castle of Rothlent in Flintshire, where they besieged him. He somehow sent a message to Roger Lacy, the Constable of Chester, begging for help. Unable to find any soldiers, Lacy had the idea of gathering together a group of fiddlers, musicians and 'whores' and marching then towards a heavily armed Welsh army. One might have expected a massacre, but the Welsh army was so frightened – perhaps they thought anyone mad enough to attack an army with ballads, fiddles and ladies of the night was capable of pretty much anything – that they turned and fled. The Earl was so thrilled that he granted control of all the fiddlers, musicians, cobblers, whores and so on to Lacy. The constable soon transferred this right to Hugh de Dutton, and all future Lords of Dutton, at least with regard to the minstrels and prostitutes.

The story may be apocryphal. But gradually, a custom developed whereby the Lord of Dutton, or his representative, held a court every Midsummer's Day at St John the Baptist Church in Chester. In the locale of Chester, this was a significant event; a carnival and a clear display of the power and wealth of the Duttons of Dutton and the independence of the Palatine.[487] In 1539, however, there was unusual twist, because two of Sir Piers Dutton's daughters had got just got married, possibly the previous day, and there had been an enormous party at Dutton Hall to celebrate. (Dutton's rebuilding of the hall began soon afterwards). The pageantry began with the Dutton estate steward, riding with other family members and friends to the east gate of Chester. The records are unclear regarding whether Sir Piers Dutton personally attended in 1539. There was a herald riding ahead of them, holding a banner of their coat of arms. He was blowing a trumpet the whole time. The steward then made a public declaration that, by royal command, Sir Piers Dutton was 'protector of all and every musician and minstrel etc. whosoever either resident or resorting within or to the county palatine of Chester and within or to the city of Chester, by virtue and authority of the ancient art, custom, pre-eminence and special royalty of the predecessors of the manor of Dutton.' He commanded that every minstrel and other vagrant come forward to be licensed on pain of forfeiture of their instruments and imprisonment.

The proclamation being ended, the retinue rode to St. John the Baptist Church with all the minstrels following behind, playing their instruments. At the church, they dismounted, entered the church and knelt in the chancel to pray, all the time with music blaring in the background. When they arose, the minstrels shouted out, 'God bless the king and the heir of Dutton!' Then the whole company, still playing their instruments, made their way to the court house, where the minstrels were called to the steward and told by him:

> 'If you know of any treason against the king or prince, in this court you ought to present it. Secondly, if you have exercised your minstrelsy without the licence of the lord of this court, or by any other licence than from the lord of this court, it is here presentable; and whether any of you have profaned the Sabbath by playing upon that day unless you have had especial licence for it from the lord of this court or his steward, or whether any of you hath been drunk or the like. Thirdly, whether you have heard any scandalous words tending to the prejudice of the heir of Dutton and by whom, the jury is here to present it, and also to present the default of all such suitors as ought to have appeared that day.'[488]

Assuming they answered in the desired way, Dutton, via his steward – in return for about 4d – granted each of the minstrels their licence to play in Cheshire for the next year. In 1499, for example, Lawrence Dutton charged each minstrel 4½d and each prostitute 4d (a day's wages for a labourer).[489] Usually, Dutton, or his steward, would then invite the 'gentlemen' present to a party. But, on this occasion, the steward placed white scarves over their shoulders, probably because they would now help to celebrate a wedding.[490]

On their return from Dutton Hall to Chester, the brides and grooms were met at Flookersbrook bridge by the steward, attended by the pursuivant and standard-bearer, preceded by all the licensed musicians with white scarves across their shoulders, ranked in pairs, and playing on their instruments. This procession marched through the city to the houses of Sir Piers Dutton's new sons-in-law, where lavish entertainments were laid on.[491] The last time the minstrel's court occurred was 1756,[492] the Manor of Dutton no longer being in the hands of the Dutton family. The ceremony was revived in 2008 by the Cheshire Museums Service in conjunction with St. John's Church as an historical re-enactment-cum-Medieval music event.[493]

The entire affair may just seem eccentric to modern readers. But this was a clear display, rather like Dutton Hall, of Sir Piers Dutton's wealth and power. He had a herald in his own livery making proclamations, the minstrels had to admit any 'treason' they might have heard against him under oath, and they all had to pay him and play for him. The events of 24th June 1539 appear to have constituted such a 'party to end all parties' that they even made it in to the annals of Cheshire history. Anybody who was anybody in Tudor Cheshire was invited to Sir Piers Dutton's celebration.

More Gang Violence

1539 was a year of celebration for Dutton. Apart from leading a commission to establish the heirs of the deceased Elizabeth Shiley,[494] he focused on his daughters' marriages and rebuilding Dutton Hall. 1540, however, was marred by tragedy: in that year Hugh Dutton, Sir Piers Dutton's eldest surviving son and his heir, died. Hugh had a young son, John, so his line would carry on, but, in terms of dominating Cheshire, Hugh's death didn't matter. The only mention of Hugh in the court records is in connection to a land dispute in 1528, but there's no evidence of violence.[495] It was Ralph who was Dutton's enforcer, the son after his own heart. This had been most clearly proven on 16th April 1537 when Ralph led a gang of Dutton's men to seize land that had been in the use of a gentleman called John Aldersley for ten years. Aldersley described Ralph Dutton as 'a gentleman of great power and riches'.[496] Ralph defended his actions, insisting that the land was under the jurisdiction of the Justices of Chester and that he acted on their behalf. Aldersley was left pleading with the court for redress. Of course, there were still those disputing Sir Piers Dutton's rights to various lands. In 1540, Sir William Stanley and Ralph Manning attempted to recover various lands from Dutton, including 1000 acres of forest and 1000 acres of farmland.[497]

Thomas Cromwell was also a man after Dutton's heart. In early 1540, Thomas Long wrote to Cromwell with evidence of the kind of man Dutton was.[498] Dutton's horse keeper, Thomas Ruggeley, approached Long outside St John's Church in Clerkenwell and shouted at him, 'I know thee well enough by thy yellow cap and thy blue feather; thou art one of the watch that took me such a night and set me in the stocks, and therefore I will cut thy flesh and likewise meet with all thy fellows.' Ruggeley struck Long with a long-sword, which broke over Long's right hand, maiming it. He then drew his dagger to finish him off but was stopped by John Tedder, 'upholsterer', of Holborn. If you got in Cromwell's way, he'd do you in with altogether more ceremony; after a show trial for high treason. If you got in Dutton's way, a thug would try to kill you in broad daylight.

The Fall of Cromwell and Stewardship of Halton

But 1540 was the year of Cromwell's spectacular fall from grace. Cromwell had played for much higher stakes than Dutton; to control not just one county but the whole of England. A Protestant, his undoing was his attempt to take religious reform too far and to do so too quickly. In 1538, having already closed down many of the monasteries, Cromwell turned on the churches themselves, the colourful, opulent centres of English village life. In an attack on what he saw as 'idolatry', he demanded that all of the church statues, ornate crucifixes, and pictures be either taken down or whitewashed.[499] Most scandalously of all, he shut down the most popular – and lucrative – pilgrimage site in England, the shrine to St. Thomas Beckett at Canterbury.[500] Beckett had, of course, lost his life because he upset a mentally unstable and tyrannical king[501] and this irony many not have been lost on Cromwell as he later ascended the scaffold. Pilgrimages were extremely popular, a kind of holiday for the masses, and very lucrative for taverns and shops along the pilgrimage route.[502] Cromwell attacked them as irreligious, infuriating many traditionalists. His further demand, that a large English language Bible be positioned in every church, led to further problems: ordinary but literate people finding passages in the Bible which indicated that rich people should give all their money away or couldn't get into Heaven.[503] Cromwell's extremism was leading to political chaos and the conservative, Catholic faction of old noble families, led by the Duke of Norfolk, was gaining power at court as Henry VIII was becoming increasingly irked by what his chief minister was causing. Norfolk also resented Cromwell for dissolving the priory which included his ancestral mausoleum.

Sensing the change, and fearing the way in which Henry VIII was being beguiled by traditionalist Catholics, Cromwell acted pre-emptively and had the ringleaders – Sir Geoffrey Pole, Sir Edward Neville (Steward of Halton), and Sir Nicholas Carew – executed for treason in late 1538. This meant that, in February 1539, Dutton became Steward of Halton himself.[504] With many Catholic enemies, Cromwell then made a mistake. In order to ensure an alliance with the German states, Cromwell arranged that Henry should marry Anne of Cleves. This would be useful because it was looking as if there would be an alliance between France and Austria and Anne's father was an enemy of the Holy Roman Emperor, Charles V; an Austrian. Henry met Anne, to whom he was engaged on the basis of a very flattering portrait by Hans Holbein, in January 1540, without revealing who he was. He did not find her attractive, supposedly referring to her as the 'Flanders mare', but Henry could not get out of the marriage without offending the Germans, so he had to go through with it. This led to further less than appetizing discoveries: she had 'sagging breasts'[505] and terrible body odour. The marriage was never consummated. In February 1540, Anne praised the king as a kind husband saying: 'When he comes to bed he kisses me, and he takes me by the hand, and bids me 'Good night, sweetheart'; and in the morning kisses me and bids 'Farewell, darling.' Lady Rutland responded: 'Madam, there must be more than this, or it will be long ere we have a duke of York, which all this realm most desires.'[506]

Henry began to show an interest in the 18-year-old Catherine Howard (c.1521-1542),[507] niece of the Duke of Norfolk, which so alarmed Cromwell that he revealed Henry's sexual preferences to Anne in order to make her more attractive. But the marriage fell apart, the Franco-Austrian alliance never happened and Cromwell was damaged. He had put his master through humiliation for nothing. Cromwell's Catholic and aristocratic enemies at court, who had always hated the Protestant son of a Putney blacksmith, saw their chance. Led by the Duke of Norfolk, the council had Cromwell charged with protecting Anabaptists and other Protestant heretics, failing to enforce the Six Articles (a Catholic-inspired official religious orthodoxy that had recently been declared) and plotting against Princess Mary. In May 1540, Dutton, along with other local justices, set up the Cheshire Assizes precisely to look into cases of treason.[508] But just two months later, his ally, Cromwell, was condemned to death without trial, after a bill in the House of Lords, and executed for treason on 28th July 1540. On the scaffold at Tower Hill, he declared that he died 'in the traditional faith',[509] an interesting confession for one of England's leading reformers. Henry married the teenage Catherine Howard the same day.

The Fall of Catherine Howard

On 12th July 1540, Dutton was commissioned to lead an inquisition into the 'idiocy' of Thomas Percival of Westmorland[510] and had probably just finished this when his ally, Cromwell, was being condemned. Cromwell was one of Dutton's benefactors. Dutton probably realised that he needed to be careful. If the Catholic faction was gaining power at court, this would have ramifications in Cheshire. By 1540, Cromwell held almost all the major offices of state. He was Chancellor of the Exchequer, Secretary of State, Lord Privy Seal and Lord Great Chamberlain. Only the Lord Chancellorship, held by Sir Thomas Audley had escaped him. Upon Cromwell's removal, these offices were divided up and Norfolk was, briefly, the dominant figure. The Chancellor of the Duchy of Lancaster remained Sir John Gage (1479-1556). Gage had been an Esquire of the Body of Henry VIII at the same time as Dutton and even been knighted around the same time.[511] On 6th July 1541, Dutton wrote to him, seemingly in an attempt to besmirch yet another enemy and essentially make this enemy's life difficult. He asserted that Richard Starkey of Halton[512] frequently came to the court at Halton Castle, where he had no business being, and stole court records that implicated him. Starkey responded that he had every right to be at the court, had not stolen anything, and that Dutton had only brought the case to drain his financial resources.[513]

However, the following year Dutton would suddenly find himself with far more resources at his disposal, perhaps luckily as this was also the year that he completed Dutton Hall. Due to a series of events, the pendulum swung against the Catholic faction at court at least to some extent. Catherine Howard was interrogated about adultery by Thomas Cranmer, the Archbishop of Canterbury, on 7th November 1541. Unlike in the case of Anne Boleyn, Henry had no reason to dispose of Catherine. She was questioned because there was clear evidence of adultery with Thomas Culpepper and Francis Dereham. There were love letters in Catherine's distinctive handwriting and the sister of extreme Protestant John Lascelles (burnt at Smithfield in 1546)[514] had worked in the household of Norfolk's stepmother, the Dowager Duchess, and heard all about Catherine's sexual promiscuity. At 13, she'd had a sexual relationship with her music teacher, Henry Mannox. In 1538, she was in a relationship with Francis Dereham (c.1513-1541) and foolishly appointed him her secretary after she married Henry, raising suspicion that the relationship continued after the marriage. The king at first refused to believe the allegations against Catherine, but the evidence was very clear. Catherine was executed on 13th February 1542.[515]

Henceforth, Cranmer would be an increasingly powerful figure, trusted by Henry VIII. Clearly part of the Protestant faction, he had found reasons to justify Catherine of Aragon's divorce and drafted the pro-Protestant 'Ten Articles'. After a brief conservative backlash, he had written an introduction to the English language Bible (to be placed in every church) in 1539 and by 1541 the king had complete trust in him.[516] The Catherine Howard affair only showed how reliable Cranmer, who had interrogated Catherine and got to the bottom of it all, actually was. Indeed, it was Cranmer, on 1st November 1541, who slipped a message to Henry during mass outlining the allegations against his queen.[517]

Sheriff of Cheshire Again

By 1542, though the Catholic faction was still dominant, the execution of Catherine Howard had not helped its cause. In the five years since Dutton had been High Sheriff of Cheshire, he had built a magnificent house with his loyalty to Henry VIII carved into it, he'd been one of the county's leading Justices of the Peace, and he had diligently managed the Fee of Halton.

Dutton acted as the executor of the will of John Dutton of the New Manor (c.1500-1542), illegitimate son of Lawrence Dutton in early 1542.[518] In November 1542, he was appointed sheriff again, over Thomas Venables and Edward Fitton.[519] However, as noted, High Sheriff was a less powerful post than it had been in 1535. Indeed, a 1542 Act gave Cheshire Members of Parliament for the first time, heavily integrating it into the English realm.[520]

Chapter Nine
The Deathbed Confession

*'My wicked life is now drawing to a close
and I dread the result'*[521]

IN DECEMBER 1542, soon after he was appointed sheriff again, Dutton organized yet another inquisition post mortem.[522] Clearly, his second stint as Sheriff of Cheshire was uneventful and there is no other comment on it from the surviving royal papers. This may, in part, be because the conflict with Sir William Brereton was over. He had died in Kilkenny in Ireland in early February 1541.[523] By 1543, Dutton was the Cheshire equivalent of an elder statesman and would have had very little left to prove. More broadly, the religiously fractious kingdom was moving in his direction as well. In May 1543, the Act for the Advancement of the True Religion placed heavy restrictions on who could own or be read an English-language Bible, spear-headed by the Catholic faction. But on 12th July 1543, Henry married Catherine Parr (1512-1548), a Protestant.[524] Thereafter, he began to pursue a middle ground religious policy.

The Rough Wooing

Evidence of just how many retainers Dutton commanded, and so how powerful he was, could be seen in May 1544, during the so-called 'Rough Wooing'. Scotland was England's implacable enemy throughout the sixteenth century. Allied with France (and Turkey), it had invaded northern England in 1513, culminating in the death of James IV (1473-1513),[525] Henry VIII's brother-in-law via his sister Margaret, at the Battle of Flodden Field. This battle had also taken many members of the Cheshire gentry. The throne was inherited by the child king James V (1512-1542) and when his mother, Margaret Tudor (1489-1541), died in 1541, there ceased to be anyone of influence in Scotland arguing for peace.[526] In addition, James V refused Henry's demand to break with Rome and he further insulted Henry by refusing to meet him at York to discuss this. Henry sent troops north to Scotland, James V retaliated by sending troops over the English border, and both sides took high-ranking prisoners. But the Scots were badly defeated at the Battle of Soloway Moss, near Kelso, on 6th December and James V died a few days later, leaving the Scottish throne to his daughter Mary (1542-1587) ('Mary, Queen of Scots'[527]) who was one week old.[528]

The resultant power struggles left Scotland in a very weak position, with rival claimants to the throne jockeying for power. The official regent was the Earl of Arran, James Hamilton (1516-1575) who was next in line should the infant queen die. However, Matthew Stuart, Earl of Lennox (1516-1571), a Protestant, also had support, though a slightly weaker claim to the throne, and controlled the west of Scotland. In March 1543, he arrived in Edinburgh and, with clearly superior forces, compelled Arran to resign and accept him as regent, further arguing that Arran was actually illegitimate. Pro-English, he negotiated a marriage between Mary and Prince Edward in the so-called Treaty of Greenwich, strongly desired by the English government. This would combine the two kingdoms, under English dominance, and hopefully end the Anglo-Scottish wars. But Arran and the influential Cardinal David Beaton (1494-1546)[529] had also been negotiating a French marriage, to the Dauphin, for Queen Mary, who was herself the daughter of Mary of Guise (1515-1560), a French noblewoman.[530] This would cement the 'Auld Alliance' and was very appealing to the large anti-English faction in the Scottish parliament. Indeed, during the negotiations, Arran even became Catholic and was given a French Dukedom. On 11th December, the Scottish parliament rejected the Greenwich Treaty.

So began the 'Rough Wooing' in December 1543. War was declared on 20th December. Major hostilities began with an attack on Edinburgh on 3rd May 1544, led by the Earl of Hertford (Edward Seymour, 1500-1552, brother of Jane Seymour) and Viscount Lisle (John Dudley,

1504-1553),[531] who were later successive Lord Protectors under Edward VI.[532] Hertford had orders to burn Edinburgh and issue Henry's proclamation of 24th March 1544, which laid the blame on Cardinal Beaton's 'sinister enticement' of Arran. The Provost of Edinburgh had been ordered not to negotiate with the troops.

The next day the English forces entered through Edinburgh's Canongate and set the city on fire. Edinburgh Castle was defended by cannon fire, so Hertford burnt all the houses within the city walls.[533] With no standing army, troops were still mustered under the old feudal system whereby the king instructed his feudal tenants to send their feudal tenants as soldiers. All the major nobles and gentry sent men to fight in this war and Dutton was required to muster 100 fighters, captained by George Holford, a retainer of Dutton's to whom he paid a yearly annuity. Unfortunately, the record is 'much mutilated' so we do not know how they fared.[534]

Dutton's Death

1544 saw Dutton involved in legal disputes, asserting the authority of the Fee of Halton, and demanding a sturgeon caught within it.[535] In April 1545, Dutton was still recorded as one of the king's commissioners of the peace for Cheshire[536] and on 25th April that year he wrote to the Earl of Shrewsbury, Francis Talbot (1500-1560), apologising that Cheshire could not muster the 8000 men asked of it to help repel 'the Scots and the French.' This was because a number of able men on the list of those conscripted were already serving the Earl of Derby.[537] Around the same time Piers' son, Ralph, married Amy Townshend, daughter of Sir Robert Townshend (ca. 1500- 1555), newly appointed Chief Justice of Cheshire, something Ralph Dutton took full advantage of by using renewed violence against his enemies, knowing that he was now likely above the law.[538]

But on 18th August 1545, Edward Seymour wrote a letter to William Paget (1506-1563), the Secretary of State.[539] The abstract includes the following:

> 'Sir Piers Dutton, of Cheshire, is dead, who was rider of Delamere forest, and begs Paget to move the King that Sir

Thomas Holcroft (who here accompanies the writer) may have that office. P.S.— It is reported that Sir Thomas Lee is dead, for which Hertford (Seymour) is sorry.'[340]

Seymour was not sorry Dutton had died, but maybe they didn't know each other. We have looked at all the parallels between Cromwell and Dutton. Their way of dying was yet another.

Deathbed Confession

Dutton died at Dutton Hall 17th August 1545, according to his inquisition post mortem.[541] And Dutton seemingly died 'in the traditional faith'. According to the 1869 book *The Monastic Houses of England; Their Accusers and Defenders* by Sir Hubert Burke, Dutton confessed, on his deathbed, that he had habitually lied during his investigation into the religious houses. He stated that his allegations of debauchery against the county's holy orders were: 'most untrue in many particulars'.[542] He further told those present as he lay dying, Henry Griffin and Dr. Woolsey, that:

> 'It was the especial order of my very good friend, the Lord Cromwell, that every place and thing about the abbeys and convents which had been heretofore called sacred and holy — that is, the chapel, the abode for the holy sacrament, the chalices, and divers other things – were to be used in the same manner as common places of abode or accommodation; and things that were heretofore called holy should now be used as household goods.'[543]

Dutton confessed that Godstow nunnery, far from being debauched, was a movingly holy place: 'They were so much under the influence of confession and frequent communion that the young men sent to take a list of their property were wholly unable to overcome them in order to prove that they were amorous whores.'[544] Burke paraphrases that Dutton: '...felt great remorse for the character he had given the nunneries, for which there was no foundation, that he had taken presents from the nuns and acted with treachery in return. He hoped God would forgive him for these sins and others.'[545]

The source for Dutton's deathbed confession is 'Griffin's Chronicle' which Sir Hubert Burke described as 'a very scarce Black Letter book',[546] meaning a book printed in Gothic type face. It is so rare that there does not appear to be a copy in the British Library nor the Bodleian Library at Oxford University, so we simply have to trust that Sir Hubert Burke was telling the truth. Assuming that he was telling the truth, Dutton died a Catholic. Dutton's confession, in front of 'four men', was quoted by the anonymous writer of an article in the 1883 edition of *The Lamp* magazine. According to this source, Dutton told those assembled at his deathbed that: 'I acted with immense treachery to the convent where my own three sisters were located. They were good holy women and they knew no wrong. My wicked life is now drawing to a close and I dread the result.'[547] There is no surviving record of Dutton's funeral but, as it cost £100, it must have been a very lavish affair.[548] This would seem to be further testimony to his dying Catholic as Protestants would often deliberately request simple funerals.[549]

Aftermath and Inquisition Post-Mortem

Dutton bequeathed the Manor of Dutton to his grandson and heir, who, aged just eight, became a royal ward.[550] He left Hatton to Ralph, who was also to be the guardian of the infant Lord of Dutton's interests as well as the guardian of his own unmarried sisters. However, Ralph Dutton obviously didn't think his inheritance was sufficient and was concerned that his stepmother might even leave Dutton Hall and take valuable possessions with her. On 31st August 1545, he marched into Dutton Hall, having broken down the door, with a gang of 38 other men 'of evil disposition, nothing dreading God' and took chests of money and pretty much everything of value in the house, including Dame Juliana Dutton's clothes. She complained to the Court of Star Chamber that:

> 'Being a very young man greatly given to games and pastimes, and very prodigal in excessive expenses, it is likely *(Ralph Dutton)* may in a short time utterly waste and consume these goods. The said riotous persons have left your subject no vestures to wear upon her body saving only one gown and one kirtle of very coarse black ... which she wore at the time they took the goods from her.'

Ralph Dutton replied that he and his followers were owed money by Sir Piers Dutton, his funeral expenses to the tune of £100 had to be paid, and that he had offered to return the clothes but his step-mother had refused to meet him.[551] There were further disputes in the wake of Sir Piers Dutton's death. Juliana sued Ralph in the Court of Chancery to take possession of lands in Essex and Hertfordshire, formerly belonging to her husband Henry Patmore, which Piers had 'wrongly' taken possession of.[552] Piers' daughters Alice and Margaret sued Ralph for withholding their dowries, claiming that they could not marry as a consequence. It has been suggested that their quarrel with Ralph is the reason why one of the sisters ultimately never married.[553]

On 5th November 1545, Dutton's inquisition post mortem was held at Chester, led by Sir Henry Delves. Dutton's land holdings were so extensive that the document is 150 folios in length. His land interests extended to most significant settlements in and around Cheshire, including Chester, Middlewich and Northwich. The inquiry revealed not only that Dutton had two illegitimate children but also that he had rented out the Manor of Dutton to Ralph Dutton on a 99-year lease. In 1546, Juliana sued Ralph over a long list of manors that had belonged to her husband.[554] Juliana was still alive in 1550, when she was living in Little Hadham in Hertfordshire with her son, Thomas Patmore.[555] The final inquisition into Dutton's lands and heirs was also held in 1550.[556]

Chapter Ten
Dutton's Papist Successors

'Rowland Dutton of Hatton, esquire, his mother, wife and family vehemently infected do not resort to the church and do entertain seminaries, mass priests, and others that hide themselves for popery.'[557]

SIR PIERS Dutton liquidated the Cheshire monasteries. But his descendants were to be ardent Catholics, at a time when Catholics were mercilessly persecuted.

Ralph Dutton of Hatton and Recusancy

Ralph Dutton of Hatton was a staunch Catholic. He had even married a number of his children, aged as young as four, into Catholic families, leading to divorces by the time they reached their teens.[558] As we have seen, Ralph Dutton married Amy Townshend, daughter of Sir Robert Townsend of Ludlow, another strong Roman Catholic. In 1555, under the reign of the Catholic Queen Mary (r. 1553-1558), Ralph Dutton was Sheriff of Flintshire,[559] but once Elizabeth I ascended the throne in 1558 he had little hope of holding high local office ever again. With 1559's 'Act of Uniformity' the newly-crowned Elizabeth I attempted to reach a compromise between the extreme Catholics and the fundamentalist Protestants. This ingenious piece of diplomacy was the Church of England: theologically Protestant but Catholic in terms of ritual and the general feel of things. 'I will not open windows into men's souls,' Elizabeth insisted. But, for the good of national unity, her subjects were to conform outwardly. If they did not, then they would be fined 12 shillings per month for church non-attendance. In extreme cases, they would forfeit property, and even their freedom. Failure to swear the Oath of Allegiance (accepting the monarch as head of the Church) incurred a bar from all public office. Papists who would not conform were known as recusants. Ralph Dutton was a recusant.

In 1570, Pope Pius V[560] issued a papal bull excommunicating Elizabeth I as a heretic, adding that Catholics must not obey this 'pretended' Queen, on pain of excommunication. The government, and the people, began to see all papists as an 'enemy within' that aimed to overthrow the state. Non-attendance fines were ramped-up to £20 per month (the annual income of a 'middling sort' farmer by that time), Catholic school teachers were to be jailed, those who employed them heavily fined, it would be treason to reconcile anyone with Catholicism, and a crime to attend Catholic mass.

In 1580, the Jesuits began sending missionary priests – English Catholics, ordained abroad – to reconvert the country, and especially the North. It became treason, and a capital offence, to be a Catholic priest in England and a serious crime to shelter one.[561]

In 1581, Ralph Dutton, together with his brother-in-law Robert Townshend, was investigated over their relationship with the Jesuit missionary to England Edmund Campion (1540-1581).[562] Trained in France, Campion entered England disguised as a jeweller in 1580, led a Catholic mission, especially in northern England where recusancy was strongest, and was eventually caught, tortured and hanged, drawn and quartered as a traitor. Campion was made a saint in 1970.[563] Robert Townshend's sister, Grace, was the mother of George Gilbert, who with Thomas Pound founded the 'Catholic Association' to assist Campion on his arrival in England. Gilbert had spent some time in France and Italy in 1579, where he was reconciled to the Catholic Church. On his return to England, Gilbert had founded the Association with the Pope's Blessing. The Association's members were young, propertied, single men who were thus free to devote themselves to promoting Campion's campaign. Campion arrived in England in 1580 and travelled throughout Lancashire and Cheshire. It was alleged that Campion actually stayed in Ralph Dutton's house. The Privy Council sent Sir George Calverley (1532-1582), a former MP for Cheshire and the Sheriff of Cheshire, to Ralph Dutton's Hatton home on 23rd

February 1581 to see what was going on. Calverley, who was the great-grandson of Ralph's grandfather Peter Dutton of Hatton, Junior, found only Ralph Dutton and Robert Townshend present and they denied any knowledge of Campion. As Calverley put it, 'presently I the sheriff dealt with Mr. Dutton touching his knowledge of this Campion, who I was assured would tell me his knowledge. I found he never either knew or heard of the man.'[564] The sheriff seemed to blindly trust Dutton's word. But, despite nothing being proven, 'suspicion of Catholic sympathies clung to Dutton's family'.[565]

Ralph Dutton died on 26th June 1582 and the Manor of Hatton passed to his eldest son Rowland Dutton (1550- 1605). The Queen's Commissioners, who were charged with finding and prosecuting recusants, commented that, 'Rowland Dutton of Hatton, esquire, his mother, wife and family vehemently infected do not resort to the church and do entertain seminaries, mass priests, and others that hide themselves for popery.'[566]

The Death of the Duttons of Hatton

The fate of the Manor of Hatton would probably have infuriated Sir Piers Dutton. With the death of Rowland Dutton, Hatton passed to his son Edward Dutton (1579-1621) and then to Edward's son Peter Dutton (1602-1638). Peter married a daughter of Merchant Adventurer and draper Sir Thomas Hayes (1548-1617). Hayes was married five times, had 20 surviving children, and was Lord Mayor of London in 1614.[567] Peter's son was Peter Dutton II (1625-1669) who married Catherine Reynolds. He was Sheriff of Cheshire 1652-1653, but by the time of his death, Peter Dutton was drowning in debt. After his decease, one of his tenants, Richard Tilston, testified that Peter's widow had asked him to hide items of value in his own house so that the bailiffs could not get hold of them.[568]

All of Peter's sons and daughters died young and the estate eventually passed to his daughter Dorothy Dutton (c. 1655-1701). She conveyed it to her husband, John Massey, in 1693. In 1699, the couple sold it to Hon. George Cholmondeley,[569] a member of the very family Sir Piers Dutton battled with to secure the Dutton estate.

The Death of the Duttons of Dutton

The story of the Duttons of Dutton was even more tragic. John Dutton (c.1539-1609), the young grandson of Sir Piers Dutton, unsuccessfully sued Ralph Dutton for all the Hatton lands in 1572 but lost the case.[570] Like his uncle Ralph, John Dutton was an ardent recusant. A puritan reformer, compiling a list of Cheshire recusants in about 1583, remarked of him that, 'John Dutton of Dutton, esquire, himself, his children and family (saving his wife) are very grievously infected, and he is a common entertainer of seminaries, Mass priests and such like. They come not to church. His eldest son is lately arrived from Rome and wandereth up and down the country, commending Rome...'[571] John Dutton died in 1609, aged about 70.[572]

John's son, Thomas Dutton (c.1568-1614) was Sheriff of Cheshire 1610-1611. He inherited the manor and Thomas' son, John (1594-1609), would have been the heir. John married Elizabeth Egerton, an orphan who had been raised by her grandfather, Lord Chancellor Sir Thomas Egerton (1540-1617), in 1606, aged 11. However, John Dutton died in February 1609, aged about 15, seemingly in an accident bringing his wife to Dutton Hall. Elizabeth herself died in London in 1611, aged 16, and a monument was erected to her in the church of St Martin-in-the-Fields by her grandfather, referring to her as 'a wife, a widow, and a maid'. When Thomas Dutton died the manor was inherited by his 18-year-old daughter Eleanor and passed to her husband, Viscount Kilmorey. And, so within just 70 years of Sir Piers Dutton's death, the Duttons of Dutton had died out.[573]

Historiography of Sir Piers Dutton

Historians have not been kind to Sir Piers Dutton. Most of them, in recent years, have ignored him completely, apart from J. Patrick Greene who called him 'ruthless'.[574] Anne Coltman has called Dutton 'a servile tool of the King'.[575] Eric Ives referred to Dutton's 'ostentatious absence' from the infamous incident at the Holt, as if this was deviously planned to boost his standing with Cromwell.[576] A few other modern histories of the Reformation make brief reference to Dutton,[577] while

Herbert Hughes remarks, 'they were on good terms, the King and this knight of the northern shire'.[578] Geoffrey Chesters accuses Dutton of never forgiving Sir Randolph Brereton for restricting his liberty to 'exploit persons and finance murderers'.[579] Tim Thornton, in *Cheshire and Tudor State*, however, looks at Dutton's Palatine-level career in more depth and notes that he was, along with Sir William Brereton, the 'ruler' of Cheshire.[580] As we have seen, Thornton also sees Dutton as one of the first clear Protestants in Cheshire, as evidenced by his zeal in dissolving the religious houses and prosecuting supporters of traditional Catholicism.

When Dutton was more discussed, by nineteenth century scholars, he was termed 'an arrant liar' by Sir Hubert Burke,[581] a 'plunderer' by William Mortimer,[582] 'notorious' by William Sulley,[583] and accused of plunder by T. A. Coward.[584] The writer who reviewed the family history *Memorials of the Duttons of Dutton* in *The Spectator* in 1901 insisted, 'there is no one among them who stands out as of heroic stature. The family has produced no great soldier, no eminent politician...'[585] implicitly dismissing Sir Piers Dutton.

However, James Froude referred to him in neutral terms[586] and Rupert Morris argued, with regard to the Norton Abbey uprising and possible beginnings of a Pilgrimage of Grace in Cheshire, that the 'vigorous action of the Sheriff, Sir Piers Dutton checked its spread'.[597] Similarly, Francis Gasquet praised the 'prompt' action of Dutton, but for which the rebellion may have proved 'serious'.[588]

Legacy

To the extent that historians have discussed Dutton's historical legacy, therefore, it is seemingly implied that he helped to increase the power of the Tudor state over Cheshire. He did this by suppressing the monasteries and persecuting opponents of the new religious dispensation. Indeed, it could be argued that Dutton's legacy can be seen as a modest contribution to the centralizing politics of early Tudor England. As Mayor of Chester, he helped to undermine the independence of the city of Chester. As Sheriff of Cheshire, he assisted with Cromwell's broader centralizing policies and, specifically, integrating Cheshire into the Tudor state. By helping to undermine William Brereton of Malpas, who stood in the way of this, Dutton aided Cromwell's centralizing policy. In addition, as other historians have stressed, Dutton led the dissolution of the monasteries in Cheshire, which transferred their wealth to the English crown, even putting down a rebellion against the suppression of Norton Abbey. He also lied so that other religious houses could be more swiftly suppressed, and persecuted the king's religious opponents. With these actions, he was an agent of the power of the Tudor state over the county palatine.

Further, it may be suggested that Dutton indirectly hastened the integration of Cheshire. In the wake of the Pilgrimage of Grace, the London government feared the power of provincial magnates and needed loyal people in charge who could act decisively. It also needed to ensure that magnates, in general, could not become too powerful, as William Brereton had done. The power struggle between Dutton and Sir William Brereton as well as Cheshire's general lawlessness would – in such a context – be a kind of security risk for the state as well as an illustration of the power of provincial magnates. As such, the introduction of Justices of the Peace and Members of Parliament for Cheshire are likely to have been hastened by the county's political situation, to which Dutton was so significant.

However, Dutton is little remembered today and his physical legacy is a testimony to this. There is a portrait often stated to be of him that is a 19th century copy of a portrait from around 1600.[589] It is now in the hands of the National Trust and in 1817 a print of it was published in J. H. Hanshall's *The History of the County Palatine of Chester*.[590] Hanshall claimed that the original painting was owned by a Liverpool solicitor called Mr. Gunnery.

However, the man in the portrait is clearly wearing late Elizabethan clothes, including a ruff. A very similar looking portrait, with the year 1597 actually painted on it, is believed by the National Trust to be his grandson John Dutton but is probably someone else because the coat of arms on it is not John Dutton's.[591] Indeed, the arms would indicate that the figure may be Sir Peter Warburton (1542-1628). And, even if the assumed portrait is supposed to be Sir Piers Dutton, the original was not painted in his lifetime so it may look nothing like him and

Portrait of Sir Piers Dutton, of Hatton,

On whom Henry the Eighth confirmed the Advowry of the Cheshire Minstrels.

13. Print of a portrait, supposedly of Sir Piers Dutton
(J. H. Hanshall's The History of the County Palatine of Chester).

is, anyway, highly stylized. As discussed, there is a roundel on the screen of the minstrel's gallery at Dutton Hall which would seem to be a representation of Sir Piers Dutton. The same roundel, with SPDK beneath it, was formerly above the door of Dutton Hall. But it is of cartoonish quality.

We do not have any documentation of Dutton's final wishes. His will has not survived and nor, seemingly, has the source that recorded his deathbed confession. According to one secondary source, he was buried in 'Our Lady Mary's Chapel' in the church at Great Budworth.[592] This seems likely, as his descendants in the Dutton of Dutton line were buried there as well. But, according to a description of the church by Randle Holme in 1568,[593] there was no memorial in the church to Sir Piers Dutton, so we cannot be sure where he lies.[594]

Appendix One
The Letters of Sir Piers Dutton

1. Sir Piers Dutton to Thomas Cromwell, secretary of state.
Dated at Hatton, June 21 (1535). (From state papers, domestic, Henry
VIII., vii. 368.)

DEATH OF THE ABBOT OF VALE ROYAL—RECOMMENDS A
MONK OF THE HOUSE AS HIS SUCCESSOR, WHO WILL GIVE
£100 FOR THE PRICE.

To master secretary, this to be delivered.

My duty always humbly remembered unto your good mastership.
Please it the same to be understood the abbot of Vale Royal within
the county of Chester is lately deceased (whose soul Jesu pardon!),
and in my poor mind there is a monk within the same house called
Dan Randal Wilmslow,[595] which for his discretion and learning is the
meetest[596] and most able man to succeed the same abbot in his room
of any, being within the same house; and to have you to be his good
master for his preferment thereunto. He will be contented to give your
mastership in hand and further to do you as large pleasure as any other
man shall. Wherefore[597] it may please your mastership that I may know
your pleasure, whether the monk shall repair unto you or not; and if
any labour be made for any other person to put the same in a stay for a
season, unto such time as I may speak with you myself, which I intend
shall be hastily, God willing, whoever preserve you to his pleasure.
At Hatton the 21 day of June.[598] By your own assuredly.[599]

'Perus Dutton, Kt.'

2. Sir Piers Dutton to Lord Cromwell. Dated at Dutton, August 8 (1535). (From Harl. MS., 604, fol. 60.)

ARREST OF THE ABBOT OF NORTON AND OTHERS—THE MONK RECOMMENDED FOR THE ABBACY OF VALE ROYAL IS SENT UP.

To the right honourable and his especial good master, master Cromwell,[600] secretary unto our sovereign lord the king.

Please it your good mastership my duty remembered. These to advertise you that I have taken the bodies of the abbot of Norton, Robert Jannyns and the stranger[601] a cunning smith, two of the said abbot's servants: also Randall Brereton, baron of the king's exchequer of Chester and John Hale of Chester, merchant and have them in my custody and keeping. And the rest I intend to have as speedily as I can and to be with you with them, God willing, in all convenient speed as I possibly may. Moreover I have caused Dan Randal Wilmslow, the monk of the Vale Royal to come up to you for whom I spake under your good mastership which is a good religious man discreet and well grounded in learning and hath many good qualities, most apt to be a master of a religious house than any other monk of that house. Wherefore it may please your good mastership to be his good master toward his preferment that he may be admitted master of the same. And that I did promise your mastership this said monk will accomplish accordingly. Wherefore I beseech your mastership that this bearer and the said monk may resort unto you from time to time to know your pleasure therein, ensuring you what you do for me or my friend all is your own; as knoweth our lord God who mercifully preserve you. At Dutton the 3rd day of August (1535). By yours assured

Perus Dutton Kt.
Endorsed : Sir Piers Dutton, Knight ... hath taken certain traitors.

3. September 23 (1536). (From state papers, domestic, Henry VIII., xi, 486.)

ARREST OF JOHN HESEHAM FOR TREASON AND SEDITION IN QUESTIONING THE KING'S SPIRITUAL SUPREMACY.

To the right honourable my lord privy seal, this be delivered.

Please it your honourable lordship, that where heretofore the king's pleasure was by your commandment given unto me that I should take certain persons for suspect of treason, amongst whom one John Heseham was named and specified which John at that time fled out of this country[602] that I could not meet with him and now is coming in again. And I therefore not only for that but also for divers[603] traitorous and seditious words that he hath spoken, which was that if the spiritual men had holden together the king could not have been head of the church ; and also that the bishop of Rochester and Sir Thomas Moore died martyrs in the quarrel aforesaid. I have taken him and committed him to the castle of Chester, there to abide unto the king's pleasure and yours thereabout shall be ever glad to accomplish during my life, by the grace of our lord God who preserve your good lordship in honour long to continue.

From Dutton the 23rd day of September (1536) by yours assured.

Perus Dutton, kt.
Endorsed : sir Piers Dutton, 23 September.

4. Sir Piers Dutton to Sir Thomas Audley, Lord Chancellor.
Dated at Dutton October 12 (1536). (From state papers, domestic, Henry VIII., xl, 681.)

THE COMMISSIONERS FOR THE SUPPRESSION OF NORTON ABBEY RESISTED BY THE ABBOT—THEY TAKE REFUGE IN A TOWER IN PERIL OF THEIR LIVES—SIR PIERS RESCUES THEM AND ARRESTS THE ABBOT AND CANONS.

To the right honourable and my singular good lord Sir Thomas Audley, knight, Lord Chancellor of England this be delivered.[604]

Please it your good lordship to be advertised Mr. Coombes and Mr. Bolles the king's commissioners within the county of Chester were lately at Norton within the same county for the suppressing of the abbey there. And when they had packed up such jewels and other stuff as they had there and thought upon the morrow after to depart thence, the abbot gathered a great company together to the number of two or three hundred persons, so that the said commissioners were in fear of their lives, and were fain to take a tower there and thereupon send a letter unto me ascertaining me what danger they were in and desired me to come and assist them, else they were never likely to come thence. Which letter came to me about nine of the clock in the same night upon Sunday last; and about two of the clock in the same night I came thither with such of my lovers and tenants as I had near about me and found divers fires made there as well within the gates as without and the said abbot had caused an ox and other victuals to be killed and prepared for such his company as he had then there; and it was thought in the morrow after he had come forth to have had a great number more. Notwithstanding I used some policy and came suddenly upon them so that the company that were there fled and some of them took poles and waters; and it was so dark that I could not find them; and it was thought if the matter had not been quickly handled, it would have grown to further inconvenience, to what danger God knoweth. Howbeit, I took the abbot and three of his canons and brought them to the king's castle of Halton and there committed them to ward to the constable to be kept as the king's 'rebellions' upon pain of £1,000; and afterwards saw the said commissioners with their stuff conveyed thence and William Parker the king's servant who is appointed to be the king's farmer there restored to his possession. Wherefore it may like your good lordship that the king's grace may have knowledge hereof and that his pleasure may be further known therein which I shall be always ready and glad to accomplish to the uttermost of my power as knoweth our lord God who ever preserve your good lordship with much honour. At Dutton the 12th day of October (1536) by yours assured.

Perus Dutton, kt.

Endorsed : Sir Piers Dutton showing the insurrection of the abbot of Norton made against the suppressors of his abbey and how he the said Sir Piers rescued the commissioners and took the abbot and committed him to prison.

5. Henry VIII to Sir Piers Dutton and Sir William Brereton.
Dated October 19, 28 Henry VIII. (1536). (From state papers, domestic, Henry VIII, xi. 787.)

THANKS FOR SERVICES RENDERED—THE ABBOT AND CANONS, IF THE ALLEGATIONS ARE TRUE, TO BE HANGED.

By the king,

Trusty and well-beloved we greet you well and have as well seen the letters written by you sir Piers Dutton to our right trusty and well-beloved councillor sir Thomas Audley, knight, our chancellor of England, declaring the traitorous demeanour of the late abbot and canons of the monastery of Norton, used at the being there of our commissioners for the suppression thereof and your wisdom policy and good endeavours used for the apprehension of the same, for the which we give unto you right hearty thanks and shall undoubtedly consider your faithful service to your singular rejoice and comfort hereafter. As other letters written from you sir William Brereton to our right trusty and well-beloved councillor the lord Cromwell keeper of our privy seal touching the same matter, for your good endeavours also, wherein we give unto you our right hearty thanks. For answer whereunto you shall understand that forasmuch as it appeareth that the said late abbot and canons have most traitorously used themselves against us and our realm and moved insurrection against the common quiet of the same, that if this shall appear to you to be true that then our pleasure and commandment is you shall immediately upon the sight hereof without any manner of further circumstance of law or delay cause them to be hanged, setting up their heads and quarters around the country hanged as most arrant traitors in such sundry places as ye shall think ready and for the terrible example of all others hereafter. And herein fail you not to travail with such dexterity as this matter may be finished with all possible diligence.'

Endorsed : Copies of the letters of sir Piers Dutton and to sir William Brereton 19 October.

6. Sir Piers Dutton to Lord Cromwell. Dated at Dutton November 30 (1536). (From state papers, domestic, Henry VIII., xi. 1212.)

'DECLARES WHY HE FORBORE TO HANG UP TRAITORS'—BLAMES SIR WILLIAM BRERETON.

To the right honourable and my singular good lord the lord privy seal.

My duty lowly remembered. These to advertise your good lordship where I heretofore received the king's most dread letters of commandment and high pleasure to me and sir William Brereton, knight, in these parts, deputy chamberlain, directed of and concerning the traitorous demeanour of the late abbot and canons of the monastery of Norton by them used at the late being there of his grace's commissioners after the suppression thereof, as more at large may appear unto your good lordship by a copy of the same his grace's commandment herein enclosed and by virtue thereof incontinently after we had received his said grace's commandment, we appointed a short day then ensuing for the execution of the same his grace's commandment according to the contents thereof to have been done albeit immediately afterward before the said day assigned we received sundry letters to us directed from the earl of Derby mentioning in effect a letter from the earl of Shrewsbury, lieutenant unto the king's grace, the earls of Rutland and Huntingdon, touching that the duke of Norfolk and they had stayed the commons of Yorkshire, charging the said earl of Derby in the king's gracious name to sparple[605] his company without doing any hurt or molestation to the said commons or any of them as more at large shall appear unto your good lordship by the copy of one of the same letters to me directed herein also enclosed and thereupon in consideration of the same their doings we continued and respited the accomplishment of the king's said gracious commandment until his most gracious further pleasure to us therein were known determining our-self to certify his grace of the premises and made our letter of certificate accordingly, with my hand thereunto subscribed having the said evil doers and offenders in strait endurance of imprisonment within his castle of Chester, there surely to be kept to abide his gracious pleasure and afterward the said sir William Brereton denied that to certify ; and I was always ready to execute the same according to the purport thereof what cause or mean he had so to refuse I know not. And for that, that the king's said commandment was to us both jointly directed to execute the same, I without him in no wise could yet can execute the same. Wherefore I would be glad to have knowledge of his most gracious further pleasure therein, that I may follow the same as to my duty appertaineth. Most meekly beseeching your good lordship that I may be ascertained thereof and I shall pray to God for his highness and your good lordship long to continue.

At Dutton the 30th day of November (1536). By your own assured

*Perus Dutton kt.**

Endorsed: *Sir Piers Dutton declaring why he "forbare" to hang up traitors.**

7. Earl of Derby to Sir Piers Dutton

To my right well-beloved sir Piers Dutton, knight, Sheriff of Cheshire. I commend me to yon and have received a letter from the earl of Shrewsbury, the king's lieutenant, the earl of Rutland and the earl of Huntingdon by the hands of one Berwick, herald, in these words, "My very good lord. We heartily recommend us unto your good lordship. And whereas my lord of Norfolk and we that be here have stayed the commons of Yorkshire so that every man is sparpled and retired home unto their houses and my said lord of Norfolk departed unto the king's grace. And as we be informed from my lord Darcy, your lordship with your retinue hath appointed upon Monday next coming to be at Whalley abbey, my lord the premises considered that all things is well stayed, we desire and pray yon and nevertheless in the king's name charge yon that ye sparple your company without doing any hurt or molestation to the said commons or any of them. And that ye fail not hereof at your peril. And our lord have your lordship in his governance.

Written at Doncaster the 28th day of October. Wherefore ye with your company may depart home to your own houses and to be ready to serve the king when ye shall be commanded. And I shall be a means to the king's grace to consider your pains, costs and good minds that ye have been at to serve his grace.

Written at Preston the 30th day of October (1536). Your loving friend,[606] E. Derby.

Endorsed: The copy of a letter sent from the earl of Derby to sir Piers Dutton. (State papers, domestic, Henry VIII., xi. 1212.)

8. Sir Piers Dutton to lord Cromwell. Dated at Dutton, December 15 (1536). (From state papers, domestic, Henry Vlll., xii., pi ii., 1215.)

THANKS FOR FAVOURS, PARTICULARLY OF THE SHRIEVALTY—COMPLAINS OF SIR EDWARD NEVILLE'S PROCEEDINGS IN CONNECTION WITH THE STEWARDSHIP OF HALTON AND PRAYS RELIEF.

To the right honourable and my singular good lord the lord privy seal, these be delivered.

My duty always remembered unto your good lordship, with right hearty and humble thanks of your goodness to me many times to me showed and specially that it hath pleased your good lordship to have me in your good remembrance for the sheriffwick of Cheshire. Please it you to be advertised that after the king's grace had granted the office of stewardship of Halton to sir Edward Neville, his highness commanded the said sir Edward that I should have the exercising thereof wherein saith that time I have done as my duty in the best I could to serve his grace and as I think brought it into better frame than it was afore I meddled therewith; and have prepared more men in a readiness within the same office to serve the king's grace when they be commanded than hath been accustomed aforetime. And now lately I received letters from the said sir Edward whereby I perceive he is minded to sell the same office during the nonage of John Savage, his son-in-law, which is about the time of seven years as yet to come ; and hath offers made by sir William Brereton to give him 100 marks sterling there for: whereof I marvel that another he or any other would give so much there for ; and is but 100 mark fee by year for so short a season, except it be for some other purpose than for any profit he should have thereby, so some of my adversaries would rejoice if I should be put from it so soon after my entry therein ; and it would send to my rebuke and be thought in these parts that I had committed some offence in the same. Wherefore in consideration that my house and manor of Dutton with the members of the same, do stand within the precinct and circuit of the said office; and that I thereby have done and shall be more able to do his grace the better service, it may like your good lordship to move the king's grace herein and to prefer this letter herein closed to his grace that his further pleasure may be therein known, which during my life I shall be glad to accomplish to the uttermost of my powers, God willing, who ever preserve you. At Dutton the 15th day of December (1536?) by your own assured

Piers Dutton, kt.

Endorsed : * Sir Piers Dutton's letters written the 10th (sic) day of December.

9. Sir Piers Dutton to Henry VIII. Dated at Dutton January 7 (1537). (From Harl. MS., 283, fol. 11.)

RESPECTING THE STEWARDSHIP OF HALTON, AND SIR WILLIAM NEVILLE'S AND SIR WILLIAM BRERETON'S DEALINGS THEREIN.

'To his most dread sovereign lord the king's highness.

Please it your most noble grace to have in remembrance, that after your highness had granted the office of stewardship of Halton to sir Edward Neville, your highness commanded him that I should have the exercising thereof wherein since that time I have done according to my duty the best I could to serve your grace and as I think brought it into better order than it was afore I meddled therewith; and have prepared more men in a readiness within the same office to serve your grace when it pleaseth your highness to command them otherwise than hath been accustomed aforetime. And now lately I received sundry letters from the said sir Edward Neville, wherein he doth write unto me to pay him an 100 marks for the said office and I so doing should have the exercising thereof during the nonage of John Savage his son-in-law; and in case I would not do so I should not enjoy the same and I send unto him the said 100 marks according to his letter which he would not receive, by reason of such sinister labour and offices of money as sir William Brereton hath made to the said sir Edward to have it out of my hands, for what intent he would give so much and is but 100 shillings fee by year, for so short time God knoweth; and if I should so soon after my entry therein be put from it, it would sound to my rebuke and my adversaries would greatly rejoice thereat: for it would be thought in these parts that I had committed some offence in the same. Wherefore it may like your most excellent highness, that your grace's pleasure may be therein known to the said sir Edward: that I may have and continue in the same office according to your most high commandment and the rather that I am contented to give him an 100 marks which was his own desire, as doth appear by his said letters. Graciously considering that my house and manor of Dutton, with the members thereof, stand within the precinct and circuit of the said office; and by strength thereof I have done your grace the better service and may be the more able so to do which God willing, during my life I shall accomplish to the uttermost of my power; and daily pray to God for the preservation of your most royal estate long to endure. At Dutton the 7th day of January now instant (1537?).

Your most humble subject and servant faithful.

*Perus Dutton, kt.
Endorsed : * Sir Piers Dutton.

10. Sir Piers Dutton to the king's commissioners. Undated (About March 1537). (From state papers, domestic, Henry VIII, xi. 1106.)

SIR PIERS AND HIS UNDER-SHERIFF GO TO TOWN FOR THREE MONTHS—DISHONEST DEALINGS OF THE DEPUTY UNDER-SHERIFF IN THEIR ABSENCE—LIST OF VICTIMS

To the king's commissioners:

Showeth unto your noble lordships your orator sir Piers Dutton, knight, sheriff of the county of Chester, how that the same your orator since hence michaelmas last past, having business at London resorted thither and his deputy under sheriff with him named Ralph Mainwaring and came not home till it was within Christmas last past and when your orator and his said undersheriff went to London the said undersheriff left one John Newall his clerk, to exercise the office and room of the undersheriff until their returns home which John Newall being a subtle person having the experience of that office and also having to him delivered the king's (escheats) of the amercements[607] of the hundreds there under the seal of the exchequer, made out other threats as well against such persons as the king's duties were leviable upon as to certain other persons that ought to pay none and many of those that ought to pay did threat amore, some upon their heads than they ought to pay and delivered the said threats to the persons subscribed to levy the same so that there was levied and paid unto the said John Newall the sum of 142. 5s. 1d. Extortionately taken and received over and besides the king's duties as appeareth in a schedule hereunto annexed, the names of the persons that paid the same and the sum that any of them paid, which is to the great slander and rebuke of your orator and his undersheriff: he nor his undersheriff not being a consenting nor privy thereunto nor their deed. And for the declaration of the same your headsman and his undersheriff in the premises, they being ignorant in that behalf. That it may please your lordships to command the said defendant being here present to answer and to be examined therein and upon examination thereof, if he be found guilty therein, that he may be punished according to his deserve and to make restitution to the parties to whom he had offended for God's love.

Ralph Mainwaring, the younger. Ralph Sherman. Thomas Sherman. John Sherman. William Mores. Hugh Allen. Hugh Dawson. Thomas Dawson. Thomas Barfote.

11. Sir Piers Dutton to Lord Cromwell. Dated at Dutton December 16 (1537). (From state papers, domestic, Henry VIII, xi. 1310.)

AFFRAY BETWEEN MAINWARING AND CHOLMONDLEY— ATTEMPT OF THOMAS BRERETON TO PACK A JURY UPON HIS FATHER'S INQUISITION.

To the right honourable and my singular good lord the lord privy seal, this be delivered.

Please it your good lordship to be advertised, there hath been lately a great riot and insurrection of the king's subjects within this shire of Chester made and congregate together between sir Randle Mainwaring, knight, on the one party and Richard Cholmondeley, esquire, on the other party. The manner and doing of the same this bearer can show you, to whom it may please your good lordship to give credence and that I may know the king's pleasure in the same. Furthermore, I received a letter from your lordship delivered to me by Thomas Brereton, son of

Randle Brereton, deceased, with certain names enclosed in the same to be impannelled upon an inquisition to enquire of the death of the said Randle. Sir, the same persons which he would have had upon the inquisition were his near kinsmen and friends so that the king should have sustained great loss thereby and my conscience would not serve me to have made that return. Therefore I made stay therein until you were ascertained of the same. Wherefore if any suit be made unto your lordship therein that it may please you to consider the premises. And thus the holy ghost have you in his blessed tuition. At Dutton the 15th day of December (1537). By your own assured

Perus Dutton kt.
Endorsed : 'A tumult in Cheshire'.

Notes

Prologue

1 Short chapters examining aspects of his public life have been published in Dutton, E. (2012). *The Duttons of Stanthorne Hall.* Family History Society of Cheshire and in Anon (1901). *Memorials of the Duttons of Dutton in Cheshire With Notes Respecting the Sherborne Branch of the Family.* Henry Sotheran & Co.

Chapter One: England in 1536

2 Oath composed by Robert Aske, to be sworn by the pilgrims in the Pilgrimage of Grace of 1536.

3 For a popular examination of the importance of 1536 in England, see Lipscomb, S. (2012). *1536: The Year That Changed Henry VIII.* Lion Books. See also, Shagan, E. (2003). *Popular Politics and the English Reformation.* Cambridge University Press.

4 Bernard, G. (2011). The Dissolution of the Monasteries. *History,* 96: 3, p.390.

5 For discussions of late Medieval English religiosity, see Harper-Bill, C. (1991). *Religious Belief and Ecclesiastical Careers in Late Medieval England.* Boydell & Brewer; Logan, F. D. (1996). *Runaway Religious in Medieval England, c. 1240-1540.* Cambridge University Press; or Tanner, N. (2009). *The Ages of Faith: Popular Religion in Late Medieval England.* I. B. Taurus. There is also an interesting study of religiosity among late Medieval merchants. See Kermode, J. (2002). *Medieval Merchants: York, Beverley and Hull in the Late Middle Ages.* Cambridge University Press, Ch. 5.

6 See Kreider, A. (2012). *English Chantries: The Road to Dissolution.* Wipf & Stock Publishers.

7 See Burton, J. & Ströber, K. (2008). *Monasteries and Society in the British Isles in the Later Middle Ages.* Boydell & Brewer.

8 Wood, R. (1994). Poor Widows, c. 1393-1414. In Barron, C. & Sutton, A. (Eds). *Medieval London Widows, 1300-1500.* A.&C. Black, p.62.

9 See Prescott, E. (1992). *The English Medieval Hospital, c. 1050-1640.* Seaby.

10 McIntosh, M. (1988). Local responses to the poor in late Medieval and Tudor England. *Continuity and Change,* 3: 209-245.

11 See Knowles, D. (1955). *The Religious Orders of England.* Cambridge University Press. Also, for general accounts, see Cornwall, J. (1988). *Wealth and Society in Early Sixteenth Century England.* Cambridge University Press, or Duffy, E. (1992). *The Stripping of the Altars:Traditional Religion in England, 1400-1580.* Yale University Press.

12 For a discussion of this corruption, see Heale, M. (2004). *The Dependent Priories of Medieval English Monasteries.* Boydell & Brewer. However, it should be emphasized that a significant body of opinion avers that this corruption was exaggerated as part of Tudor propaganda. See Thompson, B. (2002). Monasteries, Society and Reform in Late Medieval England. In Clark, J. (Ed). *The Religious Order in Pre-Reformation England.* Boydell & Brewer; and Bucholz, R. & Key, N. (2013). *Early Modern England, 1485-1714.* John Wiley & Sons, p.89.

13 See Smith, L. (1966). Henry VIII and the Protestant Triumph. *The American Historical Review,* 71: 4; or Mann, S. (2007). *Supremacy and Survival: How Catholics Endured the English Reformation.* Scepter Publishers. It should be noted that the extent of the significance of factionalism has been challenged. See Bernard, G. (2000). *Power Politics in Tudor England: Essays by G. W. Bernard.* Ashgate. However, it is widely accepted that factionalism was important in Henry VIII's court.

14 See Rex, R. (1996). The crisis of obedience: God's word and Henry's Reformation. *The Historical Journal,* 39: 4; or Cameron, E. (2012). *The European Reformation.* Oxford University Press.

15 The Ten Articles, 1536. http://www.luminarium.org/encyclopedia/tenarticles.htm.

16 See Daniell, D. (1994). *William Tyndale: A Biography.* Yale University Press.

17 For a full biography of John Fisher, see Rex, R. (2003). *The Theology of John Fisher.* Cambridge University Press.

18 Mann, S. (2009). *Supremacy and Survival: How Catholics Endured the English Reformation.* Scepter Publishers.

19 See Elton, G. (1982). *The Tudor Constitution.* Cambridge University Press.

20 Tyerman, C. (1996). *England and the Crusades, 1095-1588.* University of Chicago Press.

21 Tremlett, G. (2010). *Catherine of Aragon: Henry's Spanish Queen.* Faber & Faber.

22 Obviously, there are numerous biographies of Henry VIII. The most recent is, Wooding, L. (2015). *Henry VIII.* Routledge.

NOTES

23 Norton, E. (2011). *Anne Boleyn: Henry VIII's Obsession.* Amberley Publishing.

24 Breverton, T. (2014). *Everything You Ever Wanted to Know About the Tudors But Were Afraid to Ask.* Amberley Publishing.

25 Lofts, N. (2012). *Anne Boleyn: The Tragic Story of Henry VIII's Most Notorious Wife.* Amberley Publishing.

26 For a biography of Jane Seymour, see Loades, D. (2015). *Jane Seymour: Henry VIII's Favourite Wife.* Amberley Publishing.

27 See Rayne-Davis, J. & Rayne-Davis W. (2014). *Robert Aske: The Man Who Could Have Toppled Henry VIII.* United PC Verlag. On the Pilgrimage of Grace more generally, see Hoyle, R. (2001). *The Pilgrimage of Grace and the Politics of the 1530s.* Oxford University Press; Bush, M. (1996). *The Pilgrimage of Grace: A Study of the Rebel Armies of October 1536.* Manchester University Press; or Davies, C. (1987). Popular Religion and the Pilgrimage of Grace. In Fletcher, A. & Stevenson, J. (Eds). *Order and Disorder in Early Modern England.* Cambridge University Press.

28 For a discussion of Tudor enclosures, see Chapter 5.

29 Bush, M. (2009). *The Pilgrim's Complaint: A Study of Popular Thought in the Early Tudor North.* Ashgate, p.257.

30 Spring, E. (1997). *Law, Land and Family: Aristocratic Inheritance in England, 1300-1800.* University of North Carolina Press, p.48.

31 This point is noted in Erler, M. (2013). *Reading and Writing During the Dissolution: Monks, Friars and Nuns, 1530-1558.* Cambridge University Press.

32 Haigh, C. (1969). *The Last Days of the Lancashire Monastries and the Pilgrimage of Grace.* The Chetham Society, Manchester University Press, p.50.

33 Shagan, E. (2003). *Popular Politics and the English Reformation.* Cambridge University Press, p.89.

34 This was led by Sir Francis Bigod (1507-1537). See Dodds, M. (1915). *The Pilgrimage of Grace, 1536-1537 and the Exeter Conspiracy, 1538.* Cambridge University Press.

35 Bush, M. (1996). *The Pilgrimage of Grace: A Study of the Rebel Armies of October 1536.* Manchester University Press.

36 Surdhar, C. (2013). *Bloody British History: York.* The History Press.

37 Thornton, T. (2000). *Cheshire and Tudor State, 1480-1560.* The Boydell Press.

38 Letters and Papers (LP), Henry VIII, ix, 914 (22); LP, Henry VIII, xi, 1217(23). *Letters and Papers of Henry VIII* are available on *British History Online* (BHO). http://www.british-history.ac.uk/search/series/letterspapers-hen8

39 Jackson, E. (1923). *Office and Actions of the Lord Lieutenant in Tudor England.* Philadelphia.

40 Gorski, R. (2003). *The Fourteenth Century Sheriff: English Local Administration in the Late Middle Ages.* The Boydell Press.

41 Leithead, H. (2008). Cromwell, Thomas, Earl of Essex (b. in or before 1485, d. 1540). *Dictionary of National Biography.* Oxford University Press. 1917-

42 See Dutton, E. (2012). *The Duttons of Stanthorne Hall.* Family History Society of Cheshire.

43 Thornton, T. (2000). *Cheshire and the Tudor State.* The Boydell Press, p.234.

44 For a biography of Anne of Cleves, see Norton, E. (2011). *Anne of Cleves: Henry VIII's Discarded Bride.* Amberley Publishing.

45 E.g. Hutchinson, R. (2012). *Thomas Cromwell: The Rise and Fall of Henry VIII's Most Notorious Minister.* Hachette; Maynard, T. (2011). *The Crown and the Cross: The Biography of Thomas Cromwell.* LLC or Coby, J. (2013). *Thomas Cromwell: Henry VIII's Henchman.* Amberley Publishing.

46 This is based on the novel of the same name. See Mantel, H. (2009). *Wolf Hall.* HarperCollins UK.

47 Berglar, P. (2009). *Thomas More: A Lonely Voice Against the Power of the State.* Scepter Publishers.

48 Fletcher, D. (2009). *Cardinal Wolsey: A Life in Renaissance Europe.* Bloomsbury.

49 MacCulloch, D. (1998). *Thomas Cranmer: A Life.* Yale University Press.

50 Head, D. (1995). *The Ebbs and Flows of Fortune: The Life of Thomas Howard, 3rd Duke of Norfolk.* University of Georgia Press. There is also a book-length biography of his son, Henry Howard: Childs, J. (2014). *Henry VIII's Last Victim: The Life and Times of Henry Howard, Earl of Surrey.* The Bodley Press.

51 Gunn, S. (1988). *Charles Brandon, Duke of Suffolk, ca. 1484-1545.* Blackwell.

52 In addition, Anne Boleyn's brother is explored in Cherry, C. & Ridgway, C. (2014). *George Boleyn: Tudor Poet, Courtier and Diplomat.* Made Global Publishing. There are other full length biographies of figures from this period and they will be referenced if the subjects appear in this biography.

53 Youngs, D. (2008). *Humphrey Newton (1466-1536): An Early Tudor Gentleman.* The Boydell Press. Pownall is around 36 miles east of Hatton and 19 miles east of Dutton.

54 He did, however, keep a commonplace book and write poetry.

55 Richmond, C. (1981). *John Hopton: A Fifteenth Century Suffolk Gentleman.* Cambridge University Press

56 A point made by: Haigh, C. (1993). *English Reformations: Religion, Politics and Society Under the Tudors.* Clarendon Press, p.18; Kauffman, P. (2013). *Leadership and Elizabethan Culture.* Palgrave MacMillan, p.18;

and Jones, W. (1970). *The Tudor Commonwealth, 1529-1559: a study of the impact of the social and economic developments of mid-Tudor England upon contemporary concepts of the nature and duties of the commonwealth.* The Athlone Press, p.4.

57 Ridley, J. (1996). *The Tudor Age.* Overlook Press.

58 I have previously explored this in Dutton, E. (May 2015). Turf Wars: Power Struggles in the Post-Feudal Era. In *Family Tree.*

59 Round, J. (1909). *Feudal England: Historical Studies on the 11th and 12th Centuries.* Swan & Sonnenshein Ltd.

60 Valente, C. (2003). *The Theory and Practice of Revolt in Medieval England.* Aldershot: Ashgate; Gorski, R. (2003). *The Fourteenth Century Sheriff: English Local Administration in the Late Middle Ages.* The Boydell Press; Storey, R. L. (1972). The magnates, knights and gentry. In S. B. Chrimes, C. D. Ross & R. A. Griffiths (eds). *Fifteenth Century England, 1399 – 1509.* Manchester University Press.

61 See Weir, A. (2011). *Henry VIII: King and Court.* Random House.

62 Bean, J. (1989). *From Lord to Patron: Lordship in Late Medieval England.* Manchester University Press.

63 In pursuing this argument, I appreciate that there is debate over this issue. For example, Marshall notes that not all retinues led to corruption and they helped in maintaining political stability. Marshall, A. (2008). An Early Fourteenth Century Affinity. In N. Saul (Ed). *Fourteenth Century England, V.* The Boydell Press, p.12.

64 On Henry VII, see Penn, T. (2012). *The Winter King: The Dawn of Tudor England.* Penguin.

65 Ellis, S. (2014). Tudor State Formation and the Shaping of the British Isles. In Ellis, S. & Barber, S (Eds). *Conquest and Union: Fashioning a British State, 1485-1725.* Routledge.

66 See essays in Coss P. & Keen, M. (2002). *Heraldry, Pageantry and Social Display in Medieval England.* The Boydell Press.

67 Grant, A. (2006). *Henry VII.* Routledge.

68 Hanshall, J. (1817). *The History of the County Palatine of Chester.* J. Fletcher, p.23.

69 Anon. (1901). *Memorials to the Duttons of Dutton.* Henry Sotheran & Co.

70 Youngs, D. (2007). *Humphrey Newton (1466-1536): An Early Tudor Gentleman.* The Boydell Press, p.28.

71 Jones, T., R. Yeager, T. Dolan, A. Fletcher & J. Dor (2003). *Who Murdered Chaucer? A Medieval Mystery.* New York: St Martin's Press.

72 See Clayton, D. (1990). *The Administration of the County Palatine of Chester, 1442-1485.* Manchester University Press; Liddy, C. (2008). *The*

Bishopric of Durham in the Late Middle Ages: Lordship, Community and the Cult of St. Cuthbert. Boydell & Brewer; or Kenyon, D. (1991). *The Origins of Lancashire.* Manchester University Press.

73 Yates, J. (1856). *The Rights and Jurisdiction of the County Palatine of Chester, the Earls Palatine, the Chamberlain, and Other Officers.* Charles Simms & Co. p.308.

74 Thornton, T. (2000). *Cheshire and the Tudor State.* The Boydell Press, p.43.

75 Thornton, T. (2000). *Cheshire and the Tudor State.* The Boydell Press, p.50.

76 Thornton, T. (2000). *Cheshire and the Tudor State.* The Boydell Press, p.3.

77 Thornton, T. (2000). *Cheshire and the Tudor State.* The Boydell Press, p.77.

78 Thornton, T. (2000). *Cheshire and the Tudor State.* The Boydell Press, p.22.

79 Clayton, D. (1990). *The Administration of the County Palatine of Chester, 1442-1485.* Manchester University Press.

80 Clayton, D. (1990). *The Administration of the County Palatine of Chester, 1442-1485.* Manchester University Press.

81 Thornton, T. (2000). *Cheshire and the Tudor State.* The Boydell Press, Ch. 1.

82 For a biography of William Brereton, see Ives, E. (1976). *The Letters and Accounts of William Brereton of Malpas.* Manchester: Record Society of Lancashire and Cheshire.

83 Thornton, T. (2000). *Cheshire and the Tudor State.* The Boydell Press, p.85.

84 Buchan, G. H. (1984). *A Brief History of the Duttons of Dutton.* MS. http://www.dunton.org/duttonhall/buchan.html (Accessed 15 February 2015).

85 Buchan, G. H. (1984). *A Brief History of the Duttons of Dutton.* MS. http://www.dunton.org/duttonhall/buchan.html (Accessed 15 February 2015).

86 Editor. (January 1965). Dutton Hall, many miles from home has outlived its great family. *Rural Rides,* 11.

87 *Crawley News* (12 August 2010). Former school still on sale 12 months on. http://www.crawleynews.co.uk/school-sale-12-months/story-12601262-detail/story.html

88 Bush, M. L. (1984). *The English Aristocracy: A Comparative Synthesis.* Manchester University Press, pp.27-28.

89 Indeed, sources, such as the 1580 Cheshire Heraldic Visitation (which we will discuss below) and the Victorian *Burke's Landed Gentry* accepted that the Duttons could go back much further, all the way back to Rollo, 1st Duke of Normandy (846-932), or the Counts of Cotentin (descended from the brother of the 1st Duke of Normandy) depending on which source you read. From Rollo, the line continues to the 9th century Norse jarls and their ancestors, the semi-mythical Yngling Swedish kings in the Norse Sagas, and then *their* ancestors the Norse gods (or, claim other sources, the ancient

Kings of Finland from the country's *Kalevala* myth collection), War god Odin's ancestors the Trojans and their ancestors the Greek gods. See Burke, B. (1858). *A Genealogical and Heraldic Dictionary of the Landed Gentry of Great Britain and Ireland.* Harrison; Peacham, H. (1634). *The Complete Gentleman,* London; Lysons, D. & Lysons, S. (1810). *Magna Britannia: Volume II.* T. Caddell and W. Davies; Lawson, P. H., (1968). The Duttons of Dutton, county of Chester. Chart. Chester: P. H. Lawson. Chester Records Office. See Dutton, E. (2012). *The Duttons of Stanthorne Hall.* Family History Society of Cheshire, for a detailed discussion of the pedigree.

90 Amin, N. (2015). Ednyfed Fychan, father of the Tudor Dynasty. *History Magazine,* http://www.historicuk.com/HistoryUK/HistoryofWales/Ednyfed-Fychan-father-of-the-Tudor-Dynasty/

91 Queen Elizabeth II's ancestry has been set on 'Ancestry of Elizabeth II,' http://en.wikipedia.org/wiki/Ancestry_of_Elizabeth_II (Accessed 19th March 2015)

92 Thornton, T. (2000). *Cheshire and the Tudor State.* The Boydell Press.

93 Leigh, E. (1867). *Ballads and Legends of Cheshire.* Longmans and Co.

94 Thornton, T. (2000), *Cheshire and the Tudor State.* The Boydell Press, p.234.

Chapter Two: The Rank Society

95 Chaucer, G. (1992). *Canterbury Tales.* 'General Prologue.'

96 Dutton, E. (2010). Here the status symbols clash: Social status and status expression in Finnish homes. *Suomen Antropologi,* 35: 1.

97 See Roy, W. (2001). *Making Societies: The Historical Construction of our World.* Sage.

98 Specht, H. (1981). *Chaucer's Franklin in the Canterbury Tales: The Social and Literary Background of a Chaucerian Character.* Publications of the Department of English, University of Copenhagen, p.141.

99 French, H. & Hoyle, R. (2007). *The Character of English Rural Society: Earls Colne, 1550-1750.* Manchester University Press.

100 Greenwood, A. (1988). *The Greenwood Tree in Three Continents, Or, A Fertile Family of Five Centuries, 1487-1987.* Longey Investment Trusts, p.5.

101 Bush, M. L. (1988). *Rich Noble, Poor Noble.* Manchester University Press, pp.27-28.

102 English Church History. (Oct. 1851). *The Churchman's Penny Magazine.*

103 Feldman, S. (2011). *The Apocryphal William Shakespeare.* Indianapolis: Dog Ear Publishing.

104 Bence-Jones, M. & Montgomery-Massingbird, H. (1979). *The British Aristocracy.* Constable Books.

105 Grazebrook, G. (1889). Introduction. In Grazebrook, G. & Rylands, J. (Eds). *The Visitation of Shropshire Taken in the Year 1623, Part I.* Harleian Society, p.xxiii.

106 Corfield, P. (1996). The Rivals: Landed and Other Gentlemen. In N. B. Harte and R. Quinault, (Eds). *Land and Society in Britain, 1700 – 1914.* Manchester University Press.

107 For a full biography of Sir Thomas Smith, see Strype, J. (1820). *The Life of the Learned Sir Thomas Smith, Kt, DCL: Principal Secretary of State to King Edward the Sixth and Queen Elizabeth.* Clarendon Press.

108 Quoted in Wilson, J. (2008). *Life in Shakespeare's England.* Cosimo Inc., p.5.

109 Quoted in Lawrence, J. (1827). *On the nobility of the British gentry, or the political ranks and dignities of the British Empire, compared with those on the Continent.* T. Hookham, Simpson & Marshall, p.22.

110 See Lawrence, J. (1827). *On the nobility of the British gentry, or the political ranks and dignities of the British Empire, compared with those on the Continent.* T. Hookham, Simpson & Marshall.

111 In Cheshire this marked distinction never developed, though some of the barons were higher than others in the sense that they deputed for the Earl. Moreover, the Cheshire barons and her other gentry were all just 'gentry' when they were beyond Cheshire's borders. If Cheshire had been part of the English state then it seems likely that its own barons, including the Duttons of Dutton, would have become peers of the realm.

112 Dodds, B. (2008). Patterns of Decline: Arable Production in England, France and Castile, 1370–1450. In B. Dodds & R. Britnell. (Eds). *Agriculture and Rural Society After the Black Death: Common Themes and Regional Variations.* University of Hertfordshire Press.

113 See Poos, L. (2004). *A Rural Society After the Black Death: Essex, 1350-1525.* Cambridge University Press.

114 Coss, P. (2006). An Age of Deference. In Horrox, R. & Ormrod, W. (Eds). *A Social History of England, 1200–1500.* Cambridge University Press.

115 Coss, P. (2003). *The Origins of the English Gentry.* Cambridge University Press.

116 Bush, M. L. (1988). *Rich Noble, Poor Noble.* Manchester University Press.

117 See essays in Clark, L. (Ed.). (2005). *Of Mice and Men: Image, Belief and Regulation in Late Medieval England.* The Boydell Press.

118 Heinze, R. (1976). *The Proclamations of the Tudor Kings.* Cambridge University Press, p.24.

119 Public service included sitting on Grand Juries to see whether cases should go to the assizes. Failure to do so invoked a fine. Piers Dutton was fined 6s, 8d in 1525 for refusing to do jury service (TNA CHES 24/86-7).

120 Grassby, R. (1995) *The Business Community of Seventeenth Century*

England. Cambridge University Press, p.142.

121 Lockyer, R. (2005) *Tudor and Stuart Britain.* Pearson Education Ltd.

122 On Coke, see Boyer, A. (2003). *Sir Edward Coke and the Elizabethan Age.* Stanford University Press.

123 Coke, E. (1606). *Institutes of the Laws of England.* London.

124 Burn, R. (1830). *The Justice of the Peace and Parish Officer.* S. Sweet.

125 French, H. & Hoyle, R. (2007). *The Character of English Rural Society: Earls Colne, 1550-1750.* Manchester: Manchester University Press, p.71.

126 Anon. (1848). Who is a Gentleman and Who is an Esquire? *The Patrician,* p.107.

127 Corfield, P. (1996). The Rivals: Landed and Other Gentlemen. N. B. Harte & R. Quinault. (Eds). *Land and Society in Britain, 1700-1914.* Manchester University Press, p.36.

128 Heal, F. & Holmes, C. (1994). *Gentry in England and Wales, 1500 – 1700.* MacMillan, p.97.

129 Stone, L. (1966). Social Mobility in England, 1500 – 1700. *Past and Present,* 33.

130 Cressy, D. (1978). Social status and literacy in North East England, 1560-1630. *Local Population Studies,* 21: 19-23.

131 Clark, G. (2007). *A Farewell to Alms: A Brief Economic History of the World.* Princeton University Press.

132 Schmidt, A. (1961), *The Yeoman in Tudor and Stuart England.* Amherst College: The Folger Shakespeare Library.

133 Cressy, D. (1978). Social status and literacy in North East England, 1560-1630. *Local Population Studies,* 21: 19-23.

134 Cressy, D. (1978). Social status and literacy in North East England, 1560-1630. *Local Population Studies,* 21: 19-23.

135 Clark, G. (2007). *A Farewell to Alms: A Brief Economic History of the World.* Princeton: Princeton University Press.

136 Cressy, D. (1978). Social status and literacy in North East England, 1560-1630. *Local Population Studies,* 21: 19-23.

137 Houston, R. A. (1985). *Scottish Literacy and the Scottish Identity: Illiteracy and Society in Scotland and Northern England, 1600 – 1800.* Cambridge: Cambridge University Press.

138 Deanesly, M. (2002). *The Lollard Bible.* Wipf & Stock, p.161. More senior clergy, including rectors and vicars, were usually graduates. Curates and priests without a benefice (parish) were generally non-graduates. In Cheshire, 75% of the 326 priests working in the county in 1534 did not have a benefice. They 'eked out a precarious living by the celebration of occasional trentals and obits,' making them, in essence, freelance clerics. Jones, D. (1957). *The Church in Chester, 1300-1540.* Manchester University Press, p.11.

139 Oliva, M. (2014). The Nun's Priest. In Rigby, S. & Minnis, A. (Ed.). *Historians on Chaucer: The "General Prologue" to the Canterbury Tales.* Oxford: Oxford University Press, p.130.

140 Cooper, T. (1999). *The Last Generation of English Catholic Clergy: Parish Priests in the Diocese of Coventry and Lichfield in the Early Sixteenth Century.* Boydell & Brewer, p.130.

141 Wilson, S. (2003). *The Means of Naming: A Social History.* Routledge, p.263.

142 Edmund, J. (1846). *Miscellaneous Writings and Letters of Thomas Cranmer.* The University Press.

143 Thornton, T. (2000). *Cheshire and the Tudor State.* The Boydell Press, p.182.

144 Stone, L. (1966). Social Mobility in England, 1500 – 1700. *Past and Present, 33.*

145 Clark, G. (2007). *A Farewell to Alms: A Brief Economic History of the World.* Princeton University Press.

Chapter Three: Family, Youth and Prison

146 Ormerod, G. (1819). *The History of the County Palatine and City of Chester: Vol. II.* Printed for Lackington, Hughes, Harding, Maver and Jones, p.432.

147 Heal, F. & Holmes, C. (1994). *Gentry in England and Wales, 1500 – 1700.* MacMillan, pp-35-36.

148 Harleian Manuscript (Harl). 1424 and 1505. *The Visitation of Cheshire in the Year 1580: Made by Robert Glover, Somerset Herald for William Flower, Norroy King of Arms: with Numerous Additions and Continuations.* (1882). Harleian Society.

149 Greene, P. (2004). *Norton Priory: The Archaeology of a Medieval Religious House.* Cambridge University Press, p.14.

150 See Stone, H. (2002). *St. Augustine's Bones: A Microhistory.* University of Massachusetts Press.

151 *New Monthly Magazine* (1st November 1818). On the Peculiar Custom of Licensing the Minstrels of Cheshire.

152 Leycester, P. (1673). *Leycester's Historical Antiquities.* Printed by W. L. for Robert Clavell.

153 Ormerod, G. (1819). *The History of the County Palatine and City of Chester: Vol. II.* Printed for Lackington, Hughes, Harding, Maver and Jones, p.432.

154 S.C.P., Henry VIII, Vol. xiii., fos. 178-181 and 183-186. According to a case in the Court of Star Chamber in 1528: 'William Ryder, about the age of 100 years, says that Hugh Dutton of Moldsworth and Hugh Dutton of Hatton was one person and not divers. He never knew any other Hugh Dutton, which Hugh was son of Edmund etc., as above said. The said Sir Piers granted

Moldsworth to the said Hugh for term of his life for his preferment in marriage. The wife of the said Hugh was daughter to one Vernon, by whom Hugh had issue one John Dutton. Hugh dwelt at Moldsworth. The said John, during the time his father dwelt there, had issue Piers Dutton, who was eight years old when Hugh departed and went to dwell at Hatton during his life.' The Hugh Dutton who was grandfather of Piers (Peter) Dutton was born in 1432 because his grandfather definitely died in 1440. The Chester Recognizance Rolls (*Memorials of the Duttons of Dutton*, p.243) state: 1440 (11 May) Hugh de Dutton of Hatton, writ *diem clausit extremum,* on the death of.'

155 Graff, E. (1999). *What is Marriage For?* Beacon Press, p.8.

156 For a discussion of the Battle of Blore Heath, see Burne, A. (2005). *The Battle Fields of England.* Pen and Sword, Ch. 19.

157 Michael Jones presented evidence in the January 2004 Channel 4 documentary *Britain's Real Monarch* that Edward IV was in fact the illegitimate son of Cecily, Duchess of York, and an archer. The evidence has been questioned in Pendrill, C. (2004). *The Wars of the Roses and Henry VII: Turbulence, Tyranny and Tradition in England 1459-c.1513.* Heinemann, pp.71-72.

158 For an introductory history of the Wars of the Roses see Hicks, M. (2014). *The Wars of the Roses.* Osprey Publishing.

159 Hall, J. (1883). *A History of the Town and Parish of Nantwich, or Wich Malbank, in the County Palatine of Chester.* E. J. Morten.

160 Boyd D. (1998). *A Bibliographical Dictionary of Racehorse Trainers in Berkshire 1850–1939.* London.

161 Mercer, M. (2010). *The Medieval Gentry: Power, Leadership and Choice During the Wars of the Roses.* A. & C. Black, p.69.

162 Harl., 1424, fo. 62.

163 VERNON, Sir Richard (1390-1451), of Harlaston, Staffs. And Haddon, Derbys. Published in *The History of Parliament: the House of Commons 1386-1421.* (ed). J.S. Roskell, L. Clark, C. Rawcliffe. (1993). http://www.historyofparliamentonline.org/volume/1386-1421/member/vernon-sir-richard-1390-1451

164 Leycester, P. (1673). *Leycester's Historical Antiquities.* Printed by W. L. for Robert Clavell.

165 Harl. 1424, 17. Brereton of Malpas

166 E.g. Ives, E. (1976). Introduction to *The Letters and Accounts of William Brereton of Malpas.* Record Society of Lancashire and Cheshire, p.1.

167 Ives, E. (Ed). (1976). *The Letters and Accounts of William Brereton of Malpas.* Record Society of Lancashire and Cheshire. A Knight Banneret who led a company of troops under his own banner.

168 Ives, E. W. (1992). The Fall of Anne Boleyn Reconsidered. *The English Historical Review,* 107 (424): 651–664.

169 See Hicks, M. (2012). *The Fifteenth Century Inquisitions Post Mortem: A Companion.* The Boydell Press, for a detailed discussion of this practice.

170 See *Memorials of the Duttons of Dutton,* 'Duttoniana:' 'Chester Recognizance Rolls,' as below.

171 See *Memorials of the Duttons of Dutton,* 'Duttoniana:' 'Chester Recognizance Rolls.' 11th October 1403: appointed commissioner of array in Eddisbury.

172 See *Memorials of the Duttons of Dutton,* 'Duttoniana:' 'Chester Recognizance Rolls.' 11th May 1440: Writ on the death of Hugh de Dutton.

173 See *Memorials of the Duttons of Dutton,* 'Duttoniana:' 'Chester Recognizance Rolls.' 17th February 1418/19: 'John de Dutton and his wife Margaret ...grant and livery to.'

174 See *Memorials of the Duttons of Dutton,* 'Duttoniana:' 'Chester Recognizance Rolls.' 13th December 1453, 12th March 1454, 25th July 1454, 17th December 1454, 16th December 1455.

175 Philips, K. (2003). *Medieval Maidens: Young Women and Gender in England, c. 1270 - c. 1540.* Manchester University Press, p.35.

176 Last mentioned: 1464: John de Dutton of Hatton, appointment as a collector of subsidy.

177 See *Memorials of the Duttons of Dutton,* 'Duttoniana:' 'Chester Recognizance Rolls.' 7th March 1464. Inquisition of Robert Grosvenor, Esq.

178 S.C.P., Henry VIII, Vol. xiii., fos. 178-181 and 183-186. These case abstracts have been published as: Stewart-Brown, R. (Ed.). (1916). *Lancashire and Cheshire Cases in the Court of Star Chamber.* The Record Society.

179 An Act of Parliament in the Confirmation of Made by Henry VIII to Sir Piers Dutton of Hatton of the Dutton property, Statutes of the Realm, 1536, c.48. This has been published in *Memorial to the Duttons of Dutton.*

180 SC 8/344/E1262

181 Writ to Thomas Wotton, Escheator of Cheshire, 4th August 1481. *(Duttoniana)* p.207.

182 1472: Writ of Livery setting forth the finding of the inquisition *(Duttoniana).*

183 6th August 1476, recognizance of £200 that one of Dutton's servants keep the peace *(Duttoniana).*

184 30th September 1488 *(Duttoniana).*

185 12th May 1503: Writ of Livery setting forth the finding of the inquisition *(Duttoniana).* It is written: 'the said Elizabeth (Grosvenor) married one Peter Dutton, and had issue one Peter; that the said Elizabeth long before the taking of the inquisition died; that the said Peter her husband died seized of the

inheritance of the said Elizabeth by the law of England, and the reversion of the same pertained to Peter Dutton kinsman and heir of the said Elizabeth; and the said Peter died on (8th April 1503), and that Peter Dutton was kinsman and heir, viz son of Peter son of the said Peter.'

186 King, D. (1778). *The History of Cheshire.* Chester, p.792.

187 Recognizance Rolls, quoted in Earwaker, J. (1890). *The History of the Ancient Parish of Sandbach.* Privately Published, p.96.

188 Urban, M. (2006). *Seventeenth Century Mother's Advice Books.* Palgrave MacMillan, p.18.

189 Peter Dutton of Hatton, junior, was compelled to pay a surety on 20th June 1489. *Annual Report of the Deputy Keeper of Public Records.* (1876). HMSO, p.550.

190 CALS Z/S/B/5a.

191 Fritze, R. & Robison, W. (2002). Marriage, Aristocratic and Gentry. In *Historical Dictionary of Late Medieval England.* Greenwood Publishing, p.340.

192 Graff, E. (1999). *What is Marriage For?* Beacon Press, p.8.

193 Fleming, P. (2001). *Family and Household in Medieval England.* Palgrave MacMillan, p.22.

194 Philips, K. (2012). *Medieval Maidens: Young Women and Gender in England, c.1270-c.1540.* Manchester University Press, p.37.

195 Ives, E. (1976). Introduction to *The Letters and Accounts of William Brereton of Malpas.* Record Society of Lancashire and Cheshire, p.1.

196 Ives, E. (1976). Introduction to *The Letters and Accounts of William Brereton of Malpas.* Record Society of Lancashire and Cheshire, p.12.

197 See 'Duttoniana.'

198 *Memorials of the Duttons of Dutton,* p.xxi. The record simply states 'Peter Dutton' but it is more likely to have been the (wealthier) father, especially as the son disappeared from the records in 1489.

199 PRO, DL 5/2, fo. 39, 47; CCR, 1500-1509, 10.

200 LP, Henry VII, 1503, m. 2d, 1.

201 Writ to Thomas Wotton, Escheator of Cheshire. 4th August 1481. Quoted in *Memorials of the Duttons of Dutton,* 'Duttoniana,' p.207.

202 Sartore, M. (2011). *Outlawry, Governance and Law in Medieval England.* PhD Thesis: University of Wisconsin or Gorski, R. (2003). *The Fourteenth Century Sheriff: English Local Administration in the Late Middle Ages.* The Boydell Press.

203 1580 Visitation is Harl. 1424 and 1505. The 1613 Visitation is Harl. 1535. These are published as Rylands, J. (Ed.) (1892). *The Visitation of Cheshire in the Year 1580.* Harleian Society and Armytage, G. & Rylands, J. (Eds.) (1909). *Pedigrees Made at the Visitation of Cheshire,* 1613. Record

Society for the Publication of Original Documents Relating to Lancashire and Cheshire.

204 BHO. J. S. Barrow, J. D. Herson, A. H. Lawes, P. J. Riden and M. V. J. Seaborne (2005). 'Mayors and sheriffs of Chester.' In *A History of the County of Chester: Volume 5 Part 2*: The City of Chester: Culture, Buildings, Institutions. (Ed). A. T. Thacker and C. P. Lewis, pp. 305-321 http://www.british-history.ac.uk/vch/ches/vol5/pt2/pp305-321 (accessed 21 March 2015).

205 Ormerod, G. (1819). *The History of the County Palatine and City of Chester: Vol. II,* London: Printed for Lackington, Hughes, Harding, Maver and Jones, p.431.

206 Orme, N. (2005). Education and recreation. In Radulescu, R. & Truelove, T. (Eds). *Gentry Culture in Late Medieval England.* Manchester University Press.

207 Editor (19th December 1964). THE DUTTONS OF DUTTON - and the ancestral home that moved south. *Rural Rides,* 11.

208 Rowland Dutton's divorce case in 1565 described him as being around the age of 15. Furnivall, F. (1897). *Child Marriages, Divorces and Ratifications in the Diocese of Chester, AD 1561-66.* Early Text Society, case 24.

209 Anon. (1901). *Memorials to the Duttons of Dutton.* Henry Sotheran and Co., p.180.

210 Harriss, G. (2009). *Shaping the Nation: England, 1300-1461.* Oxford University Press, pp.150-152 and Thompson, M. (1995). *The Medieval Hall: The Basis of Secular Domestic Life, 600-1600 AD.* Scolar Press, p.176.

211 Harriss, G. (2009). *Shaping the Nation: England, 1300-1461.* Oxford University Press, p.156.

212 Shaw, T. (2005). Music. In Radulescu, R. & Truelove, T. (Eds). *Gentry Culture in Late Medieval England.* Manchester University Press, p.160.

213 Orme, N. (2005). Education and recreation. In Radulescu, R. & Truelove, T. (Eds). *Gentry Culture in Late Medieval England.* Manchester University Press.

214 Moran, J. (2014). *The Growth of English Schooling, 1340-1548: Learning, Literacy, and Laicization in Pre-Reformation York.* Princeton University Press, p.66.

215 Lander, J. (1981), *Government and Community, England, 1450-1509.* Harvard University Press, p.160.

216 Lawson, J. & Silver, H. (2013). *A Social History of England.* Routledge, pp.70-71.

217 For the history of education in Cheshire in this period, at Stockport Grammar in particular, see Varley, B. (1946). *The History of Stockport Grammar School, Including the Life of Sir Edmond Shaa, Kt.* Manchester University Press.

218 The Isle of Man was recognized as an independent kingdom by Edward III. The 3rd of Earl of Derby did not take the title 'king,' instead terming himself 'Lord of Mann.' This title became invested in the crown in 1765. See Moore, A. (1900). *A History of the Isle of Man*. London.

219 For an examination of the Stanley family, see Coward, B. (1983). *The Stanleys, Lords Stanley, and Earls of Derby, 1385-1672: The Origins, Wealth, and Power of a Landowning Family*. Manchester University Press.

220 LP, Henry VIII, xi. 1212.

221 Venn, J. (1922) *Alumni Canterbrigienses: From Earliest Times to 1751*. Cambridge University Press; Emden, A. (1957). *A Biographical Register of the University of Oxford to AD 1500*. Clarendon Press; Emden, A. (1974). *A Biographical Register of the University of Oxford 1501 to 1540*. Clarendon Press.

222 Shaw T. (2005). Music. In Radulescu, R. & Truelove, T. (Eds). *Gentry Culture in Late Medieval England*. Manchester University Press, p.163.

223 Deanesly, M. (2002). *The Lollard Bible*. Wipf & Stock, p.161.

224 Foster, J. (1891). *Alumni Oxonienses 1500-1714*. Oxford University Press.

225 Sturgess, H. (1949). *Records of the Honorable Society of Middle Temple: Admissions 15th c. to 1944*. London.

226 Foster, J. (1889). *The Register of Admissions to Grays Inn, 1521-1889*. London and Cooke, W. (1878). *Students admitted to the Inner Temple 1547-1660*. London.

227 LP, Henry VIII, 17: 36.

228 The Inner Temple Library. Introduction, Part 1. (2015). http://www.innertemplelibrary.org.uk/temple-history/inner-temple-historyintroduction-part-1.htm

229 Ives, E. (1983). *The Common Lawyers of Pre-Reformation England: Thomas Kebell, A Case Study*. Cambridge University Press.

230 Baildon, W. (1896). *Records of the Honorable Society of Lincoln's Inn: Admissions, 1420-1799*. London.

231 Harl., 2115, 35.

232 Tompkins, M. (2006). "Let's Kill All the Lawyers!" Did Fifteenth Century Peasants Employ Lawyers When They Conveyed Customary Land? In L. Clark. *Identity and Insurgency in the Late Medieval Ages*. Boydell Press, p.75.

233 Musson, A. (2004). Legal Culture: Medieval Lawyers' Aspirations and Pretentions. In Ormrod, W. (Ed.). *Fourteenth Century England, Vol. III*. The Boydell Press, p.26.

234 Thornton, T. (2000), *Cheshire and the Tudor State*. The Boydell Press, p.234.

235 House of Commons. (1870). *Reports from Commissioners*. London, p.223.

236 Lawson, J. & Silver, H. (2013). *A Social History of England*. Routledge,

pp.70-71.

237 A 'Geoffrey Dutton' was admitted to the Mercers' Company in 1422 and a 'Thomas Dutton' in 1569. However, it is unclear how, if at all, they might related to the Duttons of Dutton or Hatton. The surviving records were searched at *Records of London's Livery Companies Online,* www.londonroll.org

238 Wallis, P. & Webb, C. (2011). The education and training of gentry sons in early modern England. *Social History,* 36: 1.

239 Pollard, A. J. (2004). *Imagining Robin Hood: The Late Medieval Stories in Historical Context.* Routledge, p.69.

240 Plummer, A. (1972). *The London Weavers Company, 1600–1970.* Routledge, p.83.

241 TNA CHES 25/17.

242 Orme, N. (2005). Education and recreation. In Radulescu, R. & Truelove, T. (Eds). *Gentry Culture in Late Medieval England.* Manchester University Press.

243 Star Chamber Proceedings (S. C. P), Henry VIII, Vol. vii., fols. 182-186.

244 Ives, E. (1976). Introduction to *The Letters and Accounts of William Brereton of Malpas.* Record Society of Lancashire and Cheshire, p.31.

245 A. P. Baggs, A. J. Kettle, S. J. Lander, A. T. Thacker & D. Wardle. (1980). 'Houses of Benedictine monks: The abbey of Chester' in C. R. Elrington & B. E. Harris (Eds.). *A History of the County of Chester: Volume 3.* London, pp.132-146. http://www.britishhistory.ac.uk/vch/ches/vol3/pp132-146 [accessed 4 February 2015].

246 Chesters suggests that Randle Brereton may have been the baseborn brother of Sir Randolph Brereton. Chesters, G. (1961). Power Politics in Cheshire, Part I. *Cheshire Round,* 1:1, p.26.

247 S.C.P., Henry VIII, Vol. vii., fols. 182-186.

248 TNA, STAC 2/12 - Folio 165-166.

249 Inquisitions 1518, No. 4. *Memorials of the Duttons of Dutton, Duttoniana,* p.214.

Chapter Four: The Riotous Mayor

250 Harl., 2125, 206.

251 Leycester, P. (1673). *Leycester's Historical Antiquities.* Printed by W. L. for Robert Clavell.

252 Weiss, F. (1992). *Ancestral Roots of Certain American Colonists who Came to America Before 1700: The Lineage of Alfred the Great, Charlemagne, Malcolm of Scotland, Robert the Strong, and Some of Their Descendants.* Genealogical Publishing Company, p.194

253 See *1580 Visitation of Cheshire.*

254 A recent biography is, Neale, J. (2014). *Queen Elizabeth I.* Chicago Review Press.

255 See Arthurson, I. (2009). *The Perkin Warbeck Conspiracy, 1491-1499.* The History Press.

256 Youngs, D. (2007). *Humphrey Newton (1466-1536): An Early Tudor Gentleman.* The Boydell Press, p.7.

257 Cartwright, K. (2009). Dramatic theory and lucre's discretion: The plays of Henry Medwall. In M. Pinchcombe & C. Shrank (Eds). *The Oxford Handbook of Tudor Literature.* Oxford University Press.

258 LP, Henry VIII, xi, 1253. 'Raynold Ryley and Ric. Barlow, of Bowden, Cheshire, say they were in Pomfret on Saturday after St. Andrew's Day, to sell salt and herring, and saw the captains of the commons come in. Lord Darcy was lodged in the castle, and the grand captain, Robert Aske, in the Abbey. Lord Lumley lay at Mr. Henryson's, the late mayor, and there hung out his banner with the Five Wounds. Sir Robert Neville and other noblemen, whose names they durst not ask, also came in. The companies were well harnessed, every man with a malle on his back; and they had a bridge of timber, with a vice to shoot it over any arm of the sea in this realm. The hosts say they care not for Lancashire, for the lord of Lancashire (*sic*) rules all that shire; nor for Cheshire, for the rulers there, Sir William Brereton and Sir Piers Dutton, cannot agree.' 5th December 1536.

259 Thornton, T. (2000). *Cheshire and the Tudor State.* The Boydell Press, p.23.

260 Morris, R. (1893). *Chester in the Plantagenet and Tudor Reigns.* Printed for the Author, p.62.

261 TNA STAC/ 2/7/184.

262 TNA CHES 2/167, m. 5v.

263 Morris, R. (1893). *Chester in the Plantagenet and Tudor Reigns.* Printed for the Author, p.60.

264 Sanok, C. (2007). *Her Life Historical: Exemplarity and Female Saints' Lives in Late Medieval England,* University of Pennsylvania Press, p.204, ref. 1.

265 Thornton, T. (1999). Opposition Drama and the Resolution of Disputes in Early Tudor England: Cardinal Wolsey and the Abbot of Chester. In *Bulletin of the John Rylands University Library of Manchester,* 81: 1, p.27.

266 Clark, J. (2011). *The Benedictines in the Middle Ages.* The Boydell Press.

267 Though surnames were largely hereditary by the early sixteenth century, they were not entirely stable, hence the records referring to those with aliases. See Redmonds, D., King, T. & Hey, D. (2011). *Surnames, DNA and Family History.* Oxford University Press, p.51.

268 Thornton, T. (1999). Opposition Drama and the Resolution of Disputes in Early Tudor England: Cardinal Wolsey and the Abbot of Chester. In *Bulletin of the John Rylands University Library of Manchester,* 81: 1.

269 See Dutton, E. (June 2015). Tracing Medieval Ancestors. *Family Tree.*

270 Harl., 2125, 206. It is also noted in the Cheshire Recognizance Rolls that: '1510 (Oct 11). Peter Dutton, of Hatton, Esq., exemplification of a memorandum of the escape of the said Peter Dutton from the castle of Chester, to which he was committed at the instance of John, Abbot of St. Werburgh' (*Memorials of the Duttons of Dutton,* p.258).

271 For a discussion of this class, see Smith, R. (2004). *The MiddlingSort and the Politics of Social Reformation: Colchester, 1570-1640.* Peter Lang.

272 'Later medieval Chester 1230-1550: City government and politics, 1350-1550.' In *A History of the County of Chester: Volume 5.* Part 1, the City of Chester: General History and Topography. (Ed). C. P. Lewis & A. T. Thacker (London, 2003), pp.58-64 http://www.britishhistory.ac.uk/vch/ches/vol5/pt1/pp58-64 [accessed 4 February 2015].

273 'Later medieval Chester 1230-1550: City government and politics, 1350-1550.' In *A History of the County of Chester: Volume 5.* Part 1, the City of Chester: General History and Topography. (Ed). C. P. Lewis & A. T. Thacker (London, 2003), pp.58-64 http://www.britishhistory.ac.uk/vch/ches/vol5/pt1/pp58-64 [accessed 4 February 2015].

274 Thornton, T. (1999). Opposition Drama and the Resolution of Disputes in Early Tudor England: Cardinal Wolsey and the Abbot of Chester' in *Bulletin of the John Rylands University Library of Manchester,* 81: 1, p.28.

275 By the sixteenth century, a 'clerk' could refer to a lay officer of the church, such as a 'singing clerk,' as well as to a priest or 'clerk in holy orders.' It is more likely that this person was a lay officer. See Room, A. (1998). *Dunces, Gourmands and Petticoats: 1,300 Words Whose Meanings Have Changed Through the Ages.* McGraw-Hill, p.61.

276 CALS ZS/B/5 g.

277 Thornton, T. (2000). *Cheshire and the Tudor State.* The Boydell Press, p.187.

278 Thornton, T. (2000), *Cheshire and the Tudor State.* The Boydell Press, p.200.

279 King, D. (1656). *The Vale Royal of England or the County Palatine of Chester Illustrated.* John Streater, p.192.

280 C.A.L.S., ZCX 3, f. 51.

281 Harl., 2093, 3.

282 Dutton was almost certainly not yet knighted at this point.

283 Harl., 2125, 206.

284 Harl., 2125, 206.

285 C 1/416/28.

286 This is noted in Henry Gee's will of 1545. CALS. EDA 2/1, Pg188.

287 Thornton, T. (2000). *Cheshire and the Tudor State.* Boydell & Brewer, p.208.

288 TNA E 314/42/7.

NOTES

Chapter 5: Criminal and Courtier

[289] S.C.P., Henry VIII, Vol. v., No. 162.

[290] Recognizances for Repayment of Loans. 28th May 1516.

[291] LP, Henry VIII, viii. 7th April 1535. Harl. 1968, fo. 20.

[292] Thornton, T. (2000). *Cheshire and the Tudor State.* The Boydell Press, p.96.

[293] Froude, J. (2009). *Mary Tudor.* Continuum, p.99.

[294] Thornton, T. (2000), *Cheshire and the Tudor State.* The Boydell Press, p.111.

[295] Ahnert, R. (2013). *The Rise of Prison Literature in the Sixteenth Century.* Cambridge University Press, p.15.

[296] TNA, STAC 2/12, folios 165-166.

[297] Some time between 1518 and 1529, Dutton did, however, sue John Fletcher who had given a verbal surety to cover the debt of his brother Randolph Fletcher. C1/496/18.

[298] It is unclear exactly who Sir John Dutton was but it was not uncommon in the period for the illegitimate sons of gentry to be trained as priests (Carlton, K. & Thornton, T. (2011). Illegitimacy and Authority in the North of England, 1450 – 1640. *Northern History,* XLVIII: I). As such, he may possibly have been Sir Piers Dutton's illegitimate half-brother.

[299] S.C.P., Henry VIII, xiii., fos. 178-181 and 183-186.

[300] Harl. 1424, fo. 17.

[301] S. C. P., Henry VIII, Bundle 26, no. 370.

[302] S. C. P., Henry VIII, Vol. 3, fol. 11, Bundle 17, No. 227, and 24, No. 434.

[303] *The Domesday of Inclosures, 1517-1518.* (1971). Kennikat Press, p.642.

[304] For a detailed discussion of Tudor enclosures, see Thirsk, J. (1984). *The Rural Economy of England.* A. & C. Black, Ch. VI.

[305] For a history of Bostock and the Bostock family, see McLellan, J. & Bostock, T. (2010). *Bostock: A History of a Village and its People.* Jane McLellan.

[306] S.C.P., Henry VIII, Vol. v., No. 162.

[307] LP, Henry VIII, iii, 58-72.

[308] Brock, R. (1963). *The Courtier in Early Tudor Society: Illustrated From Select Examples.* PhD Thesis: University of London.

[309] Ives, E. (1976). Introduction to *The Letters and Accounts of William Brereton of Malpas.* Record Society of Lancashire and Cheshire, p.1.

[310] Weir, A. (2002). *Henry VIII: The King and His Court.* Random House. p. 42.

[311] Thornton, T. (2000). *Cheshire and the Tudor State.* The Boydell Press, p.96.

[312] LP, Henry VIII, iii. Kings Book of Payments.

[313] Archbold, W. (1894). Neville, Ralph. In *Dictionary of National Biography.* Smith, Elder & Co.

314 LP, Henry VIII, iii. To attend the King. November 1520.

315 LP, Henry VIII, iii. Debts Due to the Crown.

316 Ives, E. (1976). *Letters and Accounts of William Brereton of Malpas.* The Record Society, p.83.

317 Bodl. MS. Dodsworth, ff. 114, v.15.

318 Brock, R. (1963). *The Courtier in Early Tudor Society: Illustrated From Select Examples.* PhD Thesis: University of London.

319 Robinson, W. (1995). Henry VIII's Household in the fifteen-twenties: the Welsh Connection. *Historical Research,* 68, 173-190, p.173.

320 Harl. MS, 433. fo. 17.

321 *Memorials of the Duttons of Dutton,* p.216.

322 Dolan, L. (2015). Child marriage in sixteenth-century northern England: the emotional undertones in the legal narratives. *Limina,* 20: 3.

323 *Memorials of the Duttons of Dutton,* p.216.

324 C/1 1469/28. This record seems, incorrectly, to say 'Margery.'

325 Inquisition post mortem praedicti Petri Dutton Militis, 37 Hen. 8, quoted in 'Duttoniana,' *Memorials of the Duttons of Dutton,* pp.214-216.

326 Thornton, T. (2000). *Cheshire and the Tudor State.* The Boydell Press, p.234.

327 Halowell Garrett, C. (1966). *The Marian Exiles.* Cambridge University Press, p.260.

328 Higgs, L. (1998). *Godliness and Governance in Tudor Colchester.* Michigan University Press, p.106.

329 C 1/416/28.

330 C 1/416/28.

331 S.C.P., Henry VIII, Vol. xiii., fos. 178-181 and 183-186.

332 British Museum. (1808). *Catalogue of the Harleian Manuscripts in the British Museum.* London, p.46 & p.82.

333 Tittler, R. (2013). *Portraits, Painters and Publics in Provincial England, 1540-1640.* Oxford: Oxford University Press, p.110.

334 Harris, N. (1825). *Catalogue of the Heralds' Visitations.* London: J. Taylor, p.120.

335 Personal correspondence, 2014.

336 British Museum. (1808). *Catalogue of the Harleian Manuscripts in the British Museum.* London, p.120.

337 CALS. EDA 2/1, Pg164.

338 McSheffrey, S. & Tanner, R. (2003). *Lollards of Coventry, 1486-1522.* Cambridge University Press.

339 Munden, A. (1997). *The Coventry Martyrs.* Coventry Archives Publication.

340 Hope, A. (2014). The Printed Book Trade in Response to Luther. In Gillespie, V. & Powell, S. (Eds). *A Companion to the Early Printed Book in*

Britain, 1476-1558. Boydell & Brewer, p.279.

341 The wife of a knight is now termed 'Lady (Surname)' and the Damehood is the female equivalent of a knighthood, conferred since 1917. However, the wives of knights only began to be termed 'Lady' in the eighteenth century. Before this time, they were 'Dames.' Mencken, H. (1948). *The American Language: An Enquiry into the Development of the English of the United States.* Alfred A. Knopf, p.560.

342 *Foxe's Book of Martyrs. Foxe's Book of Martyrs.* (1978). Ed. Forbush, W. Zondervan.

343 Higgs, L. (1998). *Godliness and Governance in Tudor Colchester.* Michigan University Press, p.107.

344 On Queen Mary, see Porter, L. (2009). *The Myth of "Bloody Mary": A Biography of Queen Mary I of England.* MacMillan.

345 Halowell Garrett, C. (1966). *The Marian Exiles.* Cambridge University Press, p.259.

346 Oxley, J. (1965). *The Reformation in Essex to the Death of Mary.* Manchester University Press, p.5.

347 Brigden, S. (1989). *London and the Reformation.* Clarendon Press.

348 Wark, K. R. (1971). *Elizabethan Recusancy in Cheshire.* The Chetham Society: Manchester University Press.

349 Thornton, T. (2000). *Cheshire and the Tudor State.* The Boydell Press, p.234.

Chapter Six: The Disputed Legacy

350 John Dutton, regarding his father Lawrence Dutton.

351 The will is transcribed in *Memorials of the Duttons of Dutton,* pp.171-174.

352 CALS EDA 2/1, Pg15b.

353 LP, Henry VIII, viii, 496.

354 This John Dutton actually had an illegitimate family himself. LP, Henry VIII, 8, 496. Beaconsall to Cromwell (April 1535). 'John Dutton, bastard son of the late Master Lawrence Dutton, keeps a young woman, by whom he has several children. He had a great sickness a year ago, and I sent one of my canons to make him promise to marry her on his recovery; which he agreed to do, but has not done. He says he will live and die as his father did; who, indeed, had many bastards, so that the land of Dutton came to Sir Piers Dutton. His father was "such a beast in his living in every point of naughtiness as never was in the whole realm." According to the 1613 Visitation (Harl. 1535, fo. 107, Duckinfield of Duckinfield), John's bastard sons were: John, Thomas, Lawrence, Robert and Henry.

355 Staves, S. (2014). Daughters and younger sons. In Brewer, J. & Staves, S.

(Eds). *Early Modern Conceptions of Property.* Routledge, p.210.

356 Carlton, K. & Thornton, T. (2011). Illegitimacy and Authority in the North of England, 1450 – 1640. *Northern History,* XLVIII: I.

357 Wright, S. M. (1983). *Derbyshire Gentry in the Fifteenth Century,* Derby: Derbyshire Record Society, p.149

358 S.C.P., Henry VIII, Vol. xiii., fos. 178-181 and 183-186.

359 Thornton, T. (2000). *Cheshire and the Tudor State.* The Boydell Press, p.202.

360 S.C.P., Henry VIII, Vol. xiii., fos. 178-181 and 183-186.

361 Court of Star Chamber Proceedings, Henry VIII, Bundle 17, no. 398.

362 Two years earlier, in 1526, Dutton himself had been appointed chief arbitrator in a land dispute between Sir William Stanley and Edward Minshull. RYCH/1362.

363 *Letters and Accounts of William Brereton,* pp.80-81.

364 LP, Henry VIII, iv. 5530.

365 Alex. (June 1791). Account of Halton Castle in Cheshire. *The Lady's Magazine.*

366 Cromwell had lent Dutton money. LP, Henry VIII, iv, 1529. 'Debts due to me, Thomas Cromwell, 1st June.'

367 Thornton, T. (2000). *Cheshire and the Tudor State.* The Boydell Press, p.200.

368 Paulet was happy to be a fervent Protestant, a fervent Catholic or moderate Anglican depending on the political mood. For a full length biography, see Scard, M. (2011). *Tudor Survivor: The Life and Times of Courtier William Paulet.* The History Press. See also, Alsop, J. & Loades, D. (1987). William Paulet, First Marquis of Winchester: A Question of Age. *The Sixteenth Century Journal* 18: 333–342.

369 Ives, E. (1976). *Letters and Accounts of William Brereton,* pp.80-81.

370 Sturgeons and whales are 'Royal Fish' and it has been mandatory to present these catches to the English monarch since 1344. See Woolrych, W. (1853). *A Treatise of the Law of Waters.* J. & J. W. Johnson.

371 Harl., 2115, fo. 33.

372 Ives, E. (1976). *Letters and Accounts of William Brereton,* Letter 26.

373 TNA SP/177. fo. 198.

374 Hanshall, J. (1817). *The History of the County Palatine of Chester.* J. Fletcher, p.379.

375 Wagner, J. & Schmid, S. (2011). *Encyclopaedia of Tudor England.* ABC-Clio. 'William Brereton.'

376 Rowland Lee to Cromwell, 10th July 1534. LP, Henry VIII, 7, 968.

377 Ellis, S. (2014). Tudor State Formation and the Shaping of the British Isles. In Ellis, S. & Barber, S. (Eds). *Conquest and Union: Fashioning a British State, 1485-1725.* Routledge or Ives, E. (1976). Introduction to *The Letters*

and Accounts of William Brereton of Malpas. Record Society of Lancashire and Cheshire.

378 Ives, E. (1976). Introduction to *The Letters and Accounts of William Brereton of Malpas.* Record Society of Lancashire and Cheshire, p.12.

379 Michon, C. (2008). Pomp and Circumstances: State Prelates Under Francis I and Henry VIII. In Richardson G. (Ed.) *The Contending Kingdoms: France and England, 1420-1700.* Ashgate, p.83.

380 Lysons, D. (1810). *Magna Britannia.* Cadwell & Davies, p.4

381 Harl. MS. 283, f. 14. B. M.

Chapter Seven: High Sheriff of Cheshire

382 Henry VIII to Sir Piers Dutton, 19th October 1536.

383 LP, Henry VIII, xii (1), 26 May 1537, 1282. Lord Chancellor Audley to Cromwell.

384 TNA STAC 2/8/274.

385 Pleas of Evidence, Ledger of Vale Royal Abbey. Folio 45 (*British History Online*).

386 Cistercian Monk. (1852). *A Concise History of the Cistercian Order.* T. Richardson & Son.

387 Geoffrey Chesters suggests that Randle Brereton may have been the illegitimate brother of Sir Randolph Brereton. Chesters, G. (1961). Power Politics in Cheshire. *Cheshire Round,* 1:1, p.26.

388 'Dan' was an honorific used for monks.

389 LP, Henry VIII, vii, 1037 (misdated as 1534).

390 LP, Henry VIII, vii, 868.

391 TNA, C 1/902/ 16-18.

392 Ackerman, J. (1843). On the Forgeries of Public Money. *Proceedings of the Numismatic Society, vol. 6,* pp. 57-82.

393 Bucholz, R. & Ward, J. (2012). *London: A Social and Cultural History.* Cambridge University Press, p.51. Indeed, by the eighteenth century, Newgate was had become a literary byword for the worst kind of prison. This is discussed in Halliday, S. (2013). *Newgate: London's Prototype of Hell.* The History Press.

394 Greene, P. (1989). *Norton Priory: The Archaeology of a Medieval Religious House.* Cambridge University Press, p.71.

395 This summary of the coining affair is taken from Chesters, G. (1961). Power Politics in Cheshire, Part II. *Cheshire Round,* 1:2, pp.45-46

396 William Brereton to Cromwell, 8th June 1537. LP Henry VIII, xii, ii, 58.

397 Ives, E. (1976). *Letters and Accounts of William Brereton of Malpas,* p.32.

398 TNA 11/27. fo. 62.

399 LP, Henry VIII, xi, 2. Sir William Brereton to Cromwell.

400 Harl. MS, 283, fo. 14.

401 See Bellamy, J. (1979). *The Tudor Law of Treason.* Routledge, Ch. 3.

402 For a discussion of the Kildare Rebellion, see Bradshaw, B. (1979). *The Irish Constitutional Revolution of the Sixteenth Century.* Cambridge University Press.

403 Dwarris, Sir F. (1848). Observations upon the history of one of the old Cheshire Families. *Archaeologia,* 33: 55-83.

404 LP, Henry VIII, x. 13th May 1536. J. Husee to Lord Lisle: 'My lord Richmond is Chamberlain of Chester and North Wales...'

405 LP, Henry VIII, xi. 12th July 1536. Robert Tatton to Wriothesley.

406 Thornton, T. (2000). *Cheshire and the Tudor State.* The Boydell Press, p.147.

407 William Brereton to Cromwell, 8th June 1537. LP, Henry VIII, xii, ii, 58.

408 A full length biography of Sir Thomas Audley has, seemingly, never been written. Were it written, it could potentially be an important contribution to the study of this period.

409 LP, Henry VIII, xii (1), 26 May 1537, 1282. Lord Chancellor Audley to Cromwell.

410 Bintoff, S. (1982). 'Audley, Thomas' In *History of Parliament: The Commons, 1509-1558.* The Boydell Press.

411 A point made by Ives, E. (1976). Introduction to *The Letters and Accounts of William Brereton of Malpas.* Record Society of Lancashire and Cheshire, p.40.

412 LP, Henry VIII, ix, 1106

413 Bordo, S. (2013). *The Creation of Anne Boleyn: A New Look at England's Most Notorious Queen.* Houghton, Mifflin & Harcourt.

414 LP, Henry VIII, 10. Lists of Person Appointed to Offices, May 1536.

415 For a full biography, see Gibbons, G. (2001). *The Political Career of Thomas Wriothesley, First Earl of Southampton 1505-1550, Henry VIII's Last Chancellor.* The Edwin Mellen Press.

416 LP, Henry VIII, 10. Lists of Person Appointed to Offices, May 1536.

417 Sir Piers Dutton to Lord Cromwell, 23rd September 1536. LP. Henry VIII, xi, 486.

418 LP, Hen. VIII, x, pp. 141, 517.

419 Greene, P. (1989). *Norton Priory: The Archaeology of a Medieval Religious House.* Cambridge University Press, p.71.

420 LP, Hen. VIII, x, p.393; xi, p.265.

421 Sir Piers Dutton to Sir Thomas Audley, Lord Chancellor. LP, Henry VIII, xi, 681.

422 LP, Henry VIII, xi, 787.

423 LP, Henry VIII, xi, 1212-2.

424 LP, Henry VIII, xi, 1212.

425 LP, Hen. VIII, xi, pp. 305–6, 413.

426 *Letters and Accounts of William Brereton of Malpas,* p.32.

427 S. H. B. (1869). *The Monastic Houses of England; Their Accusers and Defenders.* Thomas Richardson & Son, p.2.

428 Quoted in Burke, H. (1870). *The Men and Women of the English Reformation.* London, p.346.

429 Beck, J. (1969). *Tudor Cheshire.* Cheshire Community Council, p.101.

430 LP, Henry VIII, xi, 1019.

431 Chesters, G. (1966). Dissolution of the Cheshire monasteries. *Cheshire Round,* 1: 5. p.151. For further discussion of this issue, see Cox, P. (2013). *Reformation Responses in Tudor Cheshire c. 1500-1577,* Warwick University, whose stimulating PhD thesis first drew my attention to these issues.

432 LP, Henry VIII, xiv (1), 639.

433 Bennett, J. (1935) The White Friars of Chester. *Journal of the Chester and North Wales Architectural, Archaeological and Historic Society,* new series, 31, p.17.

434 CALS ZM/B/5, f. 74; ZS/B/2, ff. 45v, 86v, 87v.

435 Heath, P. (ed.) (1973). *Bishop Geoffrey Blythe's Visitations,* Staffordshire Record Society, pp. 95-104.

436 LP, Henry VIII, xii (1), 130. It has been suggested that the rivalry between Dutton and Sir William Brereton over the fate of Norton Abbey may have contributed to the crown's decision not to grant the abbey to either man. See Guinn-Chipman, S. (2015). *Religious Space in Reformation England: Contesting the Past.* Routledge.

437 L.P, Henry VIII, xi. 1106.

438 For example, in both 1475 and 1477, Lawrence Dutton was bound over to keep the peace to Hugh Done (see Recognizance Rolls in *Memorials of the Duttons of Dutton*). So there was likely a dispute between Dutton's manor and that belonging to the Done family.

439 Thornton, T. (2000). *Cheshire and the Tudor State.* The Boydell Press, p.215.

440 Harl., 283, fo. 15. B. M

441 LP, Henry VIII, xii (1). March 1537.

442 E.g. Editor. (2 January 1965). Dutton Hall, many miles from home, has outlived its great family. *Rural Rides;* Bintoff, S. (1982). 'Done, Sir John.' In *History of Parliament: The Commons, 1509-1558.* The Boydell Press; Anon. (1870). *Handbook for Shropshire, Cheshire and Lancashire.* John Murray, p.126.

443 *Memorials of the Duttons of Dutton.* (1901), p.18.

444 Ormerod, G. (1819). *The History of the County Palatine and City of*

Chester: Vol. II. Printed for Lackington, Hughes, Harding, Maver and Jones, p.432. Delves was one of the MPs for Cheshire in 1554 and his mother, Margaret, was a Brereton of Brereton.

445 LP, Henry VIII, xii, ii, 18.

446 LP, Henry VIII, Vol. 12, 2, 58, ii. Letter from Sir William Brereton to Thomas Cromwell.

447 LP, Henry VIII, vii, 597. 29th August 1537, Sir William Brereton to Thomas Cromwell.

448 William Brereton to Cromwell, LP, Henry VIII, xii (2). 597.

449 For a history of Boughton, see Wright, C. (1998). *A History of the Civil Parish of Boughton, Cheshire.* Self Published.

450 Greene, P. (1989). *Norton Priory: The Archaeology of a Medieval Religious House.* Cambridge University Press, p.70. LP, Henry VIII, xii (2) 597.

451 LP, Henry VIII, vii, 597. 29th August 1537, Sir William Brereton to Thomas Cromwell.

452 LP, Henry VIII, xii (1), 1282.

453 LP, Henry VIII, xii (2). May 1537.

454 As late as 1544, Dutton was in a dispute with a probable relative of the abbot's. John Birkenhead was Dutton's tenant and Dutton sued him for retaining deeds relating to the rented land. C1/975/76-78. John Birkenhead was Chester's clerk, clerk of the court and, from 1537, 'lieutenant justice.' Thornton, T. (2000). *Cheshire and the Tudor State.* The Boydell Press, p.92.

455 LP Henry VIII, xiii (1) 1-20. Sir William Brereton to Thomas Cromwell in 1538: 'Sir Henry Delves to whom, as sheriff of Cheshire, you wrote for the admission of Thomas Hurleton as his deputy, refuses to obey, on account of the favour he bears to Sir Piers Dutton, and says he has made your Lordship answer therein.'

456 Bintoff, S. (ed.). (1982). DELVES, Sir Henry (1498-1560), of Doddington, Cheshire. Published in *The History of Parliament: the House of Commons 1509-1558.*

457 Thornton, T. (2000). *Cheshire and the Tudor State.* The Boydell Press, p.157.

458 LP, Henry VIII, xii, 2, 1123, 1186

459 LP, Henry VIII, viii, i.

460 LP Henry VIII, 13, 27th January. Richard Hough to Cromwell. Richard Hough (1505-1573) was an ally of Cromwell's in Cheshire and was its MP in 1558.

461 LP, Henry VIII, xiii, 1. Augm. Book, 209, 3b.

462 LP, Henry VIII, xi, ii.

463 LP, Henry VIII, xi, 1310. Misdated as 1536.

464 Dutton to Cromwell. LP, Henry VIII, xi, 1310.

465 Thornton, T. (2000). *Cheshire and the Tudor State.* The Boydell Press, pp.216-221.

466 LP, Henry VIII, xiii (1), 519.

467 LP, Henry VIII, xiii, 2, 49, 50 and 56.

468 4th Feb 1539. William Brereton to Cromwell, LP, Henry VIII, xiv.

469 John Dutton of Helsby was dead by 1544 and had an adult son, Lawrence Dutton (a Chester merchant), by 1512. (TNA WALE 29/284 and TNA WALE 29/242). Accordingly, he was probably born in 1470 at the latest. In that his son has the relatively unusual name 'Lawrence' and John Dutton of Helsby cannot be descended from Lawrence Dutton (c.1474-1528) or the Lawrence Dutton, Esq., referred to in Sir Piers Dutton's court case, he may be the grandson of Lawrence Dutton, brother of John Dutton (c.1400-1464)

470 Harl. MS, 283, fo. 14.

471 See Bintoff, S. T. (1982). *The History of Parliament: The House of Commons, 1509-1558.* Boydell & Brewer. 'FitzWilliam, Sir William I.'

472 Harl. MS, 2115, fo. 88.

473 TNA PROB 11/28/90.

474 LP, Henry VIII, xiv (1). July Grants

475 LP, Henry VIII, xiv (2). 9 Oct. R. O. St. P. II. 377

476 *History of Parliament Online,* http://www.historyofparliamentonline.org/volume/1558-1603/member/brereton-sir-william-i-1520-59

477 Goody, J. (1983). *The Development of Marriage and Family in Europe.* Cambridge University Press, p.266.

Chapter Eight: Dutton Hall and Her Minstrels

478 Coward, T. (1903). *Picturesque Cheshire.* Sherratt & Hughes, p.58.

479 See Buchan, G. H., (1984), *A Brief History of the Duttons of Dutton.* MS. http://www.dunton.org/duttonhall/buchan.html (Accessed 15 February 2015).

480 Anon. (1901). *Memorials to the Duttons of Dutton.* London.

481 Coward, T. (1903). *Picturesque Cheshire.* Sherratt & Hughes, p.58.

482 Coward, T. (1903). *Picturesque Cheshire.* Sherratt & Hughes, pp.54-55.

483 It was reported in the 1880s there were two ghosts at Dutton Hall; a Roman soldier who used to gallop across the paddock in front of the house and a wraith-like figure in the minstrel's gallery. See Spectre Stricken (1882). *Ghostly Visitors: A Series of Authentic Narratives.* Religio-Philosophical Publishing.

484 Johnson, R. (2011). *All Things Medieval: An Encyclopedia of the Medieval World, Vol. 1.* ABC-Clio, p.331.

485 Thornton, T. (2000). *Cheshire and the Tudor State*. The Boydell Press, p.49.

486 Bennett, J. (1921). The Grey Friars of Chester. *Journal of the Chester and North Wales Archaeological and Historic Society,* 24: 2, p.57. A Feodary was an official of the Court of Wards and Liveries. This court would search out minors who were feudal tenants of the king and administer their estates until they reached 21. Until that time, these peers and gentry would be royal wards who would be educated in the household of the Master of the Wards. See Schurink F. (2009). The Intimacy of Manuscript of the Pleasure of Print. In Pinchcombe, M. & Schrank, C. (Eds). *The Oxford Handbook of Tudor Literature, 1485-1603.* Oxford University Press.

487 Thornton, T. (2000). *Cheshire and the Tudor State*. The Boydell Press, pp.46-48.

488 Quoted from: Leycester, P. (1673). *Leycester's Historical Antiquities.* Printed by W. L. for Robert Clavell.

489 Thornton, T. (2000). *Cheshire and the Tudor State*. The Boydell Press, p.48.

490 *New Monthly Magazine* (1st November 1818). On the Peculiar Custom of Licensing the Minstrels of Cheshire.

491 *New Monthly Magazine* (1st November 1818). On the Peculiar Custom of Licensing the Minstrels of Cheshire.

492 Thornton, T. (2000). *Cheshire and the Tudor State*. The Boydell Press, p.48.

493 *Chester Chronicle.* (20th June 2008). City event makes return.

494 LP, Henry VIII, 14, 41.

495 Lancashire Fines, 1528. m. 1, 51 *(Duttoniana).*

496 Aldersley v Dutton and others. S.C.P, Henry VIII, Bundle 19, 166.

497 *Twenty Ninth Annual Report of the Deputy Keeper of Public Records* (1868), p.157.

498 Thomas Long to Cromwell. LP, Henry VIII, xv, 43.

499 Doran, S. & Durston, C. (2003). *Prices, Pastors and People: The Church and Religion in England, 1500-1700.* Psychology Press, p.89.

500 Coby, J. (2013). *Thomas Cromwell: Henry VIII's Henchman.* Stroud: Amberley Publishing.

501 See Barber, R. (2003). *Henry Plantagenet.* The Boydell Press.

502 Jones, T., R. Yeager, T. Dolan, A. Fletcher & J. Dor (2003). *Who Murdered Chaucer? A Medieval Mystery.* New York: St Martin's Press.

503 See Rex, R. (2008). *Henry VIII and the English Reformation.* Palgrave Macmillan.

504 Harl., 2115, fo. 111.

505 Hart, K. (2010). *The Mistresses of Henry VIII.* The History Press, p.155.

506 Hart, K. (2010). *The Mistresses of Henry VIII.* The History Press, p.155.

507 For a biography of Catherine Howard, see Loades, D. (2012). *Catherine*

Howard: The Adulterous Wife of Henry VIII. Amberley Publishing.

508 LP, Henry VIII, 1540, 21-31.

509 Ground, E. (2014). *The Bedside Book of Final Words.* Amberley Publishing ('Cromwell, Thomas').

510 LP, Henry VIII, 15, 21-31.

511 Gage, Sir John (1479-1556). *Dictionary of National Biography.* Potter, D. (2002). Sir John Gage, Tudor Courtier and Soldier (1479-1556). *The English Historical Review,* 117: 1129.

512 When he died in 1569, Richard Starkey was recorded as 'Bailiff of the Court of Halton.' *Calendarium inquisitionum post mortem.* London (1827). p.376.

513 Harl., 2115, f, 87b.

514 Wriothesley, C. (1875). *A Chronicle of England.* Camden Press, p.170.

515 Pollard, A. (2004). *Thomas Cranmer and the English Reformation: 1489-1556.* Wipf & Stock.

516 MacCulloch, D. (1996). *Thomas Cranmer: A Life.* Yale University Press. p.96.

517 Pollard, A. (2004). *Thomas Cranmer and the English Reformation: 1489-1556.* Wipf & Stock.

518 CALS. Dutton, John, 1542. EDA 2/1.

519 LP, Henry VIII, 17: 75.

520 Lysons, D. & Lysons, S. (1810). *Magna Britannia: Volume II.* T. Caddell and W. Davies, p.4.

Chapter Nine: The Deathbed Confession

521 Quoted in Macauley upon the first Protestant mission in England. (1883). *The Lamp,* p.94.

522 Earwaker, J. (1890). *The History of the Ancient Parish of Sandbach.* E. J. Morten, p.204. 11th December 1542. Inquisition post mortem into the death of John Wynington of Ermitage.

523 LP, Henry VIII, xvi, 78.

524 Norton, E. (2011). *Catherine Parr.* Amberley Publishing.

525 See Macdougall, N. (2006). *James IV.* John Donald Publishers.

526 See Chapman, H. (1974). *The Sisters of Henry VIII.* Chivers; Cameron, J. & McDougall, M. (1998). *James V: The Personal Rule, 1528-1542.* Tuckwell Press.

527 For a readable biography see Frasier, A. (2014). *Mary Queen of Scots.* Random House.

528 Dawson, J. (2007). *Scotland Reformed, 1488–1587.* Edinburgh University Press.

529 Herkless, J. (2012). *Cardinal Beaton: Priest and Politician.* HardPress.

530 Marshall, R. (2001). *Mary of Guise.* NMS.

531 See The life of the John Dudley, lord protector under Edward VI, is examined in Loades, D. (1996). *John Dudley, Duke of Northumberland.* Clarendon Press.

532 See MacCulloch, D. (2001). *The Boy King: Edward VI and the Protestant Reformation.* University of California Press.

533 Frasier, A. (2014). *Mary, Queen of Scots.* Random House.

534 LP, Henry VIII, xix, 41.

535 Calendar of Pleadings, Henry VIII. D. *Ducatus Lancastriae: Calendarium inquisitionum post mortem, &c. temporibus Regum Edw. 1, Edw. III, Ric.II, Hen. V, Hen. VI, Edw. IV. Hen. VII, Hen. VIII, Edw. VI, Regin. Mar., Phil. & Mar., Eliz., Jac I, Car. I.* (1823), p.170.

536 Shrewsbury MS., N., p.27. Heralds' College. LP, Henry VIII, xx, 1, 17th April.

537 Shrewsbury MS, AP, 99. Heralds College. LP, Henry VIII, xx, 1.

538 Thornton, T. (2000). *Cheshire and the Tudor State.* The Boydell Press, p.145. Around this time Dutton also appears to have been in dispute with Sir Peter Warburton over who had the power to appoint the priest and deacon of Great Budworth church, something which had previously been controlled by Norton Abbey. The Council of the Marches decided that the priest should be elected by the parishioners and then, in 1546, Henry VIII awarded this right to Christ Church College, Oxford. CALS, DLT /B15 fol113 (Tomus Tertius).

539 For a full biography of Paget, see Gammon, S. (1973*). Statesman and Schemer: William, First Lord Paget - Tudor Minister.* London: David & Charles.

540 LP, Henry VIII, 20: 160. 18 Aug. Hertford to Paget.

541 Inquisition post mortem volume 90, no. 11. Quoted verbatim in *Memorials of the Duttons of Dutton,* pp.214-216.

542 S. H. B. (1869). *The Monastic Houses of England; Their Accusers and Defenders.* Thomas Richardson & Son, p.2.

543 S. H. B. (1869). *The Monastic Houses of England; Their Accusers and Defenders.* Thomas Richardson & Son, p.87.

544 S. H. B. (1869). *The Monastic Houses of England; Their Accusers and Defenders.* Thomas Richardson & Son, pp.29-30.

545 From 'Griffin's Chronicle. Quoted in Burke, H. (1870). *The Men and Women of the English Reformation.* London, p.346.

546 Burke, H. (1880). *Historical Portraits of the Tudor Dynasty and the Reformation Period: Vol. II.* John Hodges, p.89.

547 Quoted in Macauley upon the first Protestant mission in England. (1883). *The Lamp,* p.94. The article cited the quote from Henry Brinklow's *Complaint*

of Roderick Mors, which was published in about 1545. However, the quote cannot be found there. The author probably meant to cite Thorndale's *Memorials of the English Abbeys,* which he cited earlier on the same page. This book, as with *Griffin's Chronicle*, appears to have been lost.

548 S.C.P., Henry VIII, Vol. xiii., fo. 173,

549 Daniell, C. (2005). *Death and Burial in Medieval England, 1066-1550.* Routledge, p.51.

550 MS 650.

551 S.C.P., Henry VIII, Vol. xiii., fo. 173,

552 PRO, C. 1/116/63.

553 Harris, B. (2002). *English Aristocratic Women, 1450 – 1550* .Oxford University Press, p.92.

554 *Twenty Ninth Annual Report of the Deputy Keeper of Public Records* (1868), p.64.

555 Feet of F. Herts East. IV, Edward VI quoted in Page, W. (1902). *The Victoria History of the County of Hertford, Vol. 4.* Constable & Co.

556 *Memorials of the Duttons of Dutton,* p.216.

Chapter Ten: Dutton's Papist Successors

557 Wark, K. R. (1971). *Elizabethan Recusancy in Cheshire.* The Chetham Society: Manchester University Press, p.50.

558 Furnivall, F. (1897). *Child Marriages, Divorces and Ratifications in the Diocese of Chester, AD 1561-66.* Early Text Society, cases 23 and 24.

559 Ebblewhite, E. (1897). Flintshire Genealogical Notes. *Archaeologia Cambrensis*, XIV: LV, p.183.

560 On Pius V, see Mendham, J. (1832). *The life and pontificate of Saint Pius V: Subjoined is a reimpression of a historic deduction of the episcopal oath of allegiance of the pope, in the church of Rome.* James Duncan.

561 Walsham, A. (1999). *Church Papists: Catholicism, Conformity and Confessional Polemic in Early Modern England.* The Boydell Press.

562 Wark, K. R. (1971). *Elizabethan Recusancy in Cheshire.* The Chetham Society: Manchester University Press, p.23.

563 Kilroy, G. (2005). *Edmund Campion: Memory and Transcription.* Ashgate.

564 See Wark, K. R. (1971). *Elizabethan Recusancy in Cheshire.* The Chetham Society: Manchester University Press, pp.23-24.

565 Wark, K. R. (1971). *Elizabethan Recusancy in Cheshire.* The Chetham Society: Manchester University Press, p.24.

566 Wark, K. R. (1971). *Elizabethan Recusancy in Cheshire.* The Chetham

Society: Manchester University Press, p.50.

567 Cockayne, G. (1897). *Some Account of the Lord Mayors and Sheriffs of the City of London During the First Quarter of the Seventeenth Century, 1601-1625.* London: Phillimore & Co., pp.68-69.

568 CALS. SEE WC, 1669. Inventory of Peter Dutton of Hatton.

569 Armistead, K. (1999), Massie of Coddington I. http://www.fitzwalter.com/afh/Massie/massiehist2.htm

570 Leycester, P. (1673). *Leycester's Historical Antiquities.* Printed by W. L. for Robert Clavell.

571 S.P, 15, 27, 94. Record of suspected recusants, probably from 1583, by puritan informer. Quoted in Wark, K. R. (1971). *Elizabethan Recusancy in Cheshire.* The Chetham Society: Manchester University Press, p.49.

572 Wark, K. R. (1971). *Elizabethan Recusancy in Cheshire.* The Chetham Society: Manchester University Press, p.179.

573 *Memorials to the Duttons of Dutton* (1901), Ch. 6.

574 Greene, P. (1989). *Norton Priory: The Archaeology of a Medieval Religious House.* Cambridge University Press, p.70.

575 Coltman, A. (1977). A Comparative Study of the Breretons of Wisconsin and the Breretons of South Africa. Their Pedigrees and Biographies, Photographs and Maps. Self Published.

576 Ives, E. (1976). Introduction to *The Letters and Accounts of William Brereton of Malpas.* Record Society of Lancashire and Cheshire, p.39.

577 They invariably focus on the Norton Abbey incident. E.g. Knowles, D. (1976). *The Bare Ruined Choirs: The Dissolution of the English Monasteries,* Cambridge University Press; Elton, G. (1985). *Policy and Police: The Enforcement of the Reformation in the Age of Thomas Cromwell,* Cambridge University Press or Bernard, G. (2007). *The King's Reformation: Henry VIII and the Remaking of the English Church.* Yale University Press.

578 Hughes, H. (1966). *Cheshire and Its Welsh Border.* Dobson, p.67.

579 Chesters, G. (1961). Power Politics in Cheshire. *Cheshire Round,* 1:1, p.26.

580 Thornton, T. (2000). *Cheshire and the Tudor State.* The Boydell Press.

581 Burke, H. (1870). *The Men and Women of the English Reformation.* London, p.241.

582 Mortimer, W. (1847). *A History of the Hundred of Wirral.* Whittaker and Co, p.177.

583 Sulley, P. (1889). *The Hundred of Wirral.* B. Haram & Co, p.100.

584 Coward, T. (1903). *Picturesque Cheshire.* Sherratt & Hughes, p.55.

585 Anon (20th July 1901). *The Duttons of Dutton. The Spectator.*

586 Froude, J. (1872). *History of England: From the Fall of Wolsey to the Defeat of the Spanish Armada.* Longmans, p.322-323.

587 Morris, R. (1895). *Chester.* SPCK, p.93.

588 Gasquet, F. (1902). *Henry VIII and the English Monasteries.* J. Hodges, p.96.

589 Possibly Piers Dutton or John Dutton of Dutton (d. 1608/9). British (English) School. National Trust Inventory Number 1316181. http://www.nationaltrustcollections.org.uk/object/1316181

590 Hanshall, J. (1817). *The History of the County Palatine of Chester.* J. Fletcher p.77.

591 John Dutton of Dutton (d. 1608/9). British (English) School. National Trust Inventory Number 562417. http://www.nationaltrustcollections.org.uk/object/562417

592 Buchan, G. H. (1984). *A Brief History of the Duttons of Dutton.* MS. http://www.dunton.org/duttonhall/buchan.html (Accessed 15 February 2015).

593 Harl., 2151.

594 But Dutton does have one, more subtle, physical legacy. In pre-industrial England, how many surviving children you had was predicted by your wealth. For this reason, there is a probability of 99% that anyone with predominantly English ancestors born in 1947 or later is a descendant of King Edward III, who had ten legitimate children, most of whom had many children themselves. Most of Dutton's 13 children had children, most of them large families. Ralph Dutton, for example, had 12 children, most of whom had many children. Accordingly, if most of your ancestors before the twentieth century were from Cheshire and its environs then there's a strong probability that Sir Piers Dutton lives on through you. See Millard, A. (2010). Probability of descending from Edward III. https://community.dur.ac.uk/a.r.millard/genealogy/EdwardIIIDescent.php.

Appendix One: The Letters of Sir Piers Dutton

595 As already noted, 'Dan' was a form of address for clerics and seemingly those who were not non-graduate priests as these were given the honorific 'Sir.'

596 'Meet' means 'appropriate.'

597 'Wherefore' means 'For what reason.'

598 Dutton never puts the year on his letters.

599 'By yours own assured' was by far the more common way of signing off formal letters at the time.

600 'Master' was the form of address for a gentleman or an esquire. It did not imply, as is the case now, minority. It is interesting that Dutton makes a point of addressing Cromwell with greater formality in this letter than in the previous one. Presumably, Cromwell is 'right honourable' because he is a now a baron or soon to be made one. It has been found that in correspondence from

this period, a nobleman is addressed 'my lord' or 'right honourable' whereas 'master,' 'sir,' 'Mr.' or 'right worshipful' imply gentry. See Nevalainen, T. & Raumolin-Brunberg, H. (1995). Constraints on Politeness: The Pragmatics of Address Formulae in Early English Correspondence. In Jucker, A. (Ed). *Historical Pragmatics: Pragmatic Developments in the History of English.* John Benjamins Publishing, p.586. We can also see that Dutton terms him 'good;' he is being extra-polite, according to Nevalainen and Raumolin-Brunberg, by using this word.

601 This is used to mean a person from outside the county.

602 In a number of sources, the word 'country' appears to be used to mean 'Cheshire.'

603 Multiple, many.

604 Clearly, this is extreme politeness.

605 Dutton writes 'sparpole.' 'Sparple' means 'disperse.'

606 It can be seen that Dutton uses 'By your own assured' with Cromwell and Audley, as this is relatively formal correspondence. Derby has sent Dutton an informal letter in his capacity as a friend and is clearly very familiar in his language. He also signs off 'E. Derby,' i.e. Edward Derby.

607 This word mean 'fines.'

Bibliography

Unpublished Primary Sources

Bodl. – Bodleian Library, Oxford.
C. – Court of Chancery. The National Archive, London.
CALS – Cheshire Archives and Local Studies, Chester Record Office.
CHES – Cheshire. The National Archive, London
DL – Duchy of Lancaster. The National Archive, London.
E – Records of the Exchequer and related bodies such as the Office of First Fruits and Tenths and the Court of Augmentations. The National Archive, London.
Harl. – Harleian Manuscripts. British Library, London.
MS 650 – Warrington Library and Archive.
PROB – Probate, National Archive, London.
RYCH – Ryland Charters, Manchester University Library.
SC – Special Collections. The National Archive, London.
STAC – Court of Star Chamber. The National Archive, London.
TNA – The National Archive, London
WALE – Records relating to Wales. The National Archive, London.

Published Primary Sources

Annual Report of the Deputy Keeper of Public Records. (1876). London: HMSO.

Anon. (1901). *Memorials of the Duttons of Dutton With Notes Respecting the Sherborne Branch of the Family.* London: Henry Sotheran & Co (Contains 'Duttoniana' and letters to, by, and about Sir Piers Dutton).

Armytage, G. & Rylands, J. (Eds.) (1909). *Pedigrees Made at the Visitation of Cheshire,* 1613. Manchester: Record Society for the Publication of Original Documents Relating to Lancashire and Cheshire.

Baildon, W. (1896). *Records of the Honourable Society of Lincoln's Inn:*

Admissions, 1420-1799. London.

Burn, R. (1830). *The Justice of the Peace and Parish Officer.* London: S. Sweet.

Calendar of Pleadings, Henry VIII. D. *Ducatus Lancastriae: Calendarium inquisitionum post mortem, &c. temporibus Regum Edw. 1, Edw. III, Ric.II, Hen. V, Hen. VI, Edw. IV. Hen. VII, Hen. VIII, Edw. VI, Regin. Mar., Phil. & Mar., Eliz., Jac I, Car. I.* (1823).

Calendarium inquisitionum post mortem. (1827). London.

Chaucer, G. (1992). *Canterbury Tales.* London.

Coke, E. (1606). *Institutes of the Laws of England.* London.

Cooke, W. (1878). *Students admitted to the Inner Temple 1547-1660.* London.

Dictionary of National Biography. (Eds). Stephen, L. & Lee, S. Oxford. 1917-.

Ebblewhite, E. (1897). Flintshire Genealogical Notes. *Archaeologia Cambrensis,* XIV: LV.

Edmund, J. (1846). *Miscellaneous Writings and Letters of Thomas Cranmer.* Cambridge: The University Press.

Emden, A. (1974). *A Biographical Register of the University of Oxford 1501 to 1540.* Oxford: Clarendon Press.

Emden, A. (1957). *A Biographical Register of the University of Oxford to AD 1500.* Oxford: Clarendon Press.

Foster, J. (1891). *Alumni Oxonienses 1500-1714.* Oxford: Oxford University Press.

Foster, J. (1889). *The Register of Admissions to Grays Inn, 1521-1889.* London.

Foxe's Book of Martyrs. (1978). Ed. Forbush, W. Grand Rapids, MI: Zondervan.

Furnivall, F. (1897). *Child Marriages, Divorces and Ratifications in the Diocese of Chester, AD 1561-66.* London: Early Text Society.

House of Commons. (1870). *Reports from Commissioners.* London.

Ives, E. (Ed). (1976). *The Letters and Accounts of William Brereton of Malpas.* Manchester: Record Society of Lancashire and Cheshire.

Leigh, E. (1867). *Ballads and Legends of Cheshire.* London: Longmans and Co.

Letters and Papers of Henry VIII. British History Online. http://www.british-history.ac.uk/search/series/letterspapers- hen8

Leycester, P. (1673). *Leycester's Historical Antiquities.* Printed by W. L. for Robert Clavell.

Pleas of Evidence, Ledger of Vale Royal Abbey. Folio 45 *(British History*

Online).

Records of London's Livery Companies Online. www.londonroll.org

Rylands, J. (Ed.). (1892). *The Visitation of Cheshire in the Year 1580*. London: Harleian Society.

Stewart-Brown, R. (Ed.). (1916). *Lancashire and Cheshire Cases in the Court of Star Chamber, Volumes I and II*. The Record Society.

Sturgess, H. (1949). *Records of the Honorable Society of Middle Temple: Admissions 15th c. to 1944*. London.

The Domesday of Inclosures, 1517-1518. (1971). Kennikat Press.

The Ten Articles, 1536. http://www.luminarium.org/encyclopedia/ tenarticles. htm.

Twenty Ninth Annual Report of the Deputy Keeper of Public Records (1868). London.

Venn, J. (1922). *Alumni Canterbrigienses: From Earliest Times to 1751*. Cambridge: Cambridge University Press.

Wriothesley, C. (1875). *A Chronicle of England*. London: Camden Press.

Published Secondary Sources

Ackerman, J. (1843). On the Forgeries of Public Money. *Proceedings of the Numismatic Society, vol. 6,* pp. 57-82.

Ahnert, R. (2013). *The Rise of Prison Literature in the Sixteenth Century*. Cambridge: Cambridge University Press.

Alex. (June 1791). Account of Halton Castle in Cheshire. *The Lady's Magazine*.

Alsop, J. & Loades, D. (1987). William Paulet, First Marquis of Winchester: A Question of Age. *The Sixteenth Century Journal* 18: 333–342.

Amin, N. (2015). Ednyfed Fychan, father of the Tudor Dynasty. *History Magazine,* http://www.historicuk.com/HistoryUK/HistoryofWales/Ed nyfed-Fychan-father-of-the-Tudor-Dynasty/

Anon. (1901). *Memorials to the Duttons of Dutton With Notes Respecting the Sherborne Branch of the Family*. London: Henry Sotheran & Co.

Anon (20th July 1901). Review: *The Duttons of Dutton*. The Spectator.

Anon. (1883). Macaulcy Upon the first Protestant mission in England. *The Lamp*.

Anon. (1870). *Handbook for Shropshire, Cheshire and Lancashire*. London: John Murray.

Anon. (1848). Who is a Gentleman and Who is an Esquire? *The Patrician*.

Armistead, K. (1999). Massie of Coddington I. http://www.fitzwalter.com/

afh/Massie/massiehist2.htm Arthurson, I. (2009). *The Perkin Warbeck Conspiracy,* 1491- 1499. Stroud: The History Press.

Barber, R. (2003). *Henry Plantagenet.* Woodbridge: The Boydell Press.

Bean, J. (1989). *From Lord to Patron: Lordship in Late Medieval England.* Manchester: Manchester University Press.

Beck, J. (1969). *Tudor Cheshire.* Chester: Cheshire Community Council.

Bellamy, J. (1979). *The Tudor Law of Treason.* London: Routledge.

Bence-Jones, M. & Montgomery-Massingbird, H. (1979). *The British Aristocracy.* London: Constable Books.

Bennett, J. (1935). The White Friars of Chester. *Journal of the Chester and North Wales Architectural, Archaeological and Historic Society,* new series, 31.

Bennett, J. (1921). The Grey Friars of Chester. *Journal of the Chester and North Wales Archaeological and Historic Society*, 24: 2.

Berglar, P. (2009). *Thomas More: A Lonely Voice Against the Power of the State.* New Rochelle, NY: Scepter Publishers.

Bernard, G. (2011). The Dissolution of the Monasteries. *History*, 96: 3.

Bernard, G. (2007). *The King's Reformation: Henry VIII and the Remaking of the English Church.* New Haven, CT: Yale University Press.

Bernard, G. (2000). *Power Politics in Tudor England: Essays by G. W. Bernard.* Aldershot: Ashgate.

BHO (British History Online). A. P. Baggs, A. J. Kettle, S. J. Lander, A. T. Thacker & D. Wardle. (1980). 'Houses of Benedictine monks: The abbey of Chester' in C. R. Elrington & B. E. Harris (Eds.). *A History of the County of Chester: Volume 3.* London, pp.132-146. http://www.british-history.ac.uk/vch/ches/vol3/pp132-146 [accessed 4 February 2015].

BHO. J. S. Barrow, J. D. Herson, A. H. Lawes, P. J. Riden and M.   V . J. Seaborne (2005). 'Mayors and sheriffs of Chester.' In A *History of the County of Chester: Volume 5* Part 2: The City of Chester: Culture, Buildings, Institutions. (Ed). A. T. Thacker and C. P. Lewis, pp. 305-321   http://www.british-history.ac.uk/vch/ches/vol5/pt2/pp305- 321 (accessed 21 March 2015).

BHO. 'Later medieval Chester 1230-1550: City government and politics, 1350-1550.' In *A History of the County of Chester: Volume 5.* Part 1, the City of Chester: General History and Topography. (Ed). C. P. Lewis & A. T. Thacker (London, 2003), pp.58-64 http://www.britishhistory.ac.uk/vch/ches/vol5/pt1/pp58-64 [accessed 4 February 2015].

Bintoff, S. (1982). *History of Parliament: The House of Commons, 1509-1558.* Woodbridge: The Boydell Press.

Bordo, S. (2013). *The Creation of Anne Boleyn: A New Look at England's*

BIBLIOGRAPHY

Most Notorious Queen. Boston: Houghton, Mifflin & Harcourt.

Boyd D. (1998). *A Bibliographical Dictionary of Racehorse Trainers in Berkshire 1850–1939.* Reading.

Boyer, A. (2003). *Sir Edward Coke and the Elizabethan Age.* Stanford: Stanford University Press.

Bradshaw, B. (1979). *The Irish Constitutional Revolution of the Sixteenth Century.* Cambridge: Cambridge University Press.

Breverton, T. (2014). *Everything You Ever Wanted to Know About the Tudors But Were Afraid to Ask.* Stroud: Amberley Publishing.

Brigden, S. (1989). *London and the Reformation.* London: Clarendon Press.

British Museum. (1808). *Catalogue of the Harleian Manuscripts in the British Museum.* London.

Buchan, G. H. (1984). *A Brief History of the Duttons of Dutton.* MS. http://www.dunton.org/duttonhall/buchan.html (Accessed 15 February 2015).

Bucholz, R. & Key, N. (2013). *Early Modern England, 1485- 1714.* Hoboken, NJ: John Wiley & Sons.

Bucholz, R. & Ward, J. (2012). *London: A Social and Cultural History.* Cambridge: Cambridge University Press.

Burke, B. (1858). *A Genealogical and Heraldic Dictionary of the Landed Gentry of Great Britain and Ireland.* London: Harrison.

Burke, H. (1880). *Historical Portraits of the Tudor Dynasty and the Reformation Period: Vol. II.* London: John Hodges.

Burke, H. (1870). *The Men and Women of the English Reformation.* London: R. Washbourne.

Burne, A. (2005). *The Battle Fields of England.* Barnsley: Pen and Sword.

Burton, J. & Ströber, K. (2008). *Monasteries and Society in the British Isles in the Later Middle Ages.* Woodbridge: Boydell & Brewer.

Bush, M. (2009). *The Pilgrim's Complaint: A Study of Popular Thought in the Early Tudor North.* Farnham: Ashgate.

Bush, M. (1996). *The Pilgrimage of Grace: A Study of the Rebel Armies of October 1536.* Manchester: Manchester University Press.

Bush, M. (1988). *Rich Noble, Poor Noble.* Manchester: Manchester University Press.

Bush, M. (1984). *The English Aristocracy: A Comparative Synthesis.* Manchester: Manchester University Press.

Cameron, E. (2012). *The European Reformation.* Oxford: Oxford University Press.

Cameron, J. & McDougall, M. (1998). *James V: The Personal Rule, 1528-1542.* Edinburgh: Tuckwell Press.

Carlton, K. & Thornton, T. (2011). *Illegitimacy and Authority in the North of*

England, 1450-1640. Northern History, XLVIII: I.

Cartwright, K. (2009). Dramatic theory and lucre's discretion: The plays of Henry Medwall. In M. Pinchcombe & C. Shrank (Eds). *The Oxford Handbook of Tudor Literature.* Oxford: Oxford University Press.

Chapman, H. (1974). *The Sisters of Henry VIII.* Bath: Chivers.

Cherry, C. & Ridgway, C. (2014). *George Boleyn: Tudor Poet, Courtier and Diplomat.* Made Global Publishing.

Chester Chronicle. (20th June 2008). City event makes return.

Chesters, G. (1966). Dissolution of the Cheshire monasteries. *Cheshire Round,* 1: 5.

Chesters, G. (1961). Power Politics in Cheshire, Part I. *Cheshire Round,* 1:1.

Chesters, G. (1961). Power Politics in Cheshire, Part II. *Cheshire Round,* 1:2.

Childs, J. (2014). *Henry VIII's Last Victim: The Life and Times of Henry Howard, Earl of Surrey.* London: The Bodley Head.

Cistercian Monk. (1852). *A Concise History of the Cistercian Order.* London: T. Richardson & Son.

Clark, G. (2007). *A Farewell to Alms: A Brief Economic History of the World.* Princeton: Princeton University Press.

Clark, J. (2011). *The Benedictines in the Middle Ages.* Woodbridge: The Boydell Press.

Clark, L. (Ed.). (2005). *Of Mice and Men: Image, Belief and Regulation in Late Medieval England.* Woodbridge: The Boydell Press.

Clayton, D. (1990). *The Administration of the County Palatine of Chester, 1442-1485.* Manchester: Manchester University Press.

Coby, J. (2013). *Thomas Cromwell: Henry VIII's Henchman.* Stroud: Amberley Publishing.

Cockayne, G. (1897). *Some Account of the Lord Mayors and Sheriffs of the City of London During the First Quarter of the Seventeenth Century, 1601-1625.* London: Phillimore & Co.

Coltman, A. (1977). *A Comparative Study of the Breretons of Wisconsin and the Breretons of South Africa. Their Pedigrees and Biographies, Photographs and Maps.* Self Published.

Cooper, T. (1999). *The Last Generation of English Catholic Clergy: Parish Priests in the Diocese of Coventry and Lichfield in the Early Sixteenth Century.* Woodbridge: Boydell & Brewer.

Corfield, P. (1996). The Rivals: Landed and Other Gentlemen. In N. B. Harte and R. Quinault, (Eds). *Land and Society in Britain, 1700 – 1914.* Manchester: Manchester University Press.

Cornwall, J. (1988). *Wealth and Society in Early Sixteenth Century England.*

BIBLIOGRAPHY

Cambridge: Cambridge University Press.

Coss, P. (2006). An Age of Deference. In Horrox, R. & Ormrod, W. (Eds). *A Social History of England, 1200– 1500.* Cambridge: Cambridge University Press.

Coss, P. (2003). *The Origins of the English Gentry.* Cambridge: Cambridge University Press.

Coss, P. & Keen, M. (2002). *Heraldry, Pageantry and Social Display in Medieval England.* Woodbridge: The Boydell Press.

Coward, B. (1983). *The Stanleys, Lords Stanley, and Earls of Derby, 1385-1672: The Origins, Wealth, and Power of a Landowning Family.* Manchester: Manchester University Press.

Coward, T. (1903). *Picturesque Cheshire.* London: Sherratt & Hughes.

Crawley News (12 August 2010). Former school still on sale 12 months on. http://www.crawleynews.co.uk/school-sale-12-months/story-12601262-detail/story.html

Cressy, D. (1978). Social status and literacy in North East England, 1560-1630. *Local Population Studies,* 21: 19-23.

Daniell, C. (2005). *Death and Burial in Medieval England, 1066-1550.* London: Routledge.

Daniell, D. (1994). *William Tyndale: A Biography.* New Haven: Yale University Press.

Davies, C. (1987). Popular Religion and the Pilgrimage of Grace. In Fletcher, A. & Stevenson, J. (Eds). *Order and Disorder in Early Modern England.* Cambridge: Cambridge University Press.

Dawson, J. (2007). *Scotland Reformed, 1488–1587.* Edinburgh: Edinburgh University Press.

Deanesly, M. (2002). *The Lollard Bible.* Eugene, OR: Wipf & Stock.

Dodds, B. (2008). Patterns of Decline: Arable Production in England, France and Castile, 1370–1450. In B. Dodds & R. Britnell. (Eds). *Agriculture and Rural Society After the Black Death: Common Themes and Regional Variations.* Hatfield: University of Hertfordshire Press.

Dodds, M. (1915). *The Pilgrimage of Grace, 1536-1537 and the Exeter Conspiracy, 1538.* Cambridge: Cambridge University Press.

Dolan, L. (2015). *Child marriage in sixteenth-century northern England: the emotional undertones in the legal narratives.* Limina, 20: 3.

Doran, S. & Durston, C. (2003). *Princes, Pastors and People: The Church and Religion in England, 1500-1700.* London: Psychology Press.

Duffy, E. (1992). *The Stripping of the Altars: Traditional Religion in England, 1400-1580.* New Haven: Yale University Press.

Dutton, E. (June 2015). Tracing Medieval Ancestors. *Family Tree.*

Dutton, E. (May 2015). Turf Wars: Power Struggles in the Post-Feudal Era. In *Family Tree.*

Dutton, E. (2012). *The Duttons of Stanthorne Hall.* Macclesfield: Family History Society of Cheshire.

Dutton, E. (2010). Here the status symbols clash: Social status and status expression in Finnish homes. *Suomen Antropologi*, 35: 1.

Dwarris, Sir F. (1848). Observations upon the history of one of the old Cheshire Families. *Archaeologia*, 33: 55-83.

Earwaker, J. (1890). *The History of the Ancient Parish of Sandbach.* Privately Published.

Editor. (2 January 1965). Dutton Hall, many miles from home, has outlived its great family. *Rural Rides.*

Editor. (19 December 1964). THE DUTTONS OF DUTTON – and the ancestral home that moved south. *Rural Rides,* 11.

Ellis, S. (2014). Tudor State Formation and the Shaping of the British Isles. In Ellis, S. & Barber, S (Eds). *Conquest and Union: Fashioning a British State, 1485-1725.* London: Routledge.

Elton, G. (1985). *Policy and Police: The Enforcement of the Reformation in the Age of Thomas Cromwell.* Cambridge: Cambridge University Press.

Elton, G. (1982). *The Tudor Constitution.* Cambridge: Cambridge University Press.

English Church History. (Oct. 1851). *The Churchman's Penny Magazine.*

Erler, M. (2013). *Reading and Writing During the Dissolution: Monks, Friars and Nuns, 1530-1558.* Cambridge: Cambridge University Press.

Feldman, S. (2011). *The Apocryphal William Shakespeare.* Indianapolis: Dog Ear Publishing.

Fleming, P. (2001). *Family and Household in Medieval England.* London: Palgrave MacMillan.

Fletcher, D. (2009). *Cardinal Wolsey: A Life in Renaissance Europe.* London: Bloomsbury.

Frasier, A. (2014). *Mary, Queen of Scots.* London: Random House.

French, H. & Hoyle, R. (2007). *The Character of English Rural Society: Earls Colne, 1550-1750.* Manchester: Manchester University Press.

Fritze, R. & Robison, W. (2002). Marriage, Aristocratic and Gentry. In *Historical Dictionary of Late Medieval England.* Bolder, CO: Greenwood Publishing.

Froude, J. (2009). *Mary Tudor.* London: Continuum.

Froude, J. (1872). *History of England: From the Fall of Wolsey to the Defeat of the Spanish Armada.* London: Longmans.

Gammon, S. (1973). *Statesman and Schemer: William, First Lord Paget*

BIBLIOGRAPHY

– *Tudor Minister.* London: David & Charles.

Gasquet, F. (1902). *Henry VIII and the English Monasteries.* London: J. Hodges.

Gibbons, G. (2001). *The Political Career of Thomas Wriothesley, First Earl of Southampton 1505-1550, Henry VIII's Last Chancellor.* The Edwin Mellen Press.

Goody, J. (1983). *The Development of Marriage and Family in Europe.* Cambridge: Cambridge University Press.

Gorski, R. (2003). *The Fourteenth Century Sheriff: English Local Administration in the Late Middle Ages.* Woodbridge: The Boydell Press.

Graff, E. (1999). *What is Marriage For?* Brighton: Beacon Press.

Grant, A. (2006). *Henry VII.* London: Routledge.

Grassby, R. (1995) *The Business Community of Seventeenth Century England.* Cambridge: Cambridge University Press.

Grazebrook, G. (1889). Introduction. In Grazebrook, G. & Rylands, J. (Eds). *The Visitation of Shropshire Taken in the Year 1623, Part I.* London: Harleian Society.

Greene, P. (1989). *Norton Priory: The Archaeology of a Medieval Religious House.* Cambridge: Cambridge University Press.

Greenwood, A. (1988). *The Greenwood Tree in Three Continents, Or, A Fertile Family of Five Centuries, 1487- 1987.* Longey Investment Trusts.

Ground, E. (2014). *The Bedside Book of Final Words.* Stroud: Amberley Publishing.

Guinn-Chipman, S. (2015). *Religious Space in Reformation England: Contesting the Past.* London: Routledge.

Gunn, S. (1988). *Charles Brandon, Duke of Suffolk, ca. 1484- 1545.* London: Blackwell.

Haigh, C. (1993). *English Reformations: Religion, Politics and Society Under the Tudors.* Oxford: Clarendon Press.

Haigh, C. (1969). *The Last Days of the Lancashire Monasteries and the Pilgrimage of Grace.* The Chetham Society, Manchester University Press.

Hall, J. (1883). *A History of the Town and Parish of Nantwich, or Wich Malbank, in the County Palatine of Chester.* Nantwich: E. J. Morten.

Halliday, S. (2013). *Newgate: London's Prototype of Hell.* Stroud: The History Press.

Halowell Garrett, C. (1966). *The Marian Exiles.* Cambridge: Cambridge University Press.

Hanshall, J. (1817). *The History of the County Palatine of Chester.* London:

J. Fletcher.

Harper-Bill, C. (1991). *Religious Belief and Ecclesiastical Careers in Late Medieval England.* Woodbridge: Boydell & Brewer.

Harris, B. (2002). *English Aristocratic Women, 1450 – 1550.* Oxford: Oxford University Press.

Harris, N. (1825). *Catalogue of the Heralds' Visitations.* London: J. Taylor.

Harriss, G. (2009). *Shaping the Nation: England, 1300-1461.* Oxford: Oxford University Press

Hart, K. (2010). *The Mistresses of Henry VIII.* Stroud: The History Press.

Head, D. (1995). *The Ebbs and Flows of Fortune: The Life of Thomas Howard, 3rd Duke of Norfolk.* Atlanta, GA: University of Georgia Press.

Heath, P. (Ed.) (1973). *Bishop Geoffrey Blythe's Visitations.* Staffordshire Record Society.

Heal, F. & Holmes, C. (1994). *Gentry in England and Wales, 1500 – 1700,* London: MacMillan.

Heale, M. (2004). *The Dependent Priories of Medieval English Monasteries.* Woodbridge: Boydell & Brewer.

Heinze, R. (1976). *The Proclamations of the Tudor Kings.* Cambridge: Cambridge University Press.

Herkless, J. (2012). *Cardinal Beaton: Priest and Politician.* Edinburgh: HardPress.

Hicks, M. (2014). *The Wars of the Roses.* Oxford: Osprey Publishing.

Hicks, M. (2012). *The Fifteenth Century Inquisitions Post Mortem: A Companion.* Woodbridge: The Boydell Press.

Higgs, L. (1998). *Godliness and Governance in Tudor Colchester.* Ann Arbor: University of Michigan Press.

Hope, A. (2014). The Printed Book Trade in Response to Luther. In Gillespie, V. & Powell, S. (Eds). *A Companion to the Early Printed Book in Britain, 1476-1558.* Woodbridge: Boydell & Brewer.

Houston, R. A. (1985). *Scottish Literacy and the Scottish Identity: Illiteracy and Society in Scotland and Northern England, 1600 – 1800.* Cambridge: Cambridge University Press.

Hoyle, R. (2001). *The Pilgrimage of Grace and the Politics of the 1530s.* Oxford: Oxford University Press.

Hughes, H. (1966). *Cheshire and Its Welsh Border.* London: Dennis Dobson.

Hutchinson, R. (2012). *Thomas Cromwell: The Rise and Fall of Henry VIII's Most Notorious Minister.* London: Hachette.

Ives, E. (1992). *The Fall of Anne Boleyn Reconsidered.* The English Historical Review, 107 (424): 651–664

Ives, E. (1983). *The Common Lawyers of Pre-Reformation England: Thomas*

BIBLIOGRAPHY

Kebell, A Case Study. Cambridge: Cambridge University Press.

Ives, E. (1976). Introduction to *The Letters and Accounts of William Brereton of Malpas.* Record Society of Lancashire and Cheshire.

Jackson, E. (1923). *Office and Actions of the Lord Lieutenant in Tudor England.* Philadelphia.

Johnson, R. (2011). *All Things Medieval: An Encyclopedia of the Medieval World, Vol. 1.* New York: ABC-Clio.

Jones, D. (1957). *The Church in Chester, 1300-1540.* The Chetham Society: Manchester University Press.

Jones, T., R. Yeager, T. Dolan, A. Fletcher & J. Dor (2003). *Who Murdered Chaucer? A Medieval Mystery.* New York: St Martin's Press.

Jones, W. (1970). *The Tudor Commonwealth, 1529-1559: a study of the impact of the social and economic developments of mid-Tudor England upon contemporary concepts of the nature and duties of the commonwealth.* London: The Athlone Press.

Kauffman, P. (2013). *Leadership and Elizabethan Culture.* London: Palgrave MacMillan.

Kenyon, D. (1991). *The Origins of Lancashire.* Manchester: Manchester University Press.

Kermode, J. (2002). *Medieval Merchants: York, Beverley and Hull in the Late Middle Ages.* Cambridge: Cambridge University Press.

Kilroy, G. (2005). *Edmund Campion: Memory and Transcription.* Aldershot: Ashgate.

King, D. (1656). *The Vale Royal of England or the County Palatine of Chester Illustrated.* London: John Streater.

King, D. (1778). *The History of Cheshire.* Chester: John Poole.

Knowles, D. (1976). *The Bare Ruined Choirs: The Dissolution of the English Monasteries.* Cambridge: Cambridge University Press.

Kreider, A. (2012). *English Chantries: The Road to Dissolution.* Eugene, OR: Wipf & Stock Publishers.

Lander, J. (1981). *Government and Community: England, 1450-1509.* Cambridge, MA: Harvard University Press.

Lawrence, J. (1827). *On the Nobility of the British Gentry, or the Political Ranks and Dignities of the British Empire, Compared with those on the Continent.* London: T. Hookham, Simpson & Marshall.

Lawson, J. & Silver, H. (2013). *A Social History of England.* London: Routledge.

Lawson, P. H. (1968). The Duttons of Dutton, county of Chester. Chart. Chester: P. H. Lawson. Chester Records Office.

Leycester, P. (1673). *Leycester's Historical Antiquities.* Printed by W. L. for

Robert Clavell.

Liddy, C. (2008). *The Bishopric of Durham in the Late Middle Ages: Lordship, Community and the Cult of St. Cuthbert.* Woodbridge: Boydell & Brewer.

Lipscomb, S. (2012). *1536: The Year That Changed Henry VIII.* Lion Books.

Loades, D. (2015). *Jane Seymour: Henry VIII's Favourite Wife.* Stroud: Amberley Publishing.

Loades, D. (2012). *Catherine Howard: The Adulterous Wife of Henry VIII.* Stroud: Amberley Publishing.

Loades, D. (1996). *John Dudley, Duke of Northumberland.* Oxford: Clarendon Press.

Lockyer, R. (2005). *Tudor and Stuart Britain.* London: Pearson Education Ltd.

Logan, F. D. (1996). *Runaway Religious in Medieval England, c. 1540-1540.* Cambridge: Cambridge University Press.

Lofts, N. (2012). Anne Boleyn: *The Tragic Story of Henry VIII's Most Notorious Wife.* Stroud: Amberley Publishing.

Lysons, D. & Lysons, S. (1810). *Magna Britannia: Volume II.* London: T. Caddell and W. Davies.

MacCulloch, D. (2001). *The Boy King: Edward VI and the Protestant Reformation.* Los Angeles: University of California Press.

MacCulloch, D. (1998). *Thomas Cranmer: A Life.* New Haven: Yale University Press.

Macdougall, N. (2006). *James IV.* Edinburgh: John Donald Publishers.

Mann, S. (2009). *Supremacy and Survival: How Catholics Endured the English Reformation.* New Rochelle, NY: Scepter Publishers.

Mantel, H. (2009). *Wolf Hall.* London: HarperCollins UK.

Marshall, A. (2008). An Early Fourteenth Century Affinity. In N. Saul (Ed). *Fourteenth Century England*, V. Woodbridge: The Boydell Press.

Marshall, R. (2001). *Mary of Guise.* Totnes: NMSE.

Maynard, T. (2011). *The Crown and the Cross: The Biography of Thomas Cromwell.* New York: LLC.

McIntosh, M. (1988). Local responses to the poor in late Medieval and Tudor England. *Continuity and Change, 3:* 209-245.

McLellan, J. & Bostock, T. (2010). *Bostock: A History of a Village and its People.* Jane McLellan.

McSheffrey, S. & Tanner, R. (2003). *Lollards of Coventry, 1486-1522.* Cambridge: Cambridge University Press.

Mencken, H. (1948). *The American Language: An Enquiry into the*

BIBLIOGRAPHY

Development of the English of the United States. New York: Alfred A. Knopf.

Mendham, J. (1832). *The life and pontificate of Saint Pius V: Subjoined is a re-impression of a historic deduction of the episcopal oath of allegiance of the pope, in the church of Rome.* London: James Duncan.

Mercer, M. (2010). *The Medieval Gentry: Power, Leadership and Choice During the Wars of the Roses.* London: A. & C. Black.

Michon, C. (2008). Pomp and Circumstances: State Prelates Under Francis I and Henry VIII. In Richardson G. (Ed.) *The Contending Kingdoms: France and England, 1420- 1700.* Aldershot: Ashgate.

Millard, A. (2010). Probability of descending from Edward III. https://community.dur.ac.uk/a.r.millard/genealogy/EdwardI IIDescent.php. Durham University.

Moore, A. (1900). *A History of the Isle of Man.* London.

Moran, J. (2014). *The Growth of English Schooling, 1340- 1548: Learning, Literacy, and Laicization in Pre-Reformation York.* Princeton: Princeton University Press.

Morris, R. (1895). *Chester.* London: SPCK.

Morris, R. (1893). *Chester in the Plantagenet and Tudor Reigns.* Printed for the Author.

Mortimer, W. (1847). *A History of the Hundred of Wirral.* London: Whittaker and Co.

Munden, A. (1997). *The Coventry Martyrs.* Coventry: Coventry Archives Publication.

Musson, A. (2004). Legal Culture: Medieval Lawyers' Aspirations and Pretentions. In Ormrod, W. (Ed.). *Fourteenth Century England, Vol. III.* Woodbridge: The Boydell Press.

Neale, J. (2014). *Queen Elizabeth I.* Chicago: Chicago Review Press.

Nevalainen, T. & Raumolin-Brunberg, H. (1995). Constraints on Politeness: The Pragmatics of Address Formulae in Early English Correspondence. In Jucker, A. (Ed) *Historical Pragmatics: Pragmatic Developments in the History of English.* John Benjamins Publishing.

New Monthly Magazine (1st November 1818). On the Peculiar Custom of Licensing the Minstrels of Cheshire.

Norton, E. (2011). *Anne Boleyn: Henry VIII's Obsession.* Stroud: Amberley Publishing.

Norton, E. (2011). *Anne of Cleves: Henry VIII's Discarded Bride.* Stroud: Amberley Publishing.

Norton, E. (2011). *Catherine Parr.* Stroud: Amberley Publishing.

Oliva, M. (2014). The Nun's Priest. In Rigby, S. & Minnis, A. (Ed.). *Historians on Chaucer: The "General Prologue" to the Canterbury Tales.* Oxford: Oxford University Press.

Orme, N. (2005). Education and recreation. In Radulescu, R. & Truelove, T. (Eds). *Gentry Culture in Late Medieval England.* Manchester: Manchester University Press

Ormerod, G. (1819). *The History of the County Palatine and City of Chester: Vol. II,* London: Printed for Lackington, Hughes, Harding, Maver and Jones.

Oxley, J. (1965). *The Reformation in Essex to the Death of Mary.* Manchester: Manchester University Press.

Page, W. (1902). *The Victoria History of the County of Hertford, Vol. 4.* London: Constable & Co.

Peacham, H. (1634). *The Complete Gentleman.* London.

Pendrill, C. (2004). *The Wars of the Roses and Henry VII: Turbulence, Tyranny and Tradition in England 1459- c.1513.* London: Heinemann.

Penn, T. (2012). *The Winter King: The Dawn of Tudor England.* London: Penguin.

Philips, K. (2012). *Medieval Maidens: Young Women and Gender in England, c.1270-c.1540.* Manchester: Manchester University Press.

Plummer, A. (1972). *The London Weavers Company, 1600- 1970.* London: Routledge.

Pollard, A. J. (2004). *Imagining Robin Hood: The Late Medieval Stories in Historical Context.* London: Routledge.

Pollard, A. (2004). *Thomas Cranmer and the English Reformation: 1489-1556.* Eugene, OR: Wipf & Stock.

Poos, L. (2004). *A Rural Society After the Black Death: Essex, 1350-1525.* Cambridge: Cambridge University Press.

Porter, L. (2009). *The Myth of "Bloody Mary": A Biography of Queen Mary I of England.* London: MacMillan.

Potter, D. (2002). *Sir John Gage, Tudor Courtier and Soldier (1479-1556).* The English Historical Review, 117: 11-29.

Prescott, E. (1992). *The English Medieval Hospital, c. 1050- 1640.* London: Seaby.

Rayne-Davis, J. & Rayne-Davis W. (2014). *Robert Aske: The Man Who Could Have Toppled Henry VIII.* United PC Verlag.

Redmonds, D., King, T. & Hey, D. (2011). *Surnames, DNA and Family History.* Oxford: Oxford University Press.

Rex, R. (2008). *Henry VIII and the English Reformation.* London. Palgrave Macmillan.

Rex, R. (2003). *The Theology of John Fisher.* Cambridge: Cambridge

BIBLIOGRAPHY

University Press.

Rex, R. (1996). The crisis of obedience: God's word and Henry's Reformation. *The Historical Journal*, 39: 4.

Richmond, C. (1981). *John Hopton: A Fifteenth Century Suffolk Gentleman.* Cambridge: Cambridge University Press.

Ridley, J. (1996). *The Tudor Age.* Wooster, NY: Overlook Press.

Robinson, W. (1995). Henry VIII's Household in the fifteentwenties: the Welsh Connection. *Historical Research*, 68, 173-190.

Room, A. (1998). *Dunces, Gourmands and Petticoats: 1,300 Words Whose Meanings Have Changed Through the Ages.* New York: McGraw-Hill.

Round, J. (1909). *Feudal England: Historical Studies on the 11th and 12th Centuries.* London: Swan & Sonnenshein Ltd.

Roy, W. (2001). *Making Societies: The Historical Construction of Our World.* London: Sage.

S. H. B. (1869). T*he Monastic Houses of England: Their Accusers and Defenders.* London: Thomas Richardson & Son.

Sanok, C. (2007). *Her Life Historical: Exemplarity and Female Saints' Lives in Late Medieval England.* Philadelphia: University of Pennsylvania Press.

Scard, M. (2011). *Tudor Survivor: The Life and Times of Courtier William Paulet.* Stroud: The History Press.

Schmidt, A. (1961). *The Yeoman in Tudor and Stuart England.* Amherst College: The Folger Shakespeare Library.

Schurink F. (2009). The Intimacy of Manuscript of the Pleasure of Print. In Pinchcombe, M. & Schrank, C. (Eds). *The Oxford Handbook of Tudor Literature, 1485-1603.* Oxford: Oxford University Press.

Shagan, E. (2003). *Popular Politics and the English Reformation.* Cambridge: Cambridge University Press.

Shaw, T. (2005). Music. In Radulescu, R. & Truelove, T. (Eds). *Gentry Culture in Late Medieval England.* Manchester: Manchester University Press.

Smith, L. (1966). Henry VIII and the Protestant Triumph. *The American Historical Review,* 71: 4.

Smith, R. (2004). *The Middling Sort and the Politics of Social Reformation: Colchester, 1570-1640.* Bern: Peter Lang.

Specht, H. (1981). *Chaucer's Franklin in the Canterbury Tales: The Social and Literary Background of a Chaucerian Character.* Publications of the Department of English, University of Copenhagen.

Spectre Stricken (1882). *Ghostly Visitors: A Series of Authentic Narratives.* Religio-Philosophical Publishing.

Spring, E. (1997). *Law, Land and Family: Aristocratic Inheritance in England,*

1300-1800. Chapel Hill: University of North Carolina Press.

Surdhar, C. (2013). *Bloody British History:* York. Stroud: The History Press.

Staves, S. (2014). Daughters and younger sons. In Brewer, J. & Staves, S. (Eds). *Early Modern Conceptions of Property.* London: Routledge.

Stone, H. (2002). *St. Augustine's Bones: A Microhistory.* Boston: University of Massachusetts Press.

Stone, L. (1966). *Social Mobility in England, 1500-1700.* Past and Present, 33.

Storey, R. L. (1972). The magnates, knights and gentry. In S. B. Chrimes, C. D. Ross & R. A. Griffiths (eds). *Fifteenth Century England, 1399 – 1509.* Manchester: Manchester University Press.

Strype, J. (1820). *The Life of the Learned Sir Thomas Smith, Kt, DCL: Principal Secretary of State to King Edward the Sixth and Queen Elizabeth.* Clarendon Press.

Sulley, P. (1889). *The Hundred of Wirral.* B. Haram & Co.

Tanner, N. (2009). *The Ages of Faith: Popular Religion in Late Medieval England.* New York: I. B. Taurus.

The Inner Temple Library. Introduction, Part 1. (2015). http://www.innertemplelibrary.org.uk/temple-history/innertemple-history-introduction-part-1.htm

Thirsk, J. (1984). *The Rural Economy of England.* London: A. & C. Black.

Thompson, B. (2002). Monasteries, Society and Reform in Late Medieval England. In Clark, J. (Ed). *The Religious Order in Pre-Reformation England.* Woodbridge: Boydell & Brewer.

Thompson, M. (1995). *The Medieval Hall: The Basis of Secular Domestic Life, 600-1600 AD.* Leicester: Scolar Press.

Thornton, T. (2000). *Cheshire and Tudor State, 1480-1560.* Woodbridge: The Boydell Press.

Thornton, T. (1999). Opposition Drama and the Resolution of Disputes in Early Tudor England: Cardinal Wolsey and the Abbot of Chester. In *Bulletin of the John Rylands University Library of Manchester,* 81: 1.

Tittler, R. (2013). *Portraits, Painters and Publics in Provincial England, 1540-1640.* Oxford: Oxford University Press.

Tompkins, M. (2006). "Let's Kill All the Lawyers!" Did Fifteenth Century Peasants Employ Lawyers When They Conveyed Customary Land? In Clark, L. (Ed). *Identity and Insurgency in the Late Medieval Ages.* Woodbridge: The Boydell Press.

Tremlett, G. (2010). *Catherine of Aragon: Henry's Spanish Queen.* London: Faber & Faber.

Tyerman, C. (1996). *England and the Crusades, 1095-1588.* Chicago: University of Chicago Press.

BIBLIOGRAPHY

Urban, M. (2006). *Seventeenth Century Mothers' Advice Books.* London: Palgrave MacMillan

Valente, C. (2003). *The Theory and Practice of Revolt in Medieval England.* Aldershot: Ashgate.

Varley, B. (1946). *The History of Stockport Grammar School, Including the Life of Sir Edmond Shaa, Kt.* Manchester: Manchester University Press.

Wagner, J. & Schmid, S. (2011). *Encyclopaedia of Tudor England.* ABC-Clio.

Wallis, P. & Webb, C. (2011). The education and training of gentry sons in early modern England. *Social History,* 36: 1.

Walsham, A. (1999). *Church Papists: Catholicism, Conformity and Confessional Polemic in Early Modern England.* Woodbridge: The Boydell Press.

Wark, K. R. (1971). *Elizabethan Recusancy in Cheshire.* The Chetham Society: Manchester University Press.

Weir, A. (2011). *Henry VIII: King and Court.* London: Random House.

Weiss, F. (1992). *Ancestral Roots of Certain American Colonists who Came to America Before 1700: The Lineage of Alfred the Great, Charlemagne, Malcolm of Scotland, Robert the Strong, and Some of Their Descendants.* Baltimore: Genealogical Publishing Company.

Wilson, S. (2003). *The Means of Naming: A Social History.* London: Routledge

Wood, R. (1994). Poor Widows, c. 1393-1414. In Barron, C. & Sutton, A. (Eds). *Medieval London Widows, 1300-1500.* London: A. & C. Black.

Woolrych, W. (1853). *A Treatise of the Law of Waters.* London: J. & J. W. Johnson.

Wilson, J. (2008). *Life in Shakespeare's England.* Cosimo Inc.

Wooding, L. (2015). *Henry VIII.* London: Routledge.

Wright, C. (1998). *A History of the Civil Parish of Boughton, Cheshire.* Self Published.

Wright, S. M. (1983). *Derbyshire Gentry in the Fifteenth Century.* Derby: Derbyshire Record Society.

Yates, J. (1856). *The Rights and Jurisdiction of the County Palatine of Chester, the Earls Palatine, the Chamberlain, and Other Officers.* London: Charles Simms & Co.

Youngs, D. (2008). *Humphrey Newton (1466-1536): An Early Tudor Gentleman.* Woodbridge: The Boydell Press.

Unpublished Secondary Sources

Brock, R. (1963). *The Courtier in Early Tudor Society: Illustrated From Select Examples.* PhD Thesis: University of London.

Cox, P. (2013). *Reformation Responses in Tudor Cheshire, c.1500-1577.* PhD Thesis: University of Warwick.

Sartore, M. (2011). *Outlawry, Governance and Law in Medieval England.* PhD Thesis: University of Wisconsin.

Index

A

Abbot of St. Werburgh's 37, 38, 42
Act for the Advancement of the True
    Religion 101
Act of Uniformity 107
Act of Union 68
Adknave, John (alias Harrison) 42
Age of Deference 19, 22
Aldermen 43, 44, 45, 46
Aldersley, John 95
Allen, Hugh 125
Anne of Cleves 8, 97
ap Griffith Eyton, John 67
armigerous gentry 16, 17, 19, 20, 22
Ashmole, Elias (Windsor Herald)
    56
Aske, Robert 6, 7
Aston 24, 62, 63, 86
Aston, Richard 63
Aston, Thomas 62, 86
Audley, Sir Thomas 73, 74, 76, 98,
    116, 117
Auld Alliance 102

B

Banastre, Rauff 42
Barfote, Thomas 125
Beaton, Cardinal David 102
Beconsall, Adam 59, 80
Bible 4, 17, 57, 97, 99, 101
Bigod's rebellion 6
Billington, Agnes 46
Birkenhead, Thomas (Abbot of
    Norton) 69
Black Death 9, 19, 22, 24
Black Letter book 104

Bloxwich 52
Boleyn, Anne 5, 6, 7, 28, 67, 75, 99
Bolles, Mr. 76, 117
Bonvix, Laurence 53
Booth, John 55
border raids 93
Bostock, Anne 62, 63
Bostock, Ralph 62
Bostock, William 1, 52
Boughton 82
Brandon, Charles (Duke of Suf-
    folk) 8
Breddon, John 50
Brereton, Randle 1, 28, 38, 54, 70,
    72, 126
Brereton, Randolph 28, 29, 31, 37,
    38, 43, 46, 49, 50, 63, 64, 65,
    85, 111
Brereton, William 7, 13, 28, 31, 41,
    46, 49, 50, 53, 54, 62, 65, 66,
    67, 68, 69, 72, 73, 74, 75, 76,
    77, 78, 79, 81, 82, 83, 86, 87,
    101, 111, 112, 118, 119, 120,
    122, 123
Brereton family 12, 69, 79
Broke, Henry 70
Brook, Henry 71, 83
Browne, Simon 48
Bruen, Piers 72, 86

C

Calverley, Sir George 32, 108
Campion, Edmund 108
Canterbury Tales 16, 17
Carew, Sir Nicholas 97
Catherine of Aragon 3, 5, 6, 66,
    67, 99

Catholic 4, 6, 15, 40, 55, 58, 97, 98, 99, 100, 101, 102, 105, 107, 108, 109
Catholic Association 108
Chamberlain of Cheshire 1, 13, 14, 28, 37, 41, 45, 54, 65, 68, 69, 70, 72, 73, 75, 98
Charles V, Holy Roman Emperor 97
Chaucer 16, 19, 20
Cheshire Assizes 98
Cheshire Recognizance Rolls 28, 29
Chester 8, 11, 12, 13, 24, 26, 28, 31, 32, 35, 36, 37, 38, 39, 41, 42, 43, 44, 45, 46, 47, 48, 49, 50, 52, 54, 59, 64, 65, 68, 70, 71, 72, 73, 75, 76, 80, 82, 83, 84, 85, 86, 92, 93, 94, 95, 106, 111, 112, 113, 114, 115, 116, 117, 120, 124, 125
Chester Castle 12, 38, 39, 43, 49, 64, 65, 68, 76, 82, 83, 86
Chesters, Geoffrey 79, 111
Chief Justice of Cheshire 13, 20, 41, 45, 73, 86, 103
Cholmondeley, Hon. George 109
Cholmondeley, Richard 69, 84, 125
Church of England 107
City of Chester 32, 41, 45
clerics 22
coat armour 17, 18, 20
College of Arms 17, 20, 55, 56
Constantine, Philip 47, 71
Coombes, Mr. 76, 117
Corporation of Chester 36, 42, 43, 44, 46
Cotgrave, James 55
Cotton, Harry 50
Cotton, John 50

County Palatinate 11
Court of Chancery 106
Court of Star Chamber 1, 30, 38, 48, 49, 50, 52, 64, 105
Cranmer, Thomas 8, 22, 99
Croft, Sir Edward 86
Cromwell, Thomas 5, 6, 7, 8, 15, 58, 59, 65, 66, 67, 68, 70, 71, 73, 75, 76, 78, 79, 80, 81, 83, 84, 85, 86, 96, 97, 98, 104, 110, 111, 112, 114, 115, 118, 119, 121, 125
Culpepper. Thomas 99

D

Dauphin 102
Dawson, Hugh 125
Dawson, Thomas 125
Dayner, Richard 45
Deane, Thomas 46
Delves, Sir Henry 81, 83, 87, 106
Dereham, Francis 99
Dewar, John (2nd Baron Forteviot) 14
Digby, Reignold 53
Dissolution of the Monasteries 1, 3, 4, 6, 76, 79, 112
Domesday Book 24
Done, Richard 38, 39, 49
Done, Sir John 38, 72, 81, 83, 86
Done, William 38, 39, 49
Dudley, John (Viscount Lisle) 102
Dunham 12
Dutton, Alice 55
Dutton, Anne (daughter of Piers Dutton) 55
Dutton, Anne (daughter of Sir Thomas Dutton) 62
Dutton, Dorothy 109
Dutton, Edward 109

INDEX

Dutton, Eleanor (daughter of Sir Thomas Dutton) 62

Dutton, Elizabeth (daughter of Piers Dutton) 55

Dutton, Elizabeth (daughter of Sir Thomas Dutton) 62

Dutton, Elizabeth (illegitimate daughter of Piers Dutton) 55

Dutton, Elizabeth (née Grosvenor) 30, 55

Dutton, Hugh (c. 1370-1440) 25, 26, 30, 62, 64

Dutton, Hugh (c. 1508-1540, Piers Dutton's heir) 55, 95

Dutton, Hugh (of Moldsworth) 64

Dutton, Hugh (son of Piers' son Ralph) 34

Dutton, Isabel (daughter of Sir Thomas Dutton) 62

Dutton, John (1403-1445) 62

Dutton, John (1594-1609, son of Thomas Dutton) 110

Dutton, John (c. 1400-1464) 26, 30

Dutton, John (c. 1448-1473, 'John the Childless') 62, 64

Dutton, John (c. 1470-before 1544, of Helsby) 86

Dutton, John (c. 1500-1542, illegitimate son of Lawrence Dutton) 59, 100

Dutton, John (c. 1539-1609, grandson of Piers Dutton) 110, 112

Dutton, John (grandson of Piers Dutton) 57

Dutton, John (illegitimate son of Piers Dutton) 55

Dutton, Juliana (formerly Patmore) 55, 57, 72, 74, 83, 105

Dutton, Katherine (daughter of Piers Dutton) 55

Dutton, Lawrence (c.1474-1528, 17th Lord of Dutton) 25, 26, 59, 60, 61, 62, 64, 65, 94, 100

Dutton, Lawrence Esq (childless son of Richard Dutton) 64

Dutton, Margaret (daughter of Sir Thomas Dutton) 62

Dutton, Mary 55

Dutton, Maud 55

Dutton, Peter (Junior) 26, 28, 31, 32

Dutton, Peter (Senior) 26, 28, 31, 32, 34

Dutton, Ralph 30, 38, 39, 40, 49, 55, 95, 103, 105, 106, 107, 108, 109, 110

Dutton, Roger 32, 62

Dutton, Rowland 33, 35, 107, 109

Dutton, Sir John (priest) 22, 49

Dutton, Sir Lawrence (c. 1339-1392, 11th Lord of Dutton) 62

Dutton, Sir Thomas (1314-1381, 10th Lord of Dutton) 25, 62, 63

Dutton, Sir Thomas (c.1424-1459) 27, 61, 62, 64, 65, 67

Dutton Hall 1, 8, 14, 61, 63, 81, 88, 89, 90, 91, 92, 93, 94, 95, 99, 104, 105, 110, 113

Dutton Homestall 14

Dymmock, John 48

E

Earl of Chester 11, 12, 13, 24, 45, 93

Earl of Derby 34, 41, 78, 103, 120

Earl of Rutland 78

Earl of Shrewsbury 41, 78, 103

East Grinstead 14, 88

Eccleston 41
Edinburgh 102, 103
education of the sons of the gentry 33
Edward III 25, 27
Edward IV 27, 35, 41
Edward VI 15, 103
Elizabeth I 18, 40, 107, 108
enclosure 6, 51
esquire 16, 17, 18, 20, 23, 27, 54, 82
Esquire of the Body 53, 98
Essex 21, 50, 55, 58, 74, 106
Exchequer 13, 38, 45, 48, 86, 98

F

Fee of Halton 65, 100, 103
Felday, Piers 70, 71, 72, 73, 74, 78, 82, 84, 86
feudal system 6, 9, 10, 19, 28, 37, 65, 66, 103
Field of Cloth of Gold 53
Fisher, Bishop John 4
Fitz Nigel, William 24
Fitz Odard de Dutton, Hugh 24
Fitzroy, Henry (Duke of Richmond) 73
FitzWilliam, William (Earl of Southampton) 86
Fleet Prison 21, 49, 50
Fletcher, William 38, 49
Flintshire 13, 34, 67, 68, 93, 107
Flodden Field 101
Flookersbrook 94
Fouleshurst, Elizabeth 27
Fouleshurst, Sir Robert 27, 30, 31
Fouleshurst family 12
freeman (of the City of Chester) 36, 43, 44, 45, 46

G

Gage. Sir John 98
Gee, Henry 47
Gentleman of the Privy Chamber 53, 68
gentlemen 13, 18, 20, 21, 22, 25, 35, 46, 50, 94
gentry 2, 6, 8, 9, 10, 11, 15, 17, 18, 19, 20, 21, 22, 23, 24, 26, 28, 31, 33, 34, 35, 36, 41, 44, 45, 49, 50, 52, 55, 67, 69, 86, 102, 103
gentry studies 2, 8
Gilbert, George 108
Godstow nunnery 79, 104
Goldsmith, Ralph 70
Great Budworth 24, 57, 60, 113
Great Hall 33, 92
Griffin, Henry 104
Groom of the Privy Chamber 53
Grosvenor, Richard 55
Grosvenor, Robert 41
Grymbald, John Baptist 48
Gunnery, Mr. 112

H

Hale, Robert 70
Halton 12, 24, 28, 35, 65, 66, 68, 75, 77, 86, 96, 97, 99, 100, 103, 117, 122, 123
Halton Castle 35, 65, 66, 75, 77, 86, 99
Hamilton, James (Earl of Arran) 102
Harleian Collection 56, 57
Harware, John 70
Hatton Hall 32, 33, 82
Hawarden 52
Hayes, Sir Thomas 109

INDEX

Henry VI 12, 27
Henry VII 27, 28, 36, 40, 41, 43
Henry VIII 2, 3, 4, 5, 7, 8, 15, 19,
    21, 43, 48, 53, 54, 59, 67, 73,
    75, 77, 90, 97, 98, 99, 100,
    101, 114, 116, 118, 119, 121,
    123, 124, 125
Hertfordshire 58, 86, 106
Heseham, John 75, 116
High Sheriff (of Cheshire) 1, 7, 8,
    11, 13, 25, 34, 64, 68, 69, 75,
    79, 81, 100
Hiltley 63
Hitton, Thomas 57
Holcroft, John 87
Holcroft, Sir Thomas 104
Holfe, Thomas 71
Holford, George 103
Holme, Randle 113
Holt 52, 67, 68, 110
Hopton, John 9
Hough, Richard 84
Howard, Catherine 97, 98, 99, 100
Howard, Thomas (Duke of Norfolk)
    6, 8, 78, 86, 97, 98
Hugh Lupus 11, 12
Hurleton, John 82
Hurleton, Thomas 83
husbandmen 21
Hutchins, Thomas 49
Huxley 1, 52

I

Inner Temple 34, 35
Inns of Chancery 35
Inns of Court 33, 34, 35
inquisition post mortem 28, 30, 85,
    101, 104, 106

J

James IV 101
James V 102
Jannons, Robert 70
Jesuits 108

K

Keeper of Shotwick Park 68, 75
Kinderton 12
knight 16, 17, 19, 20, 22, 23, 54,
    82, 111, 117, 118, 119, 120,
    124, 125

L

Lady Rutland 97
Lancaster, William 45
Lascelles, John 99
Lee, Rowland 67, 84, 85
Lee, Sir Thomas 104
Leech, George 32
Leftwich, Richard 54
Legh, Eleanor 40
Legh, Robert de 40
Legh, Thomas (Lord of the Manor
    of Adlington) 40, 41
Leycester, Ralph 85
Leycester, Sir Peter 25, 28
Leycester, Thomas 31
Leyland, Sir William 65
Lieutenant Governor of the Isle of
    Man 32, 34
Little Hadham 106
Lollard 57, 58
London 6, 7, 9, 12, 22, 35, 36, 44,
    47, 48, 52, 53, 55, 56, 58, 67,
    70, 71, 72, 73, 75, 81, 84, 85,
    86, 109, 110, 112, 124
Long, Thomas 1, 96
Lord of Hatton and Dutton 26

Lord of the Manor of Dutton 11, 14, 24, 27, 30, 75
Louth Park Abbey 6

M

magnates 6, 8, 9, 11, 36, 41, 48, 68, 83, 112
Mainwaring, Ralph 48, 72, 81, 96
Mainwaring, Ralph, the younger 125
Mainwaring, Randle 84, 125
Malpas 12, 28, 29, 31, 50, 53, 62, 65, 73, 74, 75, 112
Manley, William 55
Mannox, Henry 99
Manor of Dutton 11, 14, 24, 27, 30, 61, 63, 64, 75, 95, 105, 106
Manor of Hatton 25, 30, 32, 38, 64, 109
Manor of Tattenhall 84
Manor of Weston 66
Mansell, Rees 73
Mara and Mondrom, forest of 81
Marches, The 13, 67, 68, 84, 85
Margaret Tudor 102
Mary, Queen of Scots 102
Mary of Guise 102
Massey, Robert 65
Massey, William 85
Massie, Hamlett 55
Massie family 12
Mayor of Chester 8, 45, 47, 52, 54, 82, 111
Mercers 36
merchants 16, 21, 43, 44, 45, 46
Middlewich 106
middling sort 43, 44, 108
minstrels 11, 12, 15, 33, 91, 92, 93, 94, 95
minstrels' gallery 91

Moldsworth 30, 64
Molineaux, Sir Thomas 62
Montalt 12
More, Sir Thomas 4, 8
Mores, William 125
Mullington, George 83
Mundy, Richard 57

N

Nantwich 12, 27
Nantwich Castle 27
Needham, Sir Robert 87
Neville, Ralph 53
Neville, Sir Edward 68, 97
Newborough 57
Newgate 71, 72
Newton, Humphrey 9, 11
non-armigerous gentry 16, 17, 20, 22
Northwich 24, 106
Norton Abbey 1, 7, 57, 59, 69, 72, 75, 76, 79, 80, 90, 111, 112
Norton Priory 24

O

Oath of Allegiance 108
Odard 14, 24
Open Field System 51
Ormerod, George 26
outlawry 30, 32, 38, 39, 81

P

Paget, William 103
Palatine 1, 12, 42, 66, 68, 93, 111, 112, 113
Parker, William 77, 117
Parr, Catherine 101
Patmore, Henry 47, 55, 56, 106
Patmore, Juliana (see also Juliana

Dutton) 55
Patmore, Thomas 58, 106
Paulet, Sir William 66
Penkethman, Richard 66
Percival, Thomas 98
Pilgrimage of Grace 3, 5, 6, 41, 80, 85, 111, 112
Pole, Sir Geoffrey 97
Pole, Sir William 63, 72
Pope, The 5, 17, 108
Porte, Sir John 65, 86
Pound, Thomas 108
Poyntz, William 55
Prince Richard of York 41
Princes in the Tower 41
Princess Mary 81, 98
Privy Council 67, 72, 108
pro-Catholic 4, 15, 58
pro-Protestant 4, 99
Protestant 4, 5, 8, 15, 57, 58, 65, 67, 76, 96, 98, 99, 102, 107
Protestantism 4, 8, 9, 15, 35, 57, 58, 74
Pyllyn, Thomas 92

R

Raborne, John 40, 46
Radcliffe, Sir Alex 87
Ranger of Delamere Forest 68, 75, 81
rank 15, 16, 17, 19, 20, 21, 22, 23, 36, 57
recusants 108, 109, 110
retainers 10, 11, 38, 67, 101
retinues 10, 11, 53
Reynolds, Catherine 109
Richard III 27, 41
Rider of the Forest of Delamere 65
Rotherham, Thomas 53
Rough Wooing 101, 102

roundel 91, 92
Ruggeley, Thomas 96
Ryder, William 30, 36, 64

S

Saunders, John 56
Savage, Katherine 40
Savage, Sir John 50, 52, 62, 63, 64, 66
Scotland 101, 102
See of Rome Act 4
Seymour, Edward (Earl of Hertford) 102, 103
Seymour, Jane 5, 102
Sheriff of Cheshire 1, 25, 27, 30, 48, 68, 69, 81, 83, 87, 100, 101, 108, 109, 110, 111, 120
Sheriff of Flintshire 68, 107
Sherman, John 125
Sherman, Ralph 55, 125
Sherman, Thomas 125
Shiley, Elizabeth 95
Shipbrook 12
Six Articles 98
Smith, Sir Thomas 18
Smyth, William 48
Soloway Moss 102
Southworth, Sir Christopher 62
Squire of the Body 52
St. Thomas Beckett 96
St. Werburgh's Fair 43
Stanley, Peter 85
Stanley, Sir William 31, 41, 96
Starkey, Richard 99
Stenmore, Sir Walter 70
Steward of Halton 35, 65, 66, 68, 75, 97
Steward of Halton Castle 35, 65, 66, 75
St John the Baptist Church 93

Stockport 12, 34
Stoke Brunswick School 14
Stuart, Matthew (Earl of Lennox)
    102
sturgeon 66, 103
Sulyard, Sir William 86
Swettenham, Lawrence 50

T

Talbot, Francis (Earl of Shrews-
    bury) 103
Tedder, John 96
Ten Articles 4, 99
Tilston, Richard 109
Towner, John 45
Townley, John 53
Townshend, Amy 103, 107
Townshend, Sir Robert 103
Trafford, Edmund 87
Treaty of Greenwich 102
Tudor England 9, 10, 11, 12, 16,
    21, 60, 89, 111
Tudor social system 16
Tyndale, William 4, 58

U

Under Sheriff of Cheshire 64

V

Vale Royal Abbey 69, 70, 80, 114,
    115
Venables, Gilbert 40
Venables family 12
Vernon, Jane 27
Vernon, Margaret 64
Vernon, Ralph 62
Vernon, Sir Richard 27
Vernon family 12, 64
Visitations 17, 18, 55, 56, 57

W

Warbeck, Perkin 41
Warburton, Sir John 48
Warburton, Sir Peter 112, 157
Warren family 12
Warrington Priory 25
Waverton 25, 26, 36, 37
Weston 24, 66
Whitley 24
William the Conqueror 11, 12, 24,
    40
Wilmslow, Randal 70, 114, 115
Wolf Hall 8
Wolsey, Cardinal Thomas 8, 48
Woolsey, Dr. 104
Worrall, Hugh 64
Wreygth, John 70, 71

Y

yeoman 16, 17, 21, 52, 55
York 6, 22, 27, 40, 41, 97, 102
Yorkshire 6, 7, 78, 80, 119, 120

SELECTED LOCAL HISTORY TITLES BY LÉONIE PRESS

A practice/audition CD by Andrew Nixon, giving the tunes on computer-generated "piano" is also available, price £3.50, to help those who cannot read music but want to learn the tunes

OWNERS, OCCUPIERS AND OTHERS
17th Century Northwich
TONY BOSTOCK

Northwich in the 17th century was a small market town of about six acres, concentrated on a plot of low-lying flat land at the confluence of the rivers Dane and Weaver, and surrounded by fields and meadows on the slopes of the neighbouring townships. It had been an important salt-making site since Roman times and could be described as an industrial town in a pre-industrial age. The entrepreneurs involved were subject to time-honoured complex rules that regulated when, where and how the salt could be made.

Leading local historian Tony Bostock, whose family moved to the Northwich, Witton and Leftwich area from Davenham more than 300 years ago, has used a wealth of contemporary documentary sources to build up a detailed picture of life in Northwich during the 17th century. It was a particularly interesting period of history – an era of social, economic, political and religious change that affected the lives of every individual in some way. Plague, fires, flooding and the Civil War all left their mark on the town and its inhabitants.

His painstakingly researched book looks at the residential, commercial and industrial sectors of the tiny borough, traces of which can still be discerned in its present-day layout. It examines how the town was governed and how the famous salt industry began to decline towards the end of the 17th century.

The author follows the fortunes of individual families who owned or occupied wich-houses and, using wills and inventories, describes how the people of Northwich lived and worked. Fascinating appendices, tables and family trees contain information that will be invaluable to local and family history enthusiasts.

ISBN 978-1-901253-37-5, A5, 250pp,

CHESHIRE FOLK SONGS & ASSOCIATED TRADITIONS
ROY CLINGING

Roy Clinging has been involved with folk music since the early 1970s and is a respected full time singer and concertina player with experience of clubs and festivals across the UK and in the USA. He also performs in residential homes, hospitals, day centres and schools.His book contains 60 songs from his native Cheshire, ranging from those current in the 1700s to more recent work. It is aimed at folk musicians who want to expand their repertoire and anyone else interested in this rich aspect of our cultural heritage.

The tradition of folk singing goes back in Roy's family to at least his great-grandmother. As he grew up his interest in folk music deepened and was influenced by the 'folk revival'. He became actively involved through folk clubs, festivals, country dances, morris dancing and soul-caking. In a personal defining moment, he realised that if 'souling' songs still existed there might be others.

Roy then set about collecting songs from within the old county boundaries of Cheshire – detective work that he found challenging and enjoyable. His painstaking search has led him to local and national archives, and to the collections of early folk music scholars. He has received songs from interested individuals and recorded them from local singers.

Most of the titles in this A4 book are published alongside their original tune in a singable form, others are in text form only and some have had a tune added later. A few are relatively recent compositions. Explanatory notes, with details of local traditions, accompany each one. Songs include "Cheshire Lads are Chief of Men", "The Brisk Young Widow", "The Devil and the Monk" and "Whistlebitch Well".

ISBN 978-1-901253-49-8, A4 paperback format, 144pp, 6pp illustrations, £11.99

For more info: tel 01606 75660; visit www.leoniepress.com: or email jack@leoniepress.com

SELECTED LOCAL HISTORY TITLES BY LÉONIE PRESS

KNUTSFORD PRISON
The Inside Story
DAVID WOODLEY

Prison overcrowding is nothing new – in 1811 there were so many prisoners in Cheshire that the authorities decided to build a new Sessions House, Grand Jury Room and House of Correction "in a convenient situation near the town of Nether Knutsford". Work began in 1817 and when the building was eventually finished The Countryman's Rambler commented: "...one hardly believes that such a fine place was built only for thieves."

Whether the inmates would have agreed is another matter, although the food was thought by many to be superior to that provided in the workhouse. The regime included the physical exertions of the treadmill, the drudgery of picking oakum, the pointlessness of turning a crank which "ground nothing but air", the back-breaking ordeal of moving heavy cannonballs from one pile to another and occasional floggings.

Over the years, as well as local criminals, debtors and offenders against the Game and Bastardy Laws, Knutsford Prison housed disaffected Chartists and those awaiting transportation. From 1886, until it was taken over by the Home Office as an Army detention barrack in 1915, nine executions took place on its scaffold.

Author David Woodley worked for 20 years as a prison chaplain, serving in Wormwood Scrubs, Cardiff, Risley and Styal. He has immersed himself in the prison archives and describes the work of its governors, chaplains, surgeons and visiting magistrates. He looks at the role of the warders and at the lives of the male, female and juvenile prisoners who made up the jail community.

This book provides a fascinating glimpse into an often overlooked aspect of Knutsford's social history.

ISBN 978-1-901253-27-6 100pp, A5, b+w illustrations, Price £6.99

ELIZABETH ANNE GALTON (1808-1906)
A well-connected gentlewoman
Editor: ANDREW MOILLIET

Elizabeth Anne Galton's mind was as sharp and enquiring in her nineties, when Edward VII was King, as it had been in her youth during the Regency period. Her long life fitted almost exactly into the 19th century and, in the fascinating reminiscences from which this book is taken, she chronicled its changes with an observant eye.

A list of her friends, relations and acquaintances reads like a scientific, financial and commercial 'Who's Who'. She was the daughter of an influential Birmingham banker who managed the city's affairs as High Bailiff – today's equivalent of Mayor. Through him she was related to many families of importance including the Barclays, Frys, Gurneys and Lloyds, in addition to those like the Wedgwoods whose forebears had helped to make the Industrial Revolution.

Elizabeth Anne's brother, Sir Francis Galton FRS, is regarded as the founder of the science of eugenics. Among his other accomplishments he pioneered the use of fingerprints as a method of identification. She and the great Charles Darwin shared a common grandfather, Erasmus Darwin FRS, who was the moving spirit in the famous group of scientists, the Lunar Society of Birmingham – nicknamed the "Lunaticks". These illustrious men and their friends appear in her memoirs in a very human light.

In 1838, Elizabeth Anne attended Queen Victoria's Coronation at Westminster Abbey, which she described at the time as the happiest day of her life. In 1897, as a sprightly 89-year-old, she watched Victoria's ("very long") Diamond Jubilee celebration procession as it passed through London.

ISBN 978-1-901253-36-8 256pp, A5, 33 b+w illustrations   Price £10.99

For more info: tel 01606 75660; visit www.leoniepress.com: or email jack@leoniepress.com

SELECTED LOCAL HISTORY TITLES BY LÉONIE PRESS

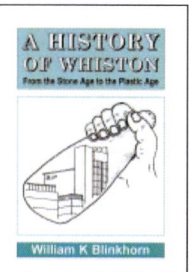

KINGSTHORPE:
A royal manor explored
TONY HORNER

This meticulously-researched work must surely be the definitive history of Kingsthorpe, Northampton – a village with ancient roots that is now a suburb but was once a proud and independent royal manor. Tony Horner's book looks at the Manor of Kingsthorpe, its situation and topography, the village land and its ownership, methods of farming, the problems of the poor and the various systems of local government employed over the years.

The author describes Kingsthorpe's population and economic history, and examines the role played by its watermills and windmills. He traces the building of schools in the village and looks in detail at the church, its Rectors and the now-demolished Rectory.

Other subjects covered include the histories and pedigrees of the main families associated with Kingsthorpe, the Hospital of St David or the Holy Trinity, and the establishment of Nonconformist churches. Village leisure pursuits are also explored.

There are transcriptions of many fascinating official documents taken from the Northamptonshire Record Office which will be invaluable for family historians, such as lists of christenings, marriages and burials in the mid-16th century, churchwardens' accounts, overseers' records, occupations, and the workhouse inventory.

Bringing the whole rich heritage of the village to life are three illustrated walks round old Kingsthorpe, which explain the significance and origins of many historic buildings or sites. Old maps show how the village used to be.

Tony Horner's maternal family moved to Kingsthorpe in 1774 and he was born there in 1932.

ISBN 978-1-901253-51-1, A5 format, 380pp, more than 80 photos, maps, plans, £12.99

A HISTORY OF WHISTON
From the Stone Age to the Plastic Age
WILLIAM K BLINKHORN

Whiston is an ancient town lying south of the road linking Liverpool and Warrington, and crossed by the Liverpool to Manchester railway. For more than 450 years it was known for its coal mines. Its recorded history begins in the 13th century but its roots are much older. A Neolithic polished stone hand-axe was discovered there in 1941 and in 1986 fragments of flint tools were found on a local farm.

William K Blinkhorn, hon. secretary of the Whiston Historical Society since it was founded in 1974, has spent years researching the town's history. In this wide-ranging book he traces the story of Whiston from its Stone Age beginnings right up to the closure of one of its most modern industries, the B.I.P. Chemicals' amino-plastics factory which had been built near the site of the Old Halsnead Pits Nos. 9 and 10.

He looks at the derivation of old place and field names; the lords of the manor and tenant lords of the manor of Whiston; taxes, tithes and land ownership; listed buildings; the effect of the plague; almshouses and charities; ale-houses and beerhouses; the care of the sick; religion and schools. There are numerous family trees of Whiston's most noted gentry.

A section devoted to the town's industries examines agriculture, coal mining, communications, watch and hand-tool making, shoe-making, blacksmithing, tanning, nailmaking, quarrying, the local brickworks, Stoves Ltd (Gas Appliances) and the production of pipes and pots.

The book is illustrated with copies of old documents and photographs, and with pen and ink illustrations by the author. The result is a fascinating and readable dip into Whiston's past.

ISBN 978-1-901253-38-2   A5, 211 pages, 75 b+w illus, 12 maps   Price £9.99

For more info: tel 01606 75660; visit www.leoniepress.com: or email jack@leoniepress.com

SELECTED LOCAL HISTORY TITLES BY LÉONIE PRESS

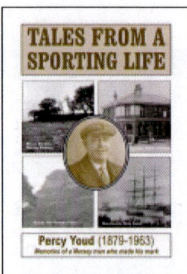

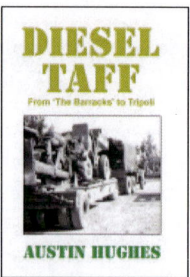

TALES FROM A SPORTING LIFE
Memories of a Mersey man who made his mark
PERCY YOUD (1879-1963)

When Percy Youd was born in Frodsham in 1879, the Manchester Ship Canal was soon to be constructed nearby. From an early age, natural ability and a marksman's eye singled him out as an outstanding shot with anything from a muzzle-loader to a 12-bore shotgun. His quarry included game in the Cheshire hills and wildfowl on the Mersey estuary. He was a fearless fist-fighter and an excellent athlete, setting a record for the gruelling Helsby Hill race – he trained on sherry – among many other sporting achievements.

Percy's first job in 1893 was at the Helsby cable works and in 1902 he moved to its sister factory at Prescot as a foreman. A few years later the company asked him to take on the Imperial Hotel on the edge of the 'Wire Works' complex. He later moved to Birkenhead. He was a keen member of the Conservative Club in Ellesmere Port and set up iin the town as an auctioneer. He led many shooting parties and his marksmanship was the subject of betting.

He organised a 100,000-name petition to try to save his Chinese friend, convicted murderer Lock Ah Tam, from the gallows and claimed friendship with Selwyn Lloyd who was MP for the Wirral.

In old age Percy wrote some of his memories down in a 22,000-word unpunctuated "lump" of vividly descriptive prose which was discovered after his death – including the script of the Frodsham 'soul-caking' play. This book contains the gently edited text, together with family portraits, old photographs and postcards, press cuttings and background information. There is also an account by his daughter of her childhood with him in the 1920s after he abducted her from his estranged wife.

ISBN 978-1-901253-30-6, 188pp, A5 format, 94 illustrations. Price £8.99.

DIESEL TAFF
From 'The Barracks' to Tripoli
AUSTIN HUGHES

Austin Hughes was born in 1922 at 'The Barracks', a flea-ridden block of houses otherwise known as Plas Maen Cottages, near Hope Mountain in North Wales. Water often had to be carried from a piped spring a mile away. After working as a baker, Austin's father became chronically ill and received parish relief. Times were hard for the family, even when they were able to move into a more comfortable home. Austin grew up as an abstemious god-fearing country lad, innocent of the world outside.

From childhood, Austin loved heavy machinery and eventually learned to use it. He graduated from driving a dumper truck to a bulldozer and was in seventh heaven. Then in October 1940 his call-up papers arrived: he had to join the Royal Engineers. This was to be an experience which changed the young Welshman's life and earned him his nick-name "Diesel Taff". By the end of the war, he'd been to 18 countries.

As a sapper, he was posted to bomb disposal in London, working on cranes and other heavy plant during the 1941 Blitz. Soon he was shipped via Brazil, Durban and Bombay to the Middle East — where he helped to build the only 'sinking bridge' in the world — and then with his pals in the 39 Mech. Equipment Pltn. R.E. he worked all types of earth moving equipment, living in the back of his wagon for four years. He led convoys bringing Polish refugees from Russia.

Imperial War Museum: *"An excellent autobiography which will be an interesting addition to our holdings."*

*'**The Sapper**' magazine*: *"A most readable worm's-eye-view of an area of the war not adequately covered elsewhere."*

ISBN 978-1-901253-14-6 224pp, 61 b+w photos, 2 maps, A5 format Price: £8.99

For more info: tel 01606 75660; visit www.leoniepress.com: or email jack@leoniepress.com